# Web Client Programming with Perl

# Web Client Programming with Perl

Clinton Wong

O'REILLY™

*Cambridge · Köln · Paris · Sebastopol · Tokyo*

**Web Client Programming with Perl**
by Clinton Wong

Copyright © 1997 O'Reilly & Associates, Inc. All rights reserved.
Printed in the United States of America.

Published by O'Reilly & Associates, Inc., 101 Morris Street, Sebastopol, CA 95472.

**Editor:** Linda Mui

**Production Editor:** Jane Ellin

**Printing History:**

       March 1997:       First Edition

Nutshell Handbook and the Nutshell Handbook logo are registered trademarks and The Java Series is a trademark of O'Reilly & Associates, Inc.

Many of the designations used by manufacturers and sellers to distinguish their products are claimed as trademarks. Where those designations appear in this book, and O'Reilly & Associates, Inc. was aware of a trademark claim, the designations have been printed in caps or initial caps.

While every precaution has been taken in the preparation of this book, the publisher assumes no responsibility for errors or omissions, or for damages resulting from the use of the information contained herein.

This book is printed on acid-free paper with 85% recycled content, 15% post-consumer waste. O'Reilly & Associates is committed to using paper with the highest recycled content available consistent with high quality.

ISBN: 1-56592-214-X

# Table of Contents

# *Preface*

The World Wide Web has been credited with bringing the Internet to the masses. The Internet was previously the stomping ground of academics and a small, elite group of computer professionals, mostly UNIX programmers and other oddball types, running obscure commands like *ftp* and *finger*, *archie* and *telnet*, and so on.

With the arrival of graphical browsers for the Web, the Internet suddenly exploded. Anyone could find things on the Web. You didn't need to be "in the know" anymore—you just needed to be properly networked. Equipped with Netscape Navigator or Internet Explorer or any other browser, everyone can now explore the Internet freely.

But graphical browsers can be limiting. The very interactivity that makes them the ideal interface for the Internet also makes them cumbersome when you want to automate a task. It's analogous to editing a document by hand when you'd like to write a script to do the work for you. Graphical browsers require you to navigate the Web manually. In an effort to diminish the amount of tedious pointing-and-clicking you do with your browser, this book shows you how to liberate yourself from the confines of your browser.

*Web Client Programming with Perl* is a behind-the-scenes look at how your web browser interacts with web servers. Readers of this book will learn how the Web works and how to write software that is more flexible, dynamic, and powerful than the typical web browser. The goal here is not to rewrite the browser, but to give you the ability to retrieve, manipulate, and redistribute web-based information in an automated fashion.

# Who This Book Is For

I like to think that this book is for everyone. But since that's a bit of an exaggeration, let's try to identify who might really enjoy this book.

This book is for software developers who want to expand into a new market niche. It provides proof-of-concept examples and a compilation of web-related technical data.

This book is for web administrators who maintain large amounts of data. Administrators can replace manual maintenance tasks with web robots to detect and correct problems with web sites. Robots perform tasks more accurately and quickly than human hands.

But to be honest, the audience that's closest to my heart is that of computer enthusiasts, tinkerers, and motivated students, who can use this book to satisfy their curiosity about how the Web works and how to make it work for them. My editor often talks about when she first learned UNIX scripting and how it opened a world of automation for her. When you learn how to write scripts, you realize that there's very little that you can't do within that universe. With this book, you can extend that confidence to the Web. If this book is successful, then for almost any web-related task you'll find yourself thinking, "Hey, I could write a script to do that!"

Unfortunately, we can't teach you everything. There are a few things that we assume that you are already familiar with:

- The concept of client/server network applications and TCP/IP.

- How the Internet works, and how to access it.

- The Perl language. Perl was chosen as the language for examples in this book due to its ability to hide complexity. Instead of dealing with C's data structures and low-level system calls, Perl introduces higher-level functions and a straightforward way of defining and using data. If you aren't already familiar with Perl, I recommend *Learning Perl* by Randal Schwartz, and *Programming Perl* (popularly known as "The Camel Book") by Larry Wall, Tom Christiansen, and Randal Schwartz. Both of these books are published by O'Reilly & Associates, Inc. There are other fine Perl books as well. Check out *http://www.perl.com* for the latest book critiques.

# Is This Book for You?

Some of you already know why you picked up this book. But others may just have a nagging feeling that it's something useful to know, though you may not be entirely sure why. At the risk of seeming self-serving, let me suggest some ways in which this book may be helpful:

- Some people just like to know how things tick. If you like to think the Web is magic, fine—but there are many who don't like to get into a car without knowing what's under the hood. For those of you who desire a better technical understanding of the Web, this book demystifies the web protocol and the browser/server interaction.

- Some people hate to waste even a minute of time. Given the choice between repeating an action over and over for an hour, or writing a script to automate it, these people will choose the script every time. Call it productivity or just stubbornness—the effect is the same. Through web automation, much time can be saved. Repetitive tasks, like tracking packages or stock prices, can be relegated to a web robot, leaving the user free to perform more fruitful activities (like eating lunch).

- If you understand your current web environment, you are more likely to recognize areas that can be improved. Instead of waiting for solutions to show up in the marketplace, you can take an active role in shaping the future direction of your own web technology. You can develop your own specialized solutions to fit specific problems.

- In today's frenzied high-tech world, knowledge isn't just power, it's money. A reasonable understanding of HTTP looks nice on the resume when you're competing for software contracts, consulting work, and jobs.

# *Organization*

This book consists of seven chapters and three appendices, as follows:

*Chapter 1, Introduction*
> Discusses basic terminology and potential uses for customized web clients.

*Chapter 2, Demystifying the Browser*
> Translates common browser tasks into HTTP transactions. By the end of the chapter, the reader will understand how web clients and servers interact, and will be able to perform these interactions manually.

*Chapter 3, Learning HTTP*
> Teaches the nuances of the HTTP protocol.

*Chapter 4, The Socket Library*
> Introduces the socket library and shows some examples of how to write simple web clients with sockets.

*Chapter 5, The LWP Library*
> Describes the LWP library that will be used for the examples in Chapters 6 and 7.

*Chapter 6, Example LWP Programs*
> A cookbook-type demonstration of several example applications.

*Chapter 7, Graphical Examples with Perl/Tk*
> A demonstration of how you can use the Tk extention to Perl to add a graphical interface to your programs.

*Appendix A, HTTP Headers*
> Contains a comprehensive listing of the headers specified by HTTP.

*Appendix B, Reference Tables*
> Lists URLs that you can use to learn more about HTTP and LWP.

*Appendix C, The Robot Exclusion Standard*
> Describes the Robot Exclusion Standard, which every good web programmer should know intimately.

# Source Code in This Book Is Online

In this book, we include many code examples. While the code is all contained within the text, many people will prefer to download examples rather than type them in by hand. You can find the complete set of source code used in this book on *ftp.ora.com* at */published/oreilly/nutshell/web-client*.

## FTP

To use FTP, you need a machine with direct access to the Internet. A sample session follows, with what you should type shown in **boldface**.

```
% ftp ftp.ora.com
Connected to ftp.ora.com.
220 FTP server (Version 6.21 Tue Mar 10 22:09:55 EST 1992) ready.
Name (ftp.ora.com:yourname): anonymous
331 Guest login ok, send domain style e-mail address as password.
Password: yourname@yourhost (use your user name and host here)
230 Guest login ok, access restrictions apply.
ftp> cd /published/oreilly/nutshell/web-client
250 CWD command successful.
ftp> binary (Very important! You must specify binary transfer for
compressed files.)
200 Type set to I.
ftp> get examples.tar.gz
200 PORT command successful.
150 Opening BINARY mode data connection for examples.tar.gz.
```

```
226 Transfer complete.
ftp> quit
221 Goodbye.
%
```

The file is a gzipped tar archive; extract the files from the archive by typing:

```
% gunzip examples.tar.gz
% tar xvf examples.tar
```

System V systems require the following *tar* command instead:

```
% tar xof examples.tar
```

## Conventions Used in This Book

We use the following formatting conventions in this book:

- *Italic* is used for command names, function names, variables, email addresses, URLs, directory and filenames, and newsgroup names. It is also used for emphasis and for the first use of a technical term.

- `Courier` is used for HTTP header names and for code.

- `Courier Italic` is used within code to show elements that should be replaced with real values.

- **`Courier Bold`** is used to show commands entered by the user.

## Request for Comments

As a reader of this book, you can help us to improve the next edition. If you find errors, inaccuracies, or typos anywhere in the book, please let us know about them. Also, if you find any misleading statements or confusing explanations, let us know. Send your bug reports and comments to:

```
O'Reilly & Associates, Inc.
101 Morris St.
Sebastopol, CA  95472
1-800-998-9938 (in the US or Canada)
1-707-829-0515 (international/local)
1-707-829-0104 (FAX)
```
*bookquestions@ora.com*

Please let us know what we can do to make the book more helpful to you. We take your comments seriously, and will do whatever we can to make this book as useful as it can be.

# Acknowledgments

The idea for this book started in early 1995 when I was a student at Purdue University. It all started when I attended a class entitled Proficient Use of WWW taught by George Vanecek, Jr. and Buster Dunsmore. It was a wonderful class that went all over the map, from HTML to HTTP to CGI to Perl programming. Other ideas for the book started when I worked at Purdue's Online Writing Lab as a web developer.

I'd like to extend a warm "thank you" to everyone who helped review the book, especially on short notice: Tom Christiansen, Larry Wall, Sean McDermott, Kirsten Klinghammer, Ed Hill, Andy Grignon, Jeff Sedayao, Michael Pelz-Sherman, and Norman Walsh. Special thanks for Kirsten and Sean for the 24-hour turnaround time, and to Tom, Larry, and Ed for being critical when someone needed to be critical.

Thanks also to Nancy Walsh for writing the Perl/Tk chapter. And thanks to all the people at O'Reilly & Associates: production editor Jane Ellin, cover designer Edie Freedman, Chris Reilley (who cleaned up the figures), Mike Sierra for Tools support, Mary Anne Weeks Mayo and Sheryl Avruch for quality control, and my editor Linda Mui.

Thanks to my parents, Chun and Liang, my sister Ginger, and my girlfriend Cynthia for their support.

# 1

# *Introduction*

So what does Web client programming mean, and what do you need to learn to do it?

A web client is an application that communicates with a web server, using Hypertext Transfer Protocol (HTTP). Hypertext Transfer Protocol is the protocol behind the World Wide Web. With every web transaction, HTTP is invoked. HTTP is behind every request for a web document or graphic, every click of a hypertext link, and every submission of a form. The Web is about distributing information over the Internet, and HTTP is the protocol used to do so.

Most web users never think about HTTP, just as most TV viewers don't think about how video images get from the studio to their home. But this book is not for the average web user. This book is for people who want to do something that available web software won't let them do.

## *Why Write Your Own Clients?*

With the proliferation of available web browsers, you might wonder why you would want to write your own client program. The answer is that by writing your own client programs, you can leap beyond the preprogrammed functionality of a browser. For example, the following scenarios are all possible:

- An urgent document is sent out via Federal Express, and the sender wants to know the status of the document the moment it becomes available. He enters the FedEx airbill tracking number into a program that notifies him of events as the FedEx server reports them. Since the document is urgent, he configures the program to contact him if the document is not delivered by the next morning.

- A system administrator would like to verify that all hyperlinks and image references are valid at her site. She runs a program to verify all documents at the site and report the results. She then finds some common mistakes in numerous documents, and runs another program to automatically fix them.

- An investor keeps a stock portfolio online and runs a program to check stock prices. The online portfolio is updated automatically as prices change, and the program can notify the investor when there is an unusual jump in a stock price.

- A college student connects his computer to the Internet via an Ethernet connection in his room. The university distributes custom software that will allow his computer to wake him up every morning with local news. Audio clips are downloaded and a web browser is launched. As the sound clips play, the browser automatically updates to display a new image that corresponds to the report. A weather map is displayed when the local weather is being announced. Images of the campus are displayed as local news is announced. National and international news briefs are presented in this automatic fashion, and the program can be configured to omit and include certain topics. The student may flunk biology, but at least he'll be the first to know who won the Bulls game.

And so on. Think about resources that you regularly visit on the Web. Maybe every morning you check the David Letterman top ten list from last night, and before you leave the office you check the weather report. Can you automate those visits? Think about that time you wanted to print an entire document that had been split up into individual files, and had to select Chapter 1, print, return to the contents page, select Chapter 2, etc. Is there a way to print the entire thing in one swoop?

Browsers are for browsing. They are wonderful tools for discovery, for traveling to far-off virtual lands. But once you know what you want, a more specialized client might be more effective for your needs.

## *The Web and HTTP*

If you don't know what the Web is, you probably picked up the wrong book. But here's some history and background, just to make sure we're all coming from the same place.

The World Wide Web was developed in 1990 by Tim Berners-Lee at the Conseil Europeen pour la Recherche Nucleaire (CERN). The inspiration behind it was simply to find a way to share results of experiments in high-energy particle physics. The central technology behind the Web was the ability to link from a document on one server to a document on another, keeping the actual location and access method of the documents invisible to the user. Certainly not the sort of thing that you'd expect to start a media circus.

So what did start the media circus? In 1993 a graphical interface to the Web, named *Mosaic,* was developed at the University of Illinois at Urbana-Champagne. At first, Mosaic ran only on UNIX systems running the X Window System, a platform that was popular with academics but unknown to practically anyone else. Yet anyone who saw Mosaic in action knew immediately that this was big news. Soon afterwards, Mac and PC versions came out, and the Web started to become immensely popular. Suddenly the buzzwords started proliferating: Information Superhighway, Internet, the Web, Mosaic, etc. (For a while all these words were used interchangeably, much to the chagrin of anyone who had been using the Internet for years.)

In 1994, a new interface to the Web called Netscape Navigator came on the (free) market, and quickly became the darling of the Net. Meanwhile, everyone and their Big Blue Brother started developing their own web sites, with no one quite sure what the Web was best used for, but convinced that they couldn't be left behind.

Most of the confusion has died down now, but not the excitement. The Web seems to have permanently captured the imagination of the world. It brings up visions of vast archives that can now be made globally available from every desktop, images and multimedia that can be distributed to every home, and... money, money, money. But the soul of the Web is pure and unchanged. When you get down to it, it's just about sending data from one machine to another— and that's what HTTP is for.

## *Browsers and URLs*

The most common interface to the World Wide Web is a *browser,* such as Mosaic, Netscape Navigator, or Internet Explorer. With a browser, you can download web documents and view them formatted on your screen.

When you request a document with your browser, you supply a web address, known as a *Universal Resource Locator* or *URL.* The URL identifies the machine that contains the document you want, and the pathname to that document on the server. The browser contacts the remote machine and requests the document you specified. After receiving the document, it formats it as needed and displays it on your browser.

For example, you might click on a hyperlink that corresponds to the URL of *http:// www.ora.com/index.html.* Your browser contacts the machine called *www.ora.com* and requests the document called *index.html.* When the document arrives, the browser formats it and displays it on your screen. If the document requires other documents to be retrieved (for example, if it includes a graphic image on the page), the browser downloads them as well. But as far as you're concerned, you just clicked on a word and a new page appeared.

## Clients and Servers

Your web browser is an example of a web *client.* The remote machine containing the document you requested is called a web *server.* The client and server communicate using a special language (a "protocol") called HTTP. Figure 1-1 demonstrates the relationship between web clients and web servers.

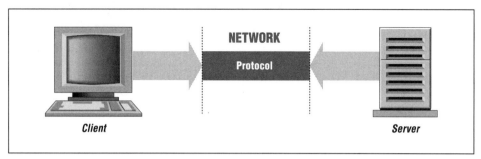

*Figure 1-1. Client and server relationship*

To keep ourselves honest, we should get a little more specific now. Although we commonly refer to the machine that contains the documents as the "server," the server isn't the hardware itself, but just a program that runs on that machine. The web server listens on a port on the network, and waits for client requests using the HTTP protocol. After the server responds to the request (using HTTP), the network connection is dropped and the browser processes the relevant data that it received, then displays it on your screen.

In practice, many clients can be using the same server at the same time, and one client can also use many servers at the same time (see Figure 1-2).

As you can see, at the core of the Web is HTTP. If you master HTTP, you can request documents from a server without needing to go through your browser. Similarly, you can return documents to web browsers without being limited to the functionality of an existing web server. HTTP programming takes you out of the realm of the everyday web user and into the world of the web power user.

Chapter 2, *Demystifying the Browser,* introduces you to simple HTTP as commonly encountered on the Web. Chapter 3, *Learning HTTP,* is a more complete reference on HTTP.

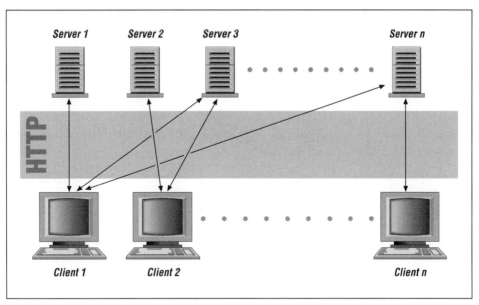

*Figure 1-2. Multiple clients and servers*

# The Programming Interface

Okay, we've told you a little about HTTP. But before your client can actually communicate with a server, it needs to establish a connection. It's like having a VCR and a TV, but no cable between them.

TCP/IP is what makes it possible for web clients and servers to speak to each other using HTTP. TCP/IP is the protocol used to send data packets across the Internet uncorrupted. Programmers need a TCP/IP programming interface, like Berkeley sockets, for their web programs to communicate.

Now, this is when we separate our audience into the lucky and the . . . less lucky.

One of the great virtues for which Perl programmers are extolled is laziness. The Perl community encourages programmers to develop modules and libraries that perform common tasks, and then to share these developments with the world at large. While you can write Perl programs that use sockets to contact the web server and then send raw HTTP requests manually, you can also use a library for Perl 5 called LWP (Library for WWW access in Perl), which basically does all the hard work for you.

Great news, huh? Only for those of us on UNIX, though. At this writing, LWP has not been fully ported to Windows 95 or Windows NT, and using Perl's socket library under NT isn't quite the same. There are some great developments from vendors like ActiveWare and Softway that might one day make NT's Perl environment look exactly as it does on UNIX. For now, however, NT users have to cope with what's out there. But on the brighter side, NT's Perl environment is getting better over time.

Also, some readers may be stuck with Perl 4, in which case LWP is off limits. Many Internet Service Providers do not support software "extras" like Perl, and thus will not upgrade the version of Perl 4 that was distributed with their operating system. Perl 4 is considered unsupported and buggy by most Perl experts, but for many readers, it's all they have.

Chapter 4, *The Socket Library*, covers sockets, and Chapter 5, *The LWP Library*, introduces you to LWP. Since most Perl programmers have LWP available to them, we wrote all the examples in Chapters 6 and 7 using LWP. However, Chapter 4 does show some examples of writing simple clients using Sockets, for those readers who cannot use LWP (or choose not to).

## *A Word of Caution*

There are some dangers in developing and configuring Web client programs. A buggy client program may overload a web server. It could cause massive amounts of network traffic. Or you might receive flame mail or lawsuits from web maintainers. Worst of all, web clients could cause data integrity problems on servers by feeding bad data to Common Gateway Interface (CGI) programs that don't bother to check for proper input. To avoid these disasters, there are a few things you can do:

- Test your code locally. The ideal environment for web development is a machine running both the web client and the web server. When you use this type of setup, communication between the client and server doesn't actually go though a network connection. Instead, communication is done locally by the operating system. If the computer dramatically slows down shortly after running your newly written client, you know there's a problem. Such a program would be even slower over a network.

- Run your own server. Many excellent servers are freely available on the Internet, and it is far better to accidentally overload your own server than the one used by your Internet Service Provider (ISP) or company.

- Give yourself options. When you finally decide to run your client program with someone else's server, leave your "verbose" options on and watch what your program is doing. Make sure you designed your program so you can stop it if it is getting out of hand.

- Ask permission. Some servers are not intended to be queried by custom-made web clients. Ask the maintainers of the server if you can run your client on their server.

- Most importantly, follow the Robot Exclusion Standard at *http://info.web-crawler.com/mak/projects/robots/norobots*. (See Appendix C for more information on the Robot Exclusion Standard.)

Basically, a home-grown web client is like an uninvited guest, and like all gate crashers, you should be polite and try not to draw too much attention to yourself. If you guzzle down all the good liquor and make a nuisance of yourself, you will be asked to leave.

# 2

# *Demystifying the Browser*

Before you start writing your own web programs, you have to become comfortable with the fact that your web browser is just another client. Lots of complex things are happening: user interface processing, network communication, operating system interaction, and HTML/graphics rendering. But all of that is gravy; without actually negotiating with web servers and retrieving documents via HTTP, the browser would be as useless as a TV without a tuner.

HTTP may sound intimidating, but it isn't as bad as you might think. Like most other Internet protocols, HTTP is text-based. If you were to look at the communication between your web browser and a web server, you would see text—and lots of it. After a few minutes of sifting through it all, you'd find out that HTTP isn't too hard to read. By the end of this chapter, you'll be able to read HTTP and have a fairly good idea of what's going on during typical everyday transactions over the Web.

The best way to understand how HTTP works is to see it in action. You actually see it in action every day, with every click of a hyperlink—it's just that the gory details are hidden from you. In this chapter, you'll see some common web transactions: retrieving a page, submitting a form, and publishing a web page. In each example, the HTTP for each transaction is printed as well. From there, you'll be able to analyze and understand how your actions with the browser are translated into HTTP. You'll learn a little bit about how HTTP is spoken between a web client and server.

After you've seen bits and pieces of HTTP in this chapter, Chapter 3, *Learning HTTP*, introduces HTTP in a more thorough manner. In Chapter 3, you'll see all the different ways that a client can request something, and all the ways a server can reply. In the end, you'll get a feel for what is possible under HTTP.

# Behind the Scenes of a Simple Document

Let's begin by visiting a hypothetical web server at *http://hypothetical.ora.com/*. Its imaginary (and intentionally sparse) web page appears in Figure 2-1.

*Figure 2-1. A hypothetical web page*

This is something you probably do every day—request a URL and then view it in your browser. But what actually happened in order for this document to appear in your browser?

## The Browser's Request

Your browser first takes in a URL and parses it. In this example, the browser is given the following URL:

```
http://hypothetical.ora.com/
```

The browser interprets the URL as follows:

*http://*

In the first part of the URL, you told the browser to use HTTP, the Hypertext Transfer Protocol.

*hypothetical.ora.com*

In the next part, you told the browser to contact a computer over the network with the hostname of *hypothetical.ora.com*.

/

> Anything after the hostname is regarded as a document path. In this example, the document path is /.

So the browser connects to *hypothetical.ora.com* using the HTTP protocol. Since no port was specified, it assumes port 80, the default port for HTTP. The message that the browser sends to the server at port 80 is:

```
GET / HTTP/1.0
Connection: Keep-Alive
User-Agent: Mozilla/3.0Gold (WinNT; I)
Host: hypothetical.ora.com
Accept: image/gif, image/x-xbitmap, image/jpeg, image/pjpeg, */*
```

Let's look at what these lines are saying:

1. The first line of this request (`GET / HTTP/1.0`) requests a document at / from the server. `HTTP/1.0` is given as the version of the HTTP protocol that the browser uses.

2. The second line tells the server to keep the TCP connection open until explicitly told to disconnect. If this header is not provided, the server has no obligation to stick around under HTTP 1.0, and disconnects after responding to the client's request. The behavior of the client and server depend on what version of HTTP is spoken. (See the discussion of persistent connections in Chapter 3 for the full scoop.)

3. In the third line, beginning with the string `User-Agent`, the client identifies itself as Mozilla (Netscape) version 3.0, running on Windows NT.

4. The fourth line tells the server what the client thinks the server's hostname is. Since the server may have multiple hostnames, the client indicates which hostname was used. In this environment, a web server can have a different document tree for each hostname it owns. If the client hasn't specified the server's hostname, the server may be unable to determine which document tree to use.

5. The fifth line tells the server what kind of documents are accepted by the browser. This is discussed more in the section "Media Types" in Chapter 3.

Together, these 5 lines constitute a *request*. Lines 2 through 5 are *request headers*.

## The Server's Response

Given a request like the one previously shown, the server looks for the file associated with "/" and returns it to the browser, preceding it with some "header information":

```
HTTP/1.0 200 OK
Date: Fri, 04 Oct 1996 14:31:51 GMT
```

```
Server: Apache/1.1.1
Content-type: text/html
Content-length: 327
Last-modified: Fri, 04 Oct 1996 14:06:11 GMT

<title>Sample Homepage</title>
<img src="/images/oreilly_mast.gif">
<h1>Welcome</h1>
Hi there, this is a simple web page.  Granted, it may not be as elegant
as some other web pages you've seen on the net, but there are
some common qualities:

<ul>
  <li> An image,
  <li> Text,
  <li> and a <a href="/example2.html"> hyperlink </a>
</ul>
```

If you look at this response, you'll see that it begins with a series of lines that specify information about the document and about the server itself. Then after a blank line, it returns the document. The series of lines before the first blank line is called the *response header*, and the part after the first blank line is called the *body* or *entity*, or *entity-body*. Let's look at the header information:

1. The first line, HTTP/1.0 200 OK, tells the client what version of the HTTP protocol the server uses. But more importantly, it says that the document has been found and is going to be transmitted.

2. The second line indicates the current date on the server. The time is expressed in Greenwich Mean Time (GMT).

3. The third line tells the client what kind of software the server is running. In this case, the server is Apache version 1.1.1.

4. The fourth line (Content-type) tells the browser the type of the document. In this case, it is HTML.

5. The fifth line tells the client how many bytes are in the entity body that follows the headers. In this case, the entity body is 327 bytes long.

6. The sixth line specifies the most recent modification time of the document requested by the client. This modification time is often used for caching purposes—so a browser may not need to request the entire HTML file again if its modification time doesn't change.

After all that, a blank line and the document text follow.

Figure 2-2 shows the transaction.

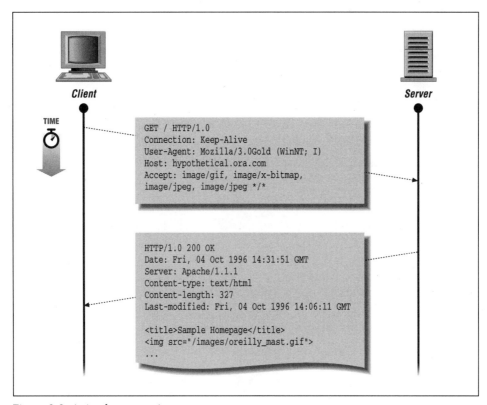

*Figure 2-2. A simple transaction*

## Parsing the HTML

The document is in HTML (as promised in the `Content-type` line). The browser retrieves the document and then formats it as needed—for example, each `<li>` item between the `<ul>` and `</ul>` is printed as a bullet and indented, the `<img>` tag displays a graphic on the screen, etc.

And while we're on the topic of the `<img>` tag, how did that graphic get on the screen? While parsing the HTML file, the browser sees:

```
<img src="/images/oreilly_mast.gif">
```

and figures out that it needs the data for the image as well. Your browser then sends a second request, such as this one, through its connection to the web server:

```
GET /images/oreilly_mast.gif HTTP/1.0
Connection: Keep-Alive
User-Agent: Mozilla/3.0Gold (WinNT; I)
Host: hypothetical.ora.com
Accept: image/gif, image/x-xbitmap, image/jpeg, image/pjpeg, */*
```

The server responds with:

```
HTTP/1.0 200 OK
Date: Fri, 04 Oct 1996 14:32:01 GMT
Server: Apache/1.1.1
Content-type: image/gif
Content-length: 9487
Last-modified: Tue, 31 Oct 1995 00:03:15 GMT

[data of GIF file]
```

Figure 2-3 shows the complete transaction, with the image requested as well as the original document.

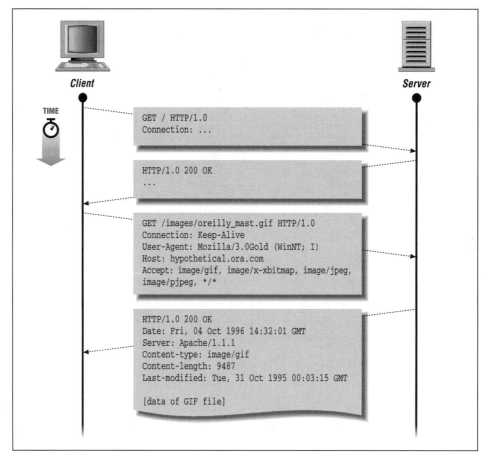

*Figure 2-3. Simple transaction with embedded image*

There are a few differences between this request/response pair and the previous one. Based on the `<img>` tag, the browser knows where the image is stored on the server. From `<img  src="/images/oreilly_mast.gif">`, the browser requests a document at a different location than "/":

```
GET /images/oreilly_mast.gif HTTP/1.0
```

The server's response is basically the same, except that the content type is different:

```
Content-type: image/gif
```

From the declared content type, the browser knows what kind of image it will receive and can render it as required. The browser shouldn't guess the content type based on the document path; it is up to the server to tell the client.

The important thing to note here is that the HTML formatting and image rendering are done at the browser end. All the server does is return documents; the browser is responsible for how they look to the user.

## *Clicking on a Hyperlink*

When you click on a hyperlink, the client and server go through something similar to what happened when we visited *http://hypothetical.ora.com/*. For example, when you click on the hyperlink from the previous example, the browser looks at its associated HTML:

```
<a href="/example2.html"> hyperlink </a>
```

From there, it knows that the next location to retrieve is */example2.html*. The browser then sends the following to *hypothetical.ora.com*:

```
GET /example2.html HTTP/1.0
Connection: Keep-Alive
User-Agent: Mozilla/3.0Gold (WinNT; I)
Host: hypothetical.ora.com
Accept: image/gif, image/x-xbitmap, image/jpeg, image/pjpeg, */*
```

The server responds with:

```
HTTP/1.0 200 OK
Date: Fri, 04 Oct 1996 14:32:14 GMT
Server: Apache/1.1.1
Content-type: text/html
Content-length: 431
Last-modified: Thu, 03 Oct 1996 08:39:45 GMT

[HTML data]
```

And the browser displays the new HTML page on the user's screen.

# *Retrieving a Document Manually*

Now that you see what a browser does, it's time for the most empowering statement in this book: There's nothing in these transactions that you can't do yourself. And you don't need to write a program—you can just do it by hand, using the standard *telnet* client and a little knowledge of HTTP.

Telnet to *www.ora.com* at port 80. From a UNIX shell prompt:*

```
% telnet www.ora.com 80
Trying 198.112.208.23 ...
Connected to www.ora.com.
Escape character is '^]'.
```

(The second argument for *telnet* specifies the port number to use. By default, *telnet* uses port 23. Most web servers use port 80.)

Now type in a GET command† for the document root:

```
GET / HTTP/1.0
```

Press ENTER twice, and you receive what a browser would receive:

```
HTTP/1.0 200 OK
Server: WN/1.15.1
Date: Mon, 30 Sep 1996 14:14:20 GMT
Last-modified: Fri, 20 Sep 1996 17:04:18 GMT
Content-type: text/html
Title: O'Reilly &amp; Associates
Link: <mailto:webmaster@ora.com>; rev="Made"

<HTML>
<HEAD>
<LINK REV=MADE HREF="mailto:webmaster@ora.com">
   .
   .
   .
```

When the document is finished, your shell prompt should return. The server has closed the connection.

Congratulations! What you've just done is simulate the behavior of a web client.

---

\* You can use a *telnet* client on something other than UNIX, but it might look different. On some non-UNIX systems, your telnet client may not show you what you're typing if you connect directly to a web server at port 80.

† Actually called a *method,* but *command* makes more sense for people who are going through this the first time around. More about this later.

# *Behind the Scenes of an HTML Form*

You've probably seen fill-out forms on the Web, in which you enter information into your browser and submit the form. Common uses for forms are guestbooks, accessing databases, or specifying keywords for a search engine.

When you fill out a form, the browser needs to send that information to the server, along with the name of the program needed to process it. The program that processes the form information is called a *CGI program*. Let's look at how a browser makes a request from a form. Let's direct our browser to contact our hypothetical server and request the document */search.html*:

```
GET /search.html HTTP/1.0
Connection: Keep-Alive
User-Agent: Mozilla/3.0Gold (WinNT; I)
Host: hypothetical.ora.com
Accept: image/gif, image/x-xbitmap, image/jpeg, image/pjpeg, */*
```

The server responds with:

```
HTTP/1.0 200 OK
Date: Fri, 04 Oct 1996 14:33:43 GMT
Server: Apache/1.1.1
Content-type: text/html
Content-length: 547
Last-modified: Tue, 01 Oct 1996 08:48:02 GMT
<title>Library Search</title>
<FORM ACTION="http://hypothetical.ora.com/cgi-bin/query" METHOD=POST>
Enter book title, author, or subject here:<p>
  <INPUT TYPE="radio" NAME="querytype" VALUE="title" CHECKED> Title<p>
  <INPUT TYPE="radio" NAME="querytype" VALUE="author"> Author<p>
  <INPUT TYPE="radio" NAME="querytype" VALUE="subject"> Subject<p>
Keywords:
<input type="text" name="queryconst" value="" size="50,2" ><p>
<BR>Press DONE to start your search.
<hr>
<input type="submit" value="Done">
<input type="reset" value="Start over">
</FORM>
```

The formatted document is shown in Figure 2-4.

Let's fill out the form and submit it, as shown in Figure 2-5.

After hitting the Done button, the browser connects to *hypothetical.ora.com* at port 80, as specified with the <FORM> tag in the HTML:

```
<FORM ACTION="http://hypothetical.ora.com/cgi-bin/query" METHOD=POST>
```

The browser then sends:

```
POST /cgi-bin/query HTTP/1.0
Referer: http://hypothetical.ora.com/search.html
```

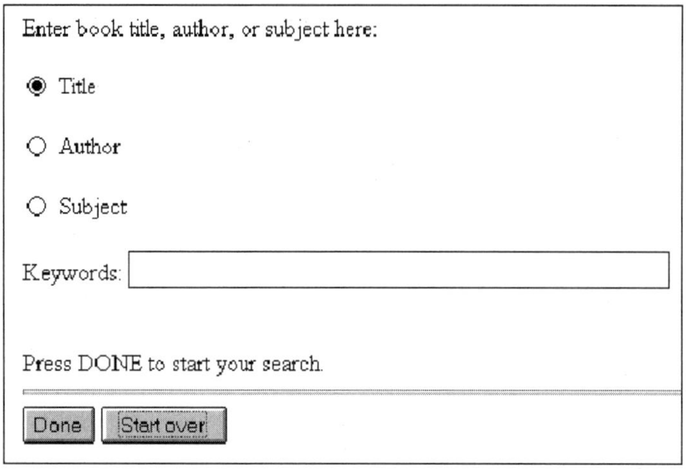

Enter book title, author, or subject here:

◉  Title

○  Author

○  Subject

Keywords: [                                                    ]


Press DONE to start your search.

[ Done ]  [ Start over ]

*Figure 2-4. A HTML form rendered in the browser*

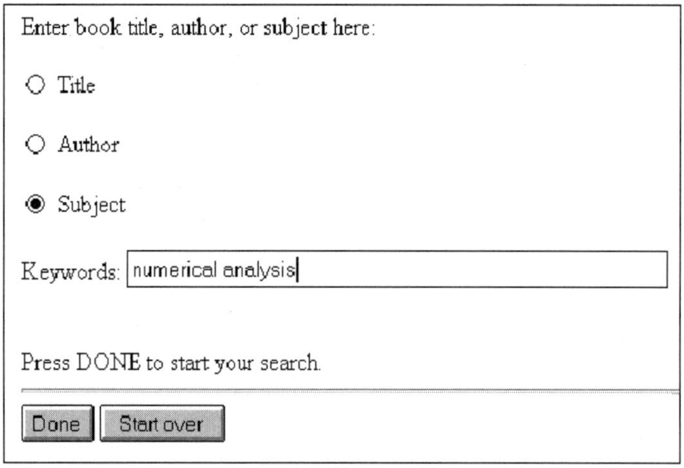

Enter book title, author, or subject here:

○  Title

○  Author

◉  Subject

Keywords: [ numerical analysis| ]


Press DONE to start your search.

[ Done ]  [ Start over ]

*Figure 2-5. Filling out the form*

```
Connection: Keep-Alive
User-Agent: Mozilla/3.0Gold (WinNT; I)
Host: hypothetical.ora.com
Accept: image/gif, image/x-xbitmap, image/jpeg, image/pjpeg, */*
Content-type: application/x-www-form-urlencoded
Content-length: 47

querytype=subject&queryconst=numerical+analysis
```

In the previous example retrieving the initial page at *hypothetical.ora.com*, we showed a series of lines that the browser output and called it a request header. Calling it a header might not have made any sense at the time, since there was no content being sent with it—if you're just requesting a document, you don't have to tell the server anything else. But since in this instance we have to tell the server what the user typed into the form, we have to use a "body" portion of the message to convey that information. So there are a few new things to note in this example:

- Instead of GET, the browser started the transaction with the string POST. GET and POST are two types of *request methods* recognized by HTTP. The most important thing that POST tells the server is that there is a body (or "entity") portion of the message to follow.

  The browser used the POST method because it was specified in the `<FORM>` tag:

  ```
  <FORM ACTION="http://hypothetical.ora.com/cgi-bin/query" METHOD=POST>
  ```

- The browser included an extra line specifying a `Content-type`. This wasn't necessary in the previous example because no content was being sent with the request. The `Content-type` line tells the server what sort of data is coming so it can determine how best to handle it. In this case, it tells the server that the data to be sent is going to be encoded using the *application/x-www-form-urlencoded* format. This format specifies how to encode special characters, and how to send multiple variables and values in forms. See Chapter 3 and Appendix B, *Reference Tables*, for more information on URL encoding.

- The browser included another line specifying a `Content-length`. Similarly, this wasn't necessary earlier because there was no content to the entity body. But there is in this example; it tells the server how much data to retrieve. In this case, the `Content-length` is 47 bytes.

- After a blank line, the entity-body is issued, reading *querytype=subject&queryconst=numerical+analysis*. (Notice that this string is exactly 47 characters, as specified in the `Content-length` line.)

Where did this *querytype=subject&queryconst=numerical+analysis* line come from? In the HTML of the form, the input field was specified with the following lines:

```
<INPUT TYPE="radio" NAME="querytype" VALUE="subject"> Subject<p>
<input type="text" name="queryconst" value="" size="50,2" >
```

The `NAME="querytype"` and `VALUE="subject"` part of the first `<INPUT>` tag was encoded as `"querytype=subject"`. The `NAME="queryconst"` part of the second `<INPUT>` tag specifies a variable name to use for whatever text is supplied in that field. We filled in that field with the words "numerical analysis." Thus, for the form data entered by the user, the browser sends:

```
querytype=subject&queryconst=numerical+analysis
```

to specify the variable and value pairs used in the form. Two or more variable/value pairs are separated with an ampersand (&). Notice that the space between "numerical" and "analysis" was replaced by a plus sign (+). Certain characters with special meaning are translated into a commonly understood format. The complete rundown of these transformations is covered in Appendix B.

At this point, the server processes the request by forwarding this information on to the CGI program. The CGI program then returns some data, and the server passes it back to the client as follows:

```
HTTP/1.0 200 OK
Date: Tue, 01 Oct 1996 14:52:06 GMT
Server: Apache/1.1.1
Content-type: text/html
Content-length: 760
Last-modified: Tue, 01 Oct 1996 12:46:15 GMT

<title>Search Results</title>
<h1>Search criteria too wide.</h1>
<h2>Refer to:</h2>
<hr>
<pre>
     1     ASYMPTOTIC EXPANSIONS
     2     BOUNDARY ELEMENT METHODS
     3     CAUCHY PROBLEM--NUMERICAL SOLUTIONS
     4     CONJUGATE DIRECTION METHODS
     5     COUPLED PROBLEMS COMPLEX SYSTEMS--NUMERICAL SOLUTIONS
     6     CURVE FITTING
     7     DEFECT CORRECTION METHODS NUMERICAL ANALYSIS
     8     DELAY DIFFERENTIAL EQUATIONS--NUMERICAL SOLUTIONS
     9     DIFFERENCE EQUATIONS--NUMERICAL SOLUTIONS
    10     DIFFERENTIAL ALGEBRAIC EQUATIONS--NUMERICAL SOLUTIONS
    11     DIFFERENTIAL EQUATIONS HYPERBOLIC--NUMERICAL SOLUTIONS
    12     DIFFERENTIAL EQUATIONS HYPOELLIPTIC--NUMERICAL SOLUTIONS
    13     DIFFERENTIAL EQUATIONS NONLINEAR--NUMERICAL SOLUTIONS
</pre>
<hr>
```

Figure 2-6 shows the results as rendered by the browser.

We'll have a more detailed discussion about posting form data and the *application/x-www-form-urlencoded* encoding method in Chapter 3, when we discuss the POST method in more detail.

# *Behind the Scenes of Publishing a Document*

If you've ever used a WYSIWYG HTML editor, you might have seen the option to publish your documents on a web server. Typically, there's an FTP option to

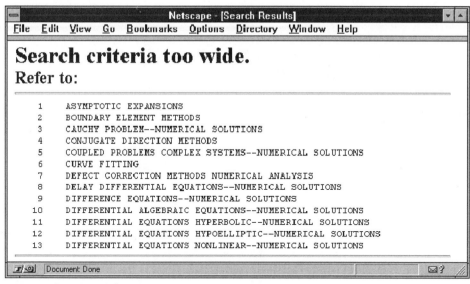

*Figure 2-6. Form results*

upload your document to the server. But on most modern publishers, there's also an HTTP upload option. How does this work?

Let's create a sample document in Navigator Gold, as in Figure 2-7.

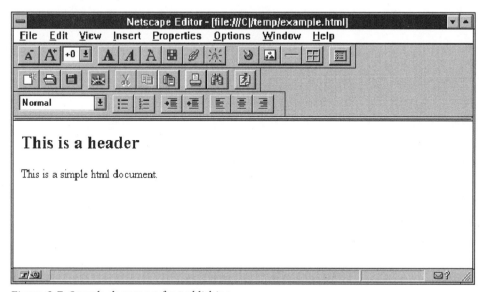

*Figure 2-7. Sample document for publishing*

After saving this file to *C:/temp/example.html*, let's publish it to the fictional site *http://publish.ora.com/*, using the dialog box shown in Figure 2-8.

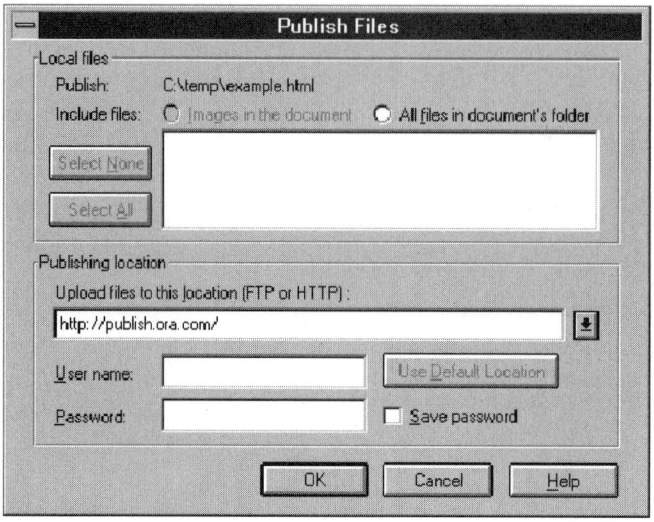

*Figure 2-8. Dialog box for publishing*

After clicking OK, the browser contacts *publish.ora.com* at port 80 and then sends:

```
PUT /example.html HTTP/1.0
Connection: Keep-Alive
User-Agent: Mozilla/3.0Gold (WinNT; I)
Pragma: no-cache
Host: publish.ora.com
Accept: image/gif, image/x-xbitmap, image/jpeg, image/pjpeg, */*
Content-Length: 307

<!DOCTYPE HTML PUBLIC "-//W3C//DTD HTML 3.2//EN">
<HTML>
<HEAD>
   <TITLE></TITLE>
   <META NAME="Author" CONTENT="">
   <META NAME="GENERATOR" CONTENT="Mozilla/3.0Gold (WinNT; I) [Netscape]">
</HEAD>
<BODY>

<H2>This is a header</H2>

<P>This is a simple html document.</P>

</BODY>
</HTML>
```

The server then responds with:

```
HTTP/1.0 201 Created
Date: Fri, 04 Oct 1996 14:31:51 GMT
```

```
Server: HypotheticalPublish/1.0
Content-type: text/html
Content-length: 30

    <h1>The file was created.</h1>
```

And now the contents of the file *C:/temp/example.html* has been transferred to the server.[*]

# *Structure of HTTP Transactions*

Now it's time to generalize. All client requests and server responses follow the same general structure, shown in Figure 2-9.

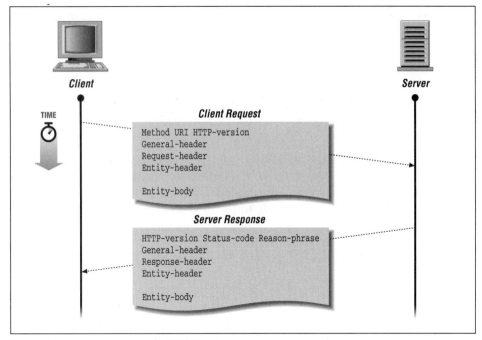

*Figure 2-9. General structure of HTTP requests*

Let's look at some queries that are modeled after examples from earlier in this chapter. Figure 2-10 shows the structure of a client request.

HTTP transactions do not need to use all the headers. In fact, it is possible to perform some HTTP requests without supplying any header information at all. A

---

[*] You might have noticed that there wasn't a `Content-type` header sent by the client. There should be one, but the software used to generate this example didn't include it. Other web publishing programs do, however. It's generally good practice for the originator of the data to specify what the data is.

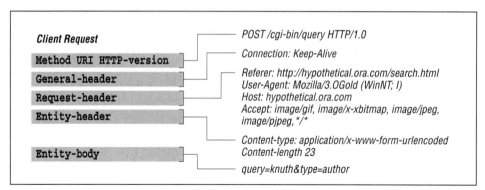

*Figure 2-10. Structure of a client request*

request of `GET / HTTP/1.0` with an empty header is sufficient for most servers to understand the client.

HTTP requests have the following general components:

1. The first line tells the client which *method* to use, which entity (document) to apply it to, and which version of HTTP the client is using. Possible methods in HTTP 1.0 are GET, POST, HEAD, PUT, LINK, UNLINK, and DELETE. HTTP 1.1 also supports the OPTIONS and TRACE methods. Not all methods need be supported by a server.

   The URL specifies the location of a document to apply the method to. Each server may have its own way of translating the URL string into some form of usable resource. For example, the URL may represent a document to transmit to the client. Or the URL may actually be a program, the output of which is sent to the client.

   Finally, the last entry on the first line specifies the version of HTTP the client is using. More about this in the next chapter.

2. General message headers are optional headers used in both the client request and server response. They indicate general information such as the current time or the path through a network that the client and server are using.

3. Request headers tell the server more information about the client. The client can identify itself and the user to the server, and specify preferred document formats that it would like to see from the server.

4. Entity headers are used when an entity (a document) is about to be sent. They specify information about the entity, such as encoding schemes, length, type, and origin.

Now for server responses. Figure 2-11 maps out the structure of a server response.

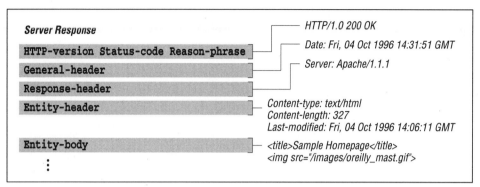

*Figure 2-11. Structure of a server response*

In the server response, the general header and entity headers are the same as those used in the client request. The entity-body is like the one used in the client request, except that it is used as a response.

The first part of the first line indicates the version of HTTP that the server is using. The server will make every attempt to conform to the most compatible version of HTTP that the client is using. The status code indicates the result of the request, and the reason phrase is a human-readable description of the status-code.

The response header tells the client about the configuration of the server. It can inform the client of what methods are supported, request authorization, or tell the client to try again later.

In the next chapter, we'll go over all the gory details of possible values and uses for HTTP entries.

# 3

# *Learning HTTP*

In the previous chapter, we went through a few examples of HTTP transactions and outlined the structure that all HTTP follows. For the most part, all web software will use an exchange similar to the HTTP we showed you in Chapter 2, *Demystifying the Browser*. But now it's time to teach you more about HTTP. Chapter 2 was like the "Spanish for Travelers" phrasebook that you got for your trip to Madrid; this chapter is the textbook for Spanish 101, required reading if you want course credit.

HTTP is defined by the HTTP specification, distributed by the World Wide Web Consortium (W3C) at *www.w3.org*. If you are writing commercial-quality HTTP applications, you should go directly to the spec, since it defines which features need to be supported for HTTP compliance. However, reading the spec is a tedious and often unpleasant experience, and readers of this book are assumed to be more casual writers of HTTP clients, so we've pared it down a bit to make HTTP more accessible for the spec-wary. This chapter includes:

- Review of the structure of HTTP transactions. This section also serves as a sort of road map to the rest of the chapter.

- Discussion of the request methods clients may use. Beyond GET, HEAD, and POST, we also give examples of the PUT, DELETE, TRACE, and OPTIONS methods.

- Summary of differences between various versions of HTTP. Clients and servers must declare which version of HTTP they use. For the most part, what you'll see is HTTP 1.0, but at least you'll know what that means. We also cover HTTP 1.1, the newest version of HTTP to date.

- Listing of server response codes, and discussion of the more common codes. These codes are the first indication of what to do with the server's response (if any), so robust client programs should be prepared to intercept them and interpret them properly.

- Coverage of HTTP headers for both clients and servers. Headers give clients the opportunity to declare who they are and what they want, and they give servers the chance to tell clients what to expect.

This is one of the longest chapters in this book, and no doubt you won't read it all in one sitting. Furthermore, if you use LWP, then you can go pretty far without knowing more than a superficial amount of HTTP. But it's all information you should know, so we recommend that you keep coming back to it. Although a few key phrases will help you get around town, fluency becomes very useful when you find yourself lost in the outskirts of the city.

## *Structure of an HTTP Transaction*

All HTTP transactions follow the same general format, as shown in Figure 3-1.

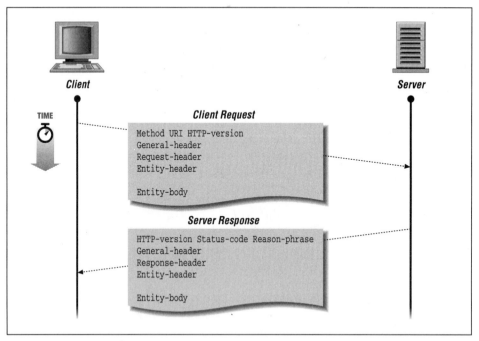

*Figure 3-1. Structure of HTTP transactions*

HTTP is a simple stateless protocol, in which the client makes a request, the server responds, and the transaction is then finished. The client initiates the transaction as follows:

1. First, the client contacts the server at a designated port number (by default, 80). Then it sends a document request by specifying an HTTP command (called a method), followed by a document address and an HTTP version number. For example:

    ```
    GET /index.html HTTP/1.0
    ```

    Here we use the GET method to request the document */index.html* using version 1.0 of HTTP. Although the most common request method is the GET method, there is also a handful of other methods that are supported by HTTP, and essentially define the scope and purpose of the transaction. In this chapter, we talk about each of the commonly used client request methods, and show you examples of their use.

    There are three versions of HTTP: 0.9, 1.0, and 1.1. At this writing, most clients and servers conform to HTTP 1.0. But HTTP 1.1 is on the horizon, and, for reasons of backward compatibility, HTTP 0.9 is still honored. We will discuss each version of HTTP and the major differences between them.

2. Next, the client sends optional header information to inform the server of the client's configuration and document preference. All header information is given line by line, each line with a header name and value. For example, a client can send its name and version number, or specify document preferences:*

    ```
    User-Agent: Mozilla/1.1N (Macintosh; I; 68K)
    Accept: */*
    Accept: image/gif
    Accept: image/x-xbitmap
    Accept: image/jpeg
    ```

    To end the header section, the client sends a blank line.

    There are many headers in HTTP. We will list all the valid headers in this chapter, but give special attention to several groupings of headers that may come in especially handy. Appendix A contains a more complete listing of HTTP headers.

3. When applicable, the client sends the data portion of the request. This data is often used by CGI programs via the POST method, or used to supply document information using the PUT method. These methods are discussed later in this chapter.

---

* More modern clients would just send one `Accept` header and separate the different values with commas.

The server responds as follows:

1. The server replies with a status line with the following three fields: the HTTP version, a status code, and description of the status. For example:

   ```
   HTTP/1.0 200 OK
   ```

   This indicates that the server uses version 1.0 of HTTP in its response, and a status code of 200 indicates that the client's request was successful and the requested data will be supplied after the headers.

   We will give a listing of each of the status codes supported by HTTP, along with a more detailed discussion of the status codes you are most likely to encounter.

2. The server supplies header information to tell the client about itself and the requested document. For example:

   ```
   Date: Saturday, 20-May-95 03:25:12 GMT
   Server: NCSA/1.3
   MIME-version: 1.0
   Content-type: text/html
   Last-modified: Wednesday, 14-Mar-95 18:15:23 GMT
   Content-length: 1029
   ```

   The header is terminated with a blank line.

3. If the client's request is successful, the requested data is sent. This data may be a copy of a file, or the response from a CGI program. If the client's request could not be fulfilled, the data may be a human-readable explanation of why the server couldn't fulfill the request.

Given this structure, a few questions come to mind:

- What request methods can a client use?
- What versions of HTTP are available?
- What headers can a client supply?
- What sort of response codes can you expect from a server, and what do you do with them?
- What headers can you expect the server to return, and what do you do with them?

We'll try to answer each of these questions in the remainder of this chapter, in approximate order. The exception to this order is client and server headers, which are discussed together, and discussed last. Many headers are shared by both clients and servers, so it didn't make sense to cover them twice; and the use of headers for both requests and responses is so closely intertwined in some cases that it seemed best to present it this way.

# Client Request Methods

A client request method is a "command" or "request" that a web client issues to a server. You can think of the method as the declaration of what the client's intentions are. There are exceptions, of course, but here are some generalizations:

- You can think of a GET request as meaning that you just want to retrieve a document.

- A HEAD request means that you just want some information about the document, but don't need the document itself.

- A POST request says that you're providing some information of your own (generally used for fill-in forms).

- PUT is used to provide a new or replacement document to be stored on the server.

- DELETE is used to remove a document on the server.

- TRACE asks that proxies declare themselves in the headers, so the client can learn the path that the document took (and thus determine where something might have been garbled or lost).

- OPTIONS is used when the client wants to know what other methods can be used for that document (or for the server at large).

We'll show some examples of each of these seven methods. Other HTTP methods that you may see (LINK, UNLINK, and PATCH) are less clearly defined, so we don't discuss them in this chapter. See the HTTP specification for more information on those methods.

## GET: Retrieve a Document

The GET method requests a document from a specific location on the server. This is the main method used for document retrieval. The response to a GET request can be generated by the server in many ways. For example, the response could come from:

- A file accessible by the web server

- The output of a CGI script or server language like NSAPI or ISAPI

- The result of a server computation, like real-time decompression of online files

- Information obtained from a hardware device, such as a video camera

In this book, we are more concerned about the data returned by a request than with the way the server generated the data. From a client's point of view, the server is a black box that takes in a method, URL, headers, and entity-body as input and generates output that clients process.

After the client uses the GET method in its request, the server responds with a status line, headers, and data requested by the client. If the server cannot process the request, due to an error or lack of authorization, the server usually sends an explanation in the entity-body of the response.

Figure 3-2 shows an example of a successful request. The client sends:

```
GET /index.html HTTP/1.0
User-Agent: Mozilla/1.1N (Macintosh; I; 68K)
Accept: */*
Accept: image/gif
Accept: image/x-xbitmap
Accept: image/jpeg
```

The server responds with:

```
HTTP/1.0 200 OK
Date: Sat, 20-May-95 03:25:12 GMT
Server: NCSA/1.3
MIME-version: 1.0
Content-type: text/html
Last-modified: Wed, 14-Mar-95 18:15:23 GMT
Content-length: 1029
```

*(body of document here)*

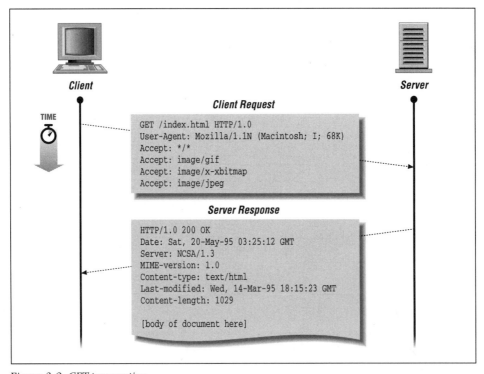

*Figure 3-2. GET transaction*

# *HEAD: Retrieve Header Information*

The HEAD method is functionally like GET, except that the server will reply with a response line and headers, but no entity-body. The headers returned by the server with the HEAD method should be exactly the same as the headers returned with a GET request. This method is often used by web clients to verify the document's existence or properties (like `Content-length` or `Content-type`), but the client has no intention of retrieving the document in the transaction. Many applications exist for the HEAD method, which make it possible to retrieve:

- Modification time of a document for caching purposes

- Size of the document, to do page layout, to estimate arrival time, or to skip the document and retrieve a smaller version of the document

- Type of the document, to allow the client to examine only documents of a certain type

- Type of server, to allow customized server queries

It is important to note that most of the header information provided by a server is optional, and may not be given by all servers. A good design in web clients is to allow flexibility in the server response and to take default actions when desired header information is not given by the server.

Figure 3-3 shows an example HTTP transaction using the HEAD method. The client sends:

```
HEAD /sample.html HTTP/1.0
User-Agent: Mozilla/1.1N (Macintosh; I; 68K)
Accept: */*
Accept: image/gif
Accept: image/x-xbitmap
Accept: image/jpeg
```

The server responds with:

```
HTTP/1.0 200 OK
Date: Sat, 20-May-95 03:25:12 GMT
Server: NCSA/1.3
MIME-version: 1.0
Content-type: text/html
Last-modified: Wed, 14-Mar-95 18:15:23 GMT
Content-length: 1029
```

(Note that the server does not return any data after the headers.)

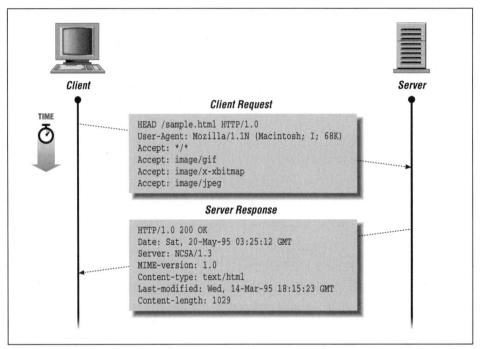

*Figure 3-3. HEAD transaction*

## POST: Send Data to the Server

The POST method allows the client to specify data to be sent to some data-handling program that the server can access. It can be used for many applications. For example, POST could be used to provide input for:

- CGI programs

- Gateways to network services, like an NNTP server

- Command-line interface programs

- Annotation of documents on the server

- Database operations

In practice, POST is used with CGI programs that happen to interface with other resources like network services and command line programs. In the future, POST may be directly interfaced with a wider variety of server resources.

In a POST request, the data sent to the server is in the entity-body of the client's request. After the server processes the POST request and headers, it may pass the entity-body to another program (specified by the URL) for processing. In some cases, a server's custom Application Programming Interface (API) may handle the data, instead of a program external to the server.

POST requests should be accompanied by a **Content-type** header, describing the format of the client's entity-body. The most commonly used format with POST is the URL-encoding scheme used for CGI applications. It allows form data to be translated into a list of variables and values. Browsers that support forms send the data in URL-encoded format. For example, given the HTML form of:

```
<title>Create New Account</title>
<center><hr><h1>Account Creation Form</h1><hr></center>


<form method="post">
<pre>
<b>
Enter user name:          <INPUT NAME="user" MAXLENGTH="20" SIZE="20">
Password:                 <INPUT NAME="pass1" TYPE="password"
                          MAXLENGTH="20" SIZE="20">
(Type it again to verify) <INPUT NAME="pass2" TYPE="password"
                          MAXLENGTH="20" SIZE="20">
</b>
</pre>
<INPUT TYPE="submit" VALUE="Create account">
<input type="reset" value="Start over">
</form>
```

the browser view looks like that in Figure 3-4.

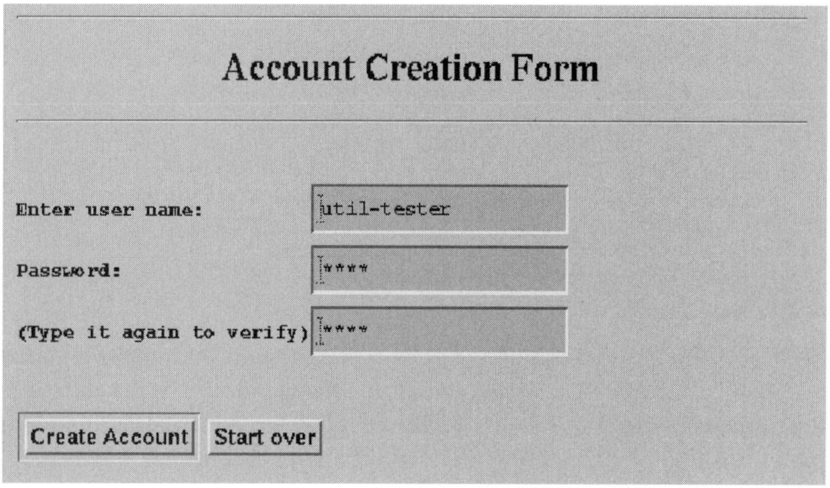

*Figure 3-4. A sample form*

Let's insert some values and submit the form. As the username, "util-tester" was entered. For the password, "1234" was entered (twice). Upon submission, the client sends:

```
POST /cgi-bin/create.pl  HTTP/1.0
Referer: file:/tmp/create.html
User-Agent: Mozilla/1.1N (X11; I; SunOS 5.3 sun4m)
Accept: */*
Accept: image/gif
Accept: image/x-xbitmap
Accept: image/jpeg
Content-type: application/x-www-form-urlencoded
Content-length: 38

user=util-tester&pass1=1234&pass2=1234
```

Note that the variables defined in the form have been associated with the values entered by the user. This information is passed to the server in URL-encoded format, described below.

The server determines that the client used a POST method, processes the URL, executes the program associated with the URL, and pipes the client's entity-body to a program specified at the address of */cgi-bin/create.pl*. The server maps this "web address" to the location of a program, usually in a designated CGI directory (in this case, */cgi-bin*). The CGI program then interprets the input as CGI data, decodes the entity body, processes it, and returns a response entity-body to the client:

```
HTTP/1.0 200 OK
Date: Sat, 20-May-95 03:25:12 GMT
Server: NCSA/1.3
MIME-version: 1.0
Content-type: text/html
Last-modified: Wed, 14-Mar-95 18:15:23 GMT
Content-length: 95

<title>User Created</title>
<h1>The util-tester account has been created</h1>
```

### URL-encoded format

Using the POST method is not the only way that forms send information. Forms can also use the GET method, and append the URL-encoded data to the URL, following a question mark. If the <FORM> tag had contained the line method="get" instead of **method="post"**, the request would have looked like this:

```
GET /cgi-bin/create.pl?user=util-tester&pass1=1234&pass2=1234 HTTP/1.0
Referer: file:/tmp/create.html
User-Agent: Mozilla/1.1N (X11; I; SunOS 5.3 sun4m)
Accept: */*
```

```
Accept: image/gif
Accept: image/x-xbitmap
Accept: image/jpeg
```

This is one reason that the data sent by a CGI program is in a special format: since it can be appended to the URL itself, it cannot contain special characters such as spaces, newlines, etc. For that reason, it is called *URL-encoded*.

The URL-encoded format, identified with a `Content-type` of *application/x-www-form-urlencoded* format by clients, is composed of a single line with variable names and values concatenated together. The variable and value are separated by an equal sign (=), and each variable/value pair is separated by an ampersand symbol (&). In the example given above, there are three variables: *user*, *pass1*, and *pass2*. The values (respectively) are: util-tester, 1234, and 1234. The encoding looks like this:

```
user=util-tester&pass1=1234&pass2=1234
```

When the client wants to send characters that normally have special meanings, like the ampersand and equal sign, the client replaces the characters with a percent sign (%) followed by an ASCII value in hexadecimal (base 16). This removes ambiguity when a special character is used. The only exception, however, is the space character (ASCII 32), which can be encoded as a plus sign (+) as well as %20. Appendix B, *Reference Tables*, contains a listing of all the ASCII characters and their CGI representations.

When the server retrieves information from a form, the server passes it to a CGI program, which then decodes it from URL-encoded format to retrieve the values entered by the user.

### File uploads with POST

POST isn't limited to the *application/x-www-form-urlencoded* content type. For example, consider the following HTML:

```
<form method="post" action="post.pl" enctype="multipart/form-data">
Enter a file to upload:<br>
<input name="thefile" type="file"><br>
<input name="done" type="submit">
</form>
```

This form allows the user to select a file and upload it to the server. Notice that the `<form>` tag contains an `enctype` attribute, specifying an encoding type of *multipart/form-data* instead of the default, *application/x-www-form-urlencoded*. This encoding type will be used by the browser as the content type when the form is submitted. As an example, suppose I create a file called *hi.txt* with the contents of

"hi there" and put it in *c:/temp/*. I use the HTML form to include the file and then hit
the submit button. My browser sends this:

```
POST /cgi-bin/post.pl HTTP/1.0
Referer: http://hypothetical.ora.com/clinton/upload.html
Connection: Keep-Alive
User-Agent: Mozilla/3.01Gold (WinNT; U)
Host: hypothetical.ora.com
Accept: image/gif, image/x-xbitmap, image/jpeg, image/pjpeg, */*
Content-type: multipart/form-data; boundary=-------------------------
11512135131576
Content-Length: 313

---------------------------11512135131576
Content-Disposition: form-data; name="done"

Submit Query
---------------------------11512135131576
Content-Disposition: form-data; name="thefile";
filename="c:\temp\hi.txt"
Content-Type: text/plain

hi there

---------------------------11512135131576--
```

The entity-body of the request is a multipart Multipurpose Internet Mail Extensions (MIME) message. See RFC 1867 for more details.

## *PUT: Store the Entity-Body at the URL*

When a client uses the PUT method, it requests that the included entity-body
should be stored on the server at the requested URL. With HTML editors, it is
possible to publish documents onto the server with a PUT method. Revisiting the
PUT example in Chapter 2, we see an HTML editor with some sample HTML in
the editor (see Figure 3-5).

The user saves the document in *C:/temp/example.html* and publishes it to *http://
publish.ora.com/* (see Figure 3-6).

When the user presses the OK button, the client contacts *publish.ora.com* at port
80 and then sends:

```
PUT /example.html HTTP/1.0
Connection: Keep-Alive
User-Agent: Mozilla/3.0Gold (WinNT; I)
Pragma: no-cache
Host: publish.ora.com
Accept: image/gif, image/x-xbitmap, image/jpeg, image/pjpeg, */*
Content-Length: 307

<!DOCTYPE HTML PUBLIC "-//W3C//DTD HTML 3.2//EN">
```

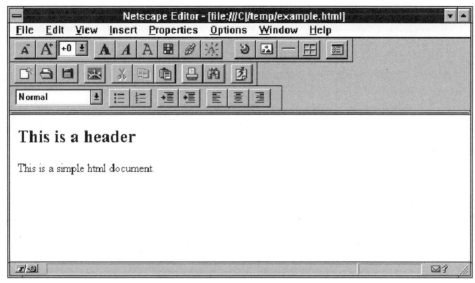

Figure 3-5. HTML editor

Figure 3-6. Publishing the document

```
<HTML>
<HEAD>
   <TITLE></TITLE>
   <META NAME="Author" CONTENT="">
   <META NAME="GENERATOR" CONTENT="Mozilla/3.0Gold (WinNT; I)
[Netscape]">
</HEAD>
<BODY>
```

```
<H2>This is a header</H2>

<P>This is a simple html document.</P>

</BODY>
</HTML>
```

The server stores the client's entity-body at */example.html* and then responds with:

```
HTTP/1.0 201 Created
Date: Fri, 04 Oct 1996 14:31:51 GMT
Server: HypotheticalPublish/1.0
Content-type: text/html
Content-length: 30

<h1>The file was created.</h1>
```

You might have noticed that there isn't a **Content-type** header sent with the browser's request in this example. It's bad style to omit the **Content-type** header. The originator of the information should describe what content type the information is. Other applications, like AOLpress for example, include a **Content-type** header when publishing data with PUT.

In practice, a web server may request authorization from the client. Most webmasters won't allow any arbitrary client to publish documents on the server. When prompted with an "authorization denied" response code, the browser will typically ask the user to enter relevant authorization information. After receiving the information from the user, the browser retransmits the request with additional headers that describe the authorization information.

## *DELETE: Remove URL*

Since PUT creates new URLs on the server, it seems appropriate to have a mechanism to delete URLs as well. The DELETE method works as you would think it would.

A client request might read:

```
DELETE /images/logo22.gif HTTP/1.1
```

The server responds with a success code upon success:

```
HTTP/1.0 200 OK
Date: Fri, 04 Oct 1996 14:31:51 GMT
Server: HypotheticalPublish/1.0
Content-type: text/html
Content-length: 21

<h1>URL deleted.</h1>
```

Needless to say, any server that supports the DELETE method is likely to request authorization before carrying through with the request.

## TRACE: View the Client's Message Through the Request Chain

The TRACE method allows a programmer to see how the client's message is modified as it passes through a series of proxy servers. The recipient of a TRACE method echoes the HTTP request headers back to the client. When the TRACE method is used with the **Max-Forwards** and **Via** headers, a client can determine the chain of intermediate proxy servers between the original client and web server. The **Max-Forwards** request header specifies the number of intermediate proxy servers allowed to pass the request. Each proxy server decrements the **Max-Forwards** value and appends its HTTP version number and hostname to the **Via** header. A proxy server that receives a **Max-Forwards** value of 0 returns the client's HTTP headers as an entity-body with the **Content-type** of *message/http*. This feature resembles *traceroute*, a UNIX program used to identify routers between two machines in an IP-based network. HTTP clients do not send an entity-body when issuing a TRACE request.

Figure 3-7 shows the progress of a TRACE request. After the client makes the request, the first proxy server receives the request, decrements the **Max-Forwards** value by one, adds itself to a **Via** header, and forwards it to the second proxy server. The second proxy server receives the request, adds itself to the **Via** header, and sends the request back, since **Max-Forwards** is now 0 (zero).

## OPTIONS: Request Other Options Available for the URL

When a client request contains the OPTIONS method, it requests a list of options for a particular resource on the server. The client can specify a URL for the OPTIONS method, or an asterisk (*) to refer to the entire server. The server then responds with a list of request methods or other options that are valid for the requested resource, using the **Allow** header for an individual resource, or the **Public** header for the entire server. Figure 3-8 shows an example of the OPTIONS method in action.

# Versions of HTTP

On the same line where the client declares its method, it also declares the URL and the version of HTTP that it conforms to. We've already discussed the available request methods, and we assume that you're already familiar with the URL. But what about the HTTP version number? For example:

```
GET /products/toothpaste/index.html HTTP/1.0
```

In this example, the client uses HTTP version 1.0.

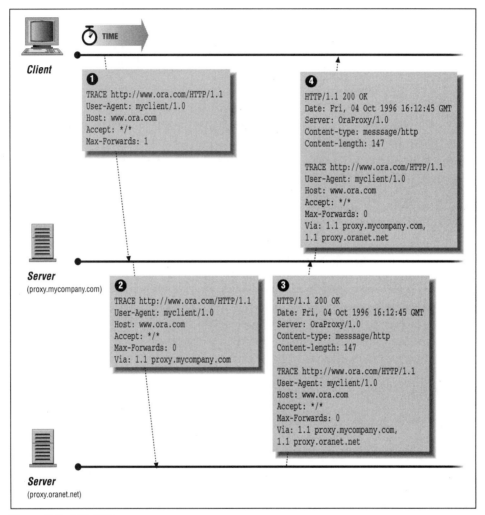

*Figure 3-7. A TRACE request*

In the server's response, the server also declares the HTTP version:

    **HTTP/1.0** 200 OK

By specifying the version number in both the client request and server response, the client and server can communicate on a common denominator, or in the worst case scenario, recognize that the transaction is not possible due to version conflicts. (For example, an HTTP/1.0 client might have a problem communicating with an HTTP/0.9 server.) If a server is capable of understanding a version of HTTP higher than 1.0, it should still be able to reply with a format that HTTP/1.0 clients can understand. Likewise, clients that understand a superset of a server's HTTP should send requests compliant with the server's version of HTTP.

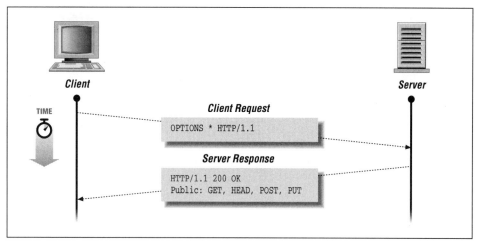

*Figure 3-8. An OPTIONS request*

While there are similarities among the different versions of HTTP, there are many differences, both subtle and glaring. Much of this discussion may not make sense to you if you aren't already familiar with HTTP headers (which are discussed at the end of this chapter). Still, let's go over some of the highlights.

## HTTP 0.9

Version 0.9 is the simplest instance of the HTTP protocol. Under HTTP 0.9, there's only one way a client can request something, and only one way a server responds. The web client connects to a server at port 80 and specifies a method and document path, as follows:

```
GET /hello.html
```

The server then returns the entity-body for */hello.html* and closes the TCP connection. If the document doesn't exist, the server just sends nothing, and the web browser will just display . . . nothing. There is no way for the server to indicate whether the document is empty or whether it doesn't exist at all. HTTP 0.9 includes no headers, version numbers, nor any opportunity for the server to include any information other than the requested entity-body itself. You can't get much simpler than this.

Since there are no headers, HTTP 0.9 doesn't have any notion of media types, so there's no need for the client or server to communicate document preferences or properties. Due to the lack of media types, the HTTP 0.9 world was completely text-based. HTTP 1.0 addressed this limitation with the addition of media types.

In practice, there is no longer any HTTP 0.9 software currently in use. For compatibility reasons, however, web servers using newer versions of HTTP need to honor requests from HTTP 0.9 clients.

## HTTP 1.0

As an upgrade to HTTP 0.9, HTTP 1.0 introduced media types, additional methods, caching mechanisms, authentication, and persistent connections.

By introducing headers, HTTP 1.0 made it possible for clients and servers to exchange "metainformation" about the document or about the software itself. For example, a client could now specify what media it could handle with the `Accept` header and a server could now declare its entity-body's media type with the `Content-type` header. This allowed the client to know what kind of data it was receiving and deal with it accordingly. With the introduction of media types, graphics could be embedded into text documents.

HTTP 1.0 also introduced simple mechanisms to allow caching of server documents. With the `Last-modified` and `If-Modified-Since` headers, a client could avoid the retransmission of cached documents that didn't change on the server. This also allowed proxy servers to cache documents, further relieving servers from the burden of transmitting data when the data is cached.

With the `Authorization` and `WWW-Authenticate` headers, server documents could be selectively denied to the general public and accessed only by those who knew the correct username and password.

## HTTP 1.1

HTTP 1.1's highlights include a better implementation of persistent connections, multihoming, entity tags, byte ranges, and digest authentication.

"Multihoming" means that a server responds to multiple hostnames, and serves from different document roots, depending on which hostname was used. To assist in server multihoming, HTTP 1.1 requires that the client include a `Host` header in all transactions.

Entity tags simplify the caching process by representing each server entity with a unique identifier called an entity tag. The `If-match` and `If-none-match` headers are used to compare two entities for equality or inequality. In HTTP 1.0, caching is based on an entity's document path and modification time. Managing the cache becomes difficult when the same document exists in multiple locations on the server. In HTTP 1.1, the document would have the same entity tag at each location. When the document changes, its entity tag also changes. In addition to entity tags, HTTP 1.1 includes the `Cache-control` header for clients and servers to specify caching behavior.

## *Proxies*

Instead of sending a request directly to a server, it is often necessary for a client to send everything through a proxy. Caching proxies are used to keep local copies of documents that would normally be very expensive to retrieve from distant or overloaded web servers. Proxies are often used with firewalls, to allow clients inside a firewall to communicate beyond it. In this case, a proxy program runs on a machine that can be accessed by computers on both the inside and outside of the firewall. Computers on the inside of a firewall initiate requests with the proxy, and the proxy then communicates to the outside world and returns the results back to the original computer. This type of proxy is used because there is no direct path from the original client computer to the server computer, due to imposed restrictions in the intermediate network between the two systems.

There is little structural difference between the request that a proxy receives and the request that the proxy server passes on to the target server. Perhaps the only important difference is that in the client's request, a full URL must be specified, instead of a relative URL. Here is a typical client request that a client would send to a proxy:

```
GET http://www.ora.com/index.html HTTP/1.0
User-Agent: Mozilla/1.1N (Macintosh; I; 68K)
Accept: */*
Accept: image/gif
Accept: image/x-xbitmap
Accept: image/jpeg
```

The proxy then examines the URL, contacts *www.ora.com*, forwards the client's request, and then returns the response from the server to the original client. When forwarding the request to the web server, the proxy would convert *http://www.ora.com/index.html* to */index.html*.

Byte ranges make it possible for HTTP 1.1 clients to retrieve only part of an entity from a server using the **Range** header. This is particularly useful when the client already has part of the entity and wishes to retrieve the remaining portion of the entity. So when a user interrupts a browser and the transfer of an embedded image is interrupted, a subsequent retrieval of the image starts where the previous transfer left off. Byte ranges also allow the client to selectively read an index of a document and jump to portions of the document without retrieving the entire document. In addition to these features, byte ranges also make it possible to have streaming multimedia, which are video or audio clips that the client reads selectively, in small increments.

In addition to HTTP 1.0's authentication mechanism, HTTP 1.1 includes digest authentication. Instead of sending the username and password in the clear, the client computes a checksum of the username, password, document location, and a unique number given by the server. If a checksum is sent, the username and password are not communicated between the client and server. Since each transaction is given a unique number, the checksum varies from transaction to transaction, and is less likely to be compromised by "playing back" authorization information captured from a previous transaction.

### Persistent connections

One of the most significant differences between HTTP 1.1 and previous versions of HTTP is that persistent connections have become the default behavior in HTTP 1.1. In versions previous to HTTP 1.1, the default behavior for HTTP transactions is for a client to contact a server, send a request, and receive a response, and then both the client and server disconnect the TCP connection. If the client needs another resource on the server, it has to reestablish another TCP connection, request the resource, and disconnect.

In practice, a client may need many resources on the same server, especially when many images are embedded within the same HTML page. By connecting and disconnecting many times, the client wastes time in network overhead. To remedy this, some HTTP 1.0 clients started to use a `Connection` header, although this header never appeared in the official HTTP 1.0 specification. This header, when used with a `keep-alive` value, specifies that the network connection should remain after the initial transaction, provided that both the client and server use the `Connection` header with the value of `keep-alive`.

These "keep-alive" connections, or *persistent* connections, became the default behavior under HTTP 1.1. After a transaction completes, the network connection remains open for another transaction. When either the client or server wishes to end the connection, the last transaction includes a `Connection` header with a `close` parameter.

## Heed the Specifications

While this book gives you a good start on learning how HTTP works, it doesn't have all the details of the full HTTP specifications. Describing all the caveats and details of HTTP 1.0 and 1.1 is, in itself, the topic of a separate book. With that in mind, if there are any questions still lingering in your mind after reading this chapter and Appendix A, *HTTP Headers*, I strongly recommend that you look at the formal protocol specifications at *http://www.w3.org/*. The formal specifications are, well, formal. But after reading this chapter, reading the protocol specs won't be that hard, since you already have many of the concepts that are talked about in the specs.

# Server Response Codes

Now that we've discussed the client's method and version numbers, let's move on to the server's responses. (We'll save discussion of client headers for last, so we can talk about them in conjunction with the related response headers.)

The initial line of the server's response indicates the HTTP version, a three-digit status code, and a human-readable description of the result. Status codes are grouped as follows:

| Code Range | Response Meaning |
|---|---|
| 100-199 | Informational |
| 200-299 | Client request successful |
| 300-399 | Client request redirected, further action necessary |
| 400-499 | Client request incomplete |
| 500-599 | Server errors |

HTTP defines only a few specific codes in each range, although these ranges will become more populated as HTTP evolves.

If a client receives a response code that it does not recognize, it should understand its basic meaning from its numerical range. While most web browsers handle codes in the 100, 200, and 300 ranges silently, some error codes in the 400 and 500 ranges are commonly reported back to the user (e.g., "404 Not Found").

## Informational (100 Range)

Previous to HTTP 1.1, the 100 range of status codes was left undefined. In HTTP 1.1, the 100 range was defined for the server to declare that it is ready for the client to continue with a request, or to declare that it will be switching to another protocol.

Since HTTP 1.1 is still relatively new, few servers are implementing the 100-level status codes at this writing. The status codes currently defined are:

| Code | Meaning |
|---|---|
| 100 Continue: | The initial part of the request has been received, and the client may continue with its request. |
| 101 Switching Protocols: | The server is complying with a client request to switch protocols to the one specified in the `Upgrade` header field. |

## Client Request Successful (200 Range)

The most common response for a successful HTTP transaction is 200 (OK), indicating that the client's request was successful, and the server's response contains the request data. If the request was a GET method, the requested information is returned in the response data section. The HEAD method is honored by returning header information about the URL. The POST method is honored by executing the POST data handler and returning a resulting entity-body.

The following is a complete list of successful response codes:

| Code | Meaning |
| --- | --- |
| 200 OK | The client's request was successful, and the server's response contains the requested data. |
| 201 Created | This status code is used whenever a new URL is created. With this result code, the **Location** header (described in Appendix A) is given by the server to specify where the new data was placed. |
| 202 Accepted | The request was accepted but not immediately acted upon. More information about the transaction may be given in the entity-body of the server's response. There is no guarantee that the server will actually honor the request, even though it may seem like a legitimate request at the time of acceptance. |
| 203 Non-Authoritative Information | The information in the entity header is from a local or third-party copy, not from the original server. |
| 204 No Content | A status code and header are given in the response, but there is no entity-body in the reply. Browsers should not update their document view upon receiving this response. This is a useful code for CGI programs to use when they accept data from a form but want the browser view to stay at the form. |
| 205 Reset Content | The browser should clear the form used for this transaction for additional input. Appropriate for data-entry CGI applications. |
| 206 Partial Content | The server is returning partial data of the size requested. Used in response to a request specifying a **Range** header. The server must specify the range included in the response with the **Content-Range** header. |

## Redirection (300 Range)

When a document has moved, the server might be configured to tell clients where it has been moved to. Clients can then retrieve the new URL silently, without the user knowing. Presumably the client may want to know whether the move is a permanent one or not, so there are two common response codes for moved documents: 301 (Moved Permanently) and 302 (Moved Temporarily).

Ideally, a 301 code would indicate to the client that, from now on, requests for this URL should be sent directly to the new one, thus avoiding unnecessary transactions in the future. Think of it like a change of address card from a friend; the post office is nice enough to forward your mail to your friend's new address for the next year, but it's better to get used to the new address so your mail will get to her faster, and won't start getting returned someday.

A 302 code, on the other hand, just says that the document has moved but will return. If a 301 is a change of address card, a 302 is a note on your friend's door saying she's gone to the movies. Either way, the client should just silently make a new request for the new URL specified by the server in the `Location` header.

The following is a complete list of redirection status codes:

| Code | Meaning |
|------|---------|
| 300 Multiple Choices | The requested URL refers to more than one resource. For example, the URL could refer to a document that has been translated into many languages. The entity-body returned by the server could have a list of more specific data about how to choose the correct resource. The client should allow the user to select from the list of URLs returned by the server, where appropriate. |
| 301 Moved Permanently | The requested URL is no longer used by the server, and the operation specified in the request was not performed. The new location for the requested document is specified in the `Location` header. All future requests for the document should use the new URL. |
| 302 Moved Temporarily | The requested URL has moved, but only temporarily. The `Location` header points to the new location. Immediately after receiving this status code, the client should use the new URL to resolve the request, but the old URL should be used for all future requests. |
| 303 See Other | The requested URL can be found at a different URL (specified in the `Location` header) and should be retrieved by a GET on that resource. |
| 304 Not Modified | This is the response code to an `If-Modified-Since` header, where the URL has not been modified since the specified date. The entity-body is not sent, and the client should use its own local copy. |
| 305 Use Proxy | The requested URL must be accessed through the proxy in the `Location` header. |

## *Client Request Incomplete (400 Range)*

Sometimes the server just can't process the request. Either something was wrong with the document, or something was wrong with the request itself. By far, the server status code that web users are most familiar with is 404 (Not Found), the code returned when the requested document does not exist. This isn't because it's the most common code that servers return, but because it's one of the few codes that the client passes to the user rather than intercepting and handling it in its own way.

For example, when the server sends a 401 (Unauthorized) code, the client does not pass the code directly to the user. Instead, it triggers the client to prompt the user for a username and password, and then resend the request with that information supplied. With the 401 status code, the server supplies the WWW-Authenticate header to specify the authentication scheme and realm it needs authorization for, and the client returns the username and password for that scheme and realm in the Authorization header.

When testing clients you have written yourself, watch out for code 400 (Bad Request), indicating a syntax error in your client's request, and code 405 (Method Not Allowed), which declares that the method the client used for the document is not valid. (Along with the 405 code, the server sends an Allow header, listing the accepted methods for the document.)

The 408 (Request Time-out) code means that the client's request wasn't completed, and the server gave up waiting for the client to finish. A client might receive this code if it did not supply the entity-body properly, or (under HTTP 1.1) if it neglected to supply a Connection: Close header.

The following is a complete listing of status codes implying that the client's request was faulty:

| Code | Meaning |
| --- | --- |
| 400 Bad Request | This response code indicates that the server detected a syntax error in the client's request. |
| 401 Unauthorized | The result code is given along with the WWW-Authenticate header to indicate that the request lacked proper authorization, and the client should supply proper authorization when requesting this URL again. See the description of the Authorization header in this chapter for more information on how authorization works in HTTP. |
| 402 Payment Required | This code is not yet implemented in HTTP. |
| 403 Forbidden | The request was denied for a reason the server does not want to (or has no means to) indicate to the client. |
| 404 Not Found | The document at the specified URL does not exist. |
| 405 Method Not Allowed | This code is given with the Allow header and indicates that the method used by the client is not supported for this URL. |
| 406 Not Acceptable | The URL specified by the client exists, but not in a format preferred by the client. Along with this code, the server provides the Content-Language, Content-Encoding, and Content-type headers. |

| Code | Meaning |
|------|---------|
| 407 Proxy Authentication Required | The proxy server needs to authorize the request before forwarding it. Used with the `Proxy-Authenticate` header. |
| 408 Request Time-out | This response code means the client did not produce a full request within some predetermined time (usually specified in the server's configuration), and the server is disconnecting the network connection. |
| 409 Conflict | This code indicates that the request conflicts with another request or with the server's configuration. Information about the conflict should be returned in the data portion of the reply. For example, this response code could be given when a client's request would cause integrity problems in a database. |
| 410 Gone | This code indicates that the requested URL no longer exists and has been permanently removed from the server. |
| 411 Length Required | The server will not accept the request without a `Content-Length` header supplied in the request. |
| 412 Precondition Failed | The condition specified by one or more `If...` headers in the request evaluated to false. |
| 413 Request Entity Too Large | The server will not process the request because its entity-body is too large. |
| 414 Request Too Long | The server will not process the request because its request URL is too large. |
| 415 Unsupported Media Type | The server will not process the request because its entity-body is in an unsupported format. |

## Server Error (500 Range)

Occasionally, the error might be with the server itself—or, more commonly, with the CGI portion of the server. CGI programmers are painfully familiar with the 500 (Internal Server Error) code, which frequently means that their program crashed. One error that client programmers should pay attention to is 503 (Service Unavailable), which means that their request cannot be performed right now, but the `Retry-After` header (if supplied) indicates when the client might try again.

The following is a complete listing of response codes implying a server error:

| Code | Meaning |
|------|---------|
| 500 Internal Server Error | This code indicates that a part of the server (for example, a CGI program) has crashed or encountered a configuration error. |
| 501 Not Implemented | This code indicates that the client requested an action that cannot be performed by the server. |
| 502 Bad Gateway | This code indicates that the server (or proxy) encountered invalid responses from another server (or proxy). |

| Code | Meaning |
|------|---------|
| 503 Service Unavailable | This code means that the service is temporarily unavailable, but should be restored in the future. If the server knows when it will be available again, a `Retry-After` header may also be supplied. |
| 504 Gateway Time-out | This response is like 408 (Request Time-out) except that a gateway or proxy has timed out. |
| 505 HTTP Version Not Supported | The server will not support the HTTP protocol version used in the request. |

# HTTP Headers

Now we're ready for the meat of HTTP: the headers that clients and servers can use to exchange information about the data, or about the software itself.

If the Web were just a matter of retrieving documents blindly, then HTTP 0.9 would have been sufficient for all our needs. But as it turns out, there's a whole set of information we'd like to exchange in addition to the documents themselves. A client might ask the server, "What kind of document are you sending?" Or, "I already have an older copy of this document—do I need to bother you for a new one?"

A server may want to know, "Who are you?" Or, "Who sent you here?" Or, "How am I supposed to know you're allowed to be here?"

All this extra ("meta-") information is passed between the client and server using HTTP headers. The headers are specified immediately after the initial line of the transaction (which is used for the client request or server response line). Any number of headers can be specified, followed by a blank line and then the entity-body itself (if any).

HTTP makes a distinction between four different types of headers:

- *General headers* indicate general information such as the date, or whether the connection should be maintained. They are used by both clients and servers.

- *Request headers* are used only for client requests. They convey the client's configuration and desired document format to the server.

- *Response headers* are used only in server responses. They describe the server's configuration and special information about the requested URL.

- *Entity headers* describe the document format of the data being sent between client and server. Although Entity headers are most commonly used by the server when returning a requested document, they are also used by clients when using the POST or PUT methods.

Headers from all three categories may be specified in any order. Header names are case-insensitive, so the `Content-Type` header is also frequently written as `Content-type`.

In the remainder of this chapter, we'll list all the headers, and then discuss the ones that are most interesting, in context. Appendix A contains a full listing of headers, with examples for each and additional information on its syntax and purpose when applicable.

| General Headers | |
| --- | --- |
| Cache-Control | Specifies behavior for caching |
| Connection | Indicates whether network connection should close after this connection |
| Date | Specifies the current date |
| MIME-Version | Specifies the version of MIME used in the HTTP transaction |
| Pragma | Specifies directives to a proxy system |
| Transfer-Encoding | Indicates what type of transformation has been applied to the message body for safe transfer |
| Upgrade | Specifies the preferred communication protocols |
| Via | Used by gateways and proxies to indicate the protocols and hosts that processed the transaction between client and server |
| **Request Headers** | |
| Accept | Specifies media formats that the client can accept |
| Accept-Charset | Tells the server the types of character sets that the client can handle |
| Accept-Encoding | Specifies the encoding schemes that the client can accept, such as *compress* or *gzip* |
| Accept-Language | Specifies the language in which the client prefers the data |
| Authorization | Used to request restricted documents |
| Cookie | Used to convey *name=value* pairs stored for the server |
| From | Indicates the email address of the user executing the client |
| Host | Specifies the host and port number that the client connected to. This header is required for all clients in HTTP 1.1. |
| If-Modified-Since | Requests the document only if newer than the specified date |
| If-Match | Requests the document only if it matches the given entity tags |
| If-None-Match | Requests the document only if it does not match the given entity tags |
| If-Range | Requests only the portion of the document that is missing, if it has not been changed |

| If-Unmodified-Since | Requests the document only if it has not been changed since the given date |
| Max-Forwards | Limits the number of proxies or gateways that can forward the request |
| Proxy-Authorization | Used to identify client to a proxy requiring authorization |
| Range | Specifies only the specified partial portion of the document |
| Referer | Specifies the URL of the document that contained the link to this one (i.e., the previous document) |
| User-Agent | Identifies the client program |

**Response Headers**

| Accept-Ranges | Declares whether or not the server accepts range requests, and if so, what units |
| Age | Indicates the age of the document in seconds |
| Proxy-Authenticate | Declares the authentication scheme and realm for the proxy |
| Public | Contains a comma-separated list of supported methods other than those specified in HTTP/1.0 |
| Retry-After | Specifies either the number of seconds or a date after which the server becomes available again |
| Server | Specifies the name and version number of the server |
| Set-Cookie | Defines a *name=value* pair to be associated with this URL |
| Vary | Specifies that the document may vary according to the value of the specified headers |
| Warning | Gives additional information about the response, for use by caching proxies |
| WWW-Authenticate | Specifies the authorization type and the realm of the authorization |

**Entity Headers**

| Allow | Lists valid methods that can be used with a URL |
| Content-Base | Specifies the base URL for resolving relative URLs |
| Content-Encoding | Specifies the encoding scheme used for the entity |
| Content-Language | Specifies the language used in the document being returned |
| Content-Length | Specifies the length of the entity |
| Content-Location | Contains the URL for the entity, when a document might have several different locations |
| Content-MD5 | Contains a MD5 digest of the data |
| Content-Range | When a partial document is being sent in response to a Range header, specifies where the data should be inserted |
| Content-Transfer-Encoding | Identifies the transfer encoding used in the document |
| Content-Type | Specifies the media type of the entity |
| Etag | Gives an entity tag for the document |

| | |
|---|---|
| Expires | Gives a date and time that the contents may change |
| Last-Modified | Gives the date and time that the entity last changed |
| Location | Specifies the location of a created or moved document |
| URI | A more generalized version of the `Location` header |

So what do you do with all this? The remainder of the chapter discusses many of the larger topics that are managed by HTTP headers.

## *Persistent Connections*

As we touched on earlier, one of the big changes in HTTP 1.1 is that persistent connections became the default. Persistent connections mean that the network connection remains open during multiple transactions between client and server. Under both HTTP 1.0 and 1.1, the `Connection` header controls whether or not the network stays open; however, its use varies according to the version of HTTP.

The `Connection` header indicates whether the network connection will be maintained after the current transaction finishes. The `close` parameter signifies that either the client or server wishes to end the connection (i.e., this is the last transaction). The `keep-alive` parameter signifies that the client wishes to keep the connection open. Under HTTP 1.0, the default is to close connections after each transaction, so the client must use the following header in order to maintain the connection for an additional request:

```
Connection: Keep-Alive
```

Under HTTP 1.1, the default is to keep connections open until they are explicitly closed. The `Keep-Alive` option is therefore unnecessary under HTTP 1.1; however, clients must be sure to include the following header in their last transaction:

```
Connection: Close
```

or the connection will remain open until the server times out. How long it takes the server to time out depends on the server's configuration … but needless to say, it's more considerate to close the connection explicitly.

## *Media Types*

One of the most important functions of headers is to make it possible for the client to know what kind of data is being served, and thus be able to process it appropriately. If the client didn't know that the data being sent is a GIF, it wouldn't know how to render it on the screen. If it didn't know that some other data was an audio snippet, it wouldn't know to call up an external helper application. For negotiating different data types, HTTP incorporated Internet Media

Types, which look a lot like MIME types but are not exactly MIME types. Appendix B gives a listing of media types used on the Web.

The way media types work is that the client tells the server which types it can handle, using the `Accept` header. The server tries to return information in a preferred media type, and declares the type of the data using the `Content-Type` header.

The `Accept` header is used to specify the client's preference for media formats, or to tell the server that it can accept unusual document types. If this header is omitted, the server assumes that the client can accept any media type. The `Accept` header can have three general forms:

```
Accept: */*
Accept: type/*
Accept: type/subtype
```

Using the first form, `*/*`, indicates that the client can accept an entity-body of any media type. The second form, *type/**, communicates that an entity-body of a certain general class is acceptable. For example, a client may issue an `Accept: image/*` to accept images, where the type of image (GIF, JPEG, or whatever) is not important. The third form indicates that an entity-body from a certain type and subtype is acceptable. For example, a browser that can only accept GIF files may use `Accept: image/gif`.

The client specifies multiple document types that it can accept by separating the values with commas:

```
Accept: image/gif, image/x-xbitmap, image/jpeg, image/pjpeg, */*
```

Some older browsers send the same line as:

```
Accept: image/gif
Accept: image/x-xbitmap
Accept: image/jpeg
Accept: image/pjpeg
Accept: */*
```

When developing a new application, it is recommended that it conform to the newer practice of separating multiple document preferences by commas, with a single `Accept` header.

In the server's response, the `Content-type` header describes the type and subtype of the media. If the client specified an `Accept` header, the media type should conform to the values used in the `Accept` header. Clients use this information to correctly handle the media type and format of the entity-body.

A client might also use a `Content-type` header with the POST or PUT method. Most commonly, with many CGI applications, clients use a POST or PUT request with information in the entity-body, and supply a `Content-type` header to describe what data can be expected in the entity-body.

## Client Caching

If we each went to a single document once in a lifetime, or even once a day, life could be much simpler for web programmers. But in reality, we tend to return to the same documents over and over again. Simple clients can just keep retrieving data over and over again, but robust clients will prefer to store local copies of documents to improve efficiency. This is called *caching*.

On sites with proxy servers, the proxies can also work as caches. So several users on that site might all share the same copy of the document, which the proxy stores locally. If you call up a URL that someone else requested earlier this morning, the proxy can simply give you that copy, meaning that you retrieve the data much faster, help to reduce network traffic, and prevent overburdening the server containing the document's source. It's sort of like carpooling at rush hour: caches do their part to make the web a better place for all of us.*

A complication with caching, however, is that the client or proxy needs to know when the document has changed on the server. So for cache management, HTTP provides a whole set of headers. There are two general systems: one based on the age of the document, and a much newer one based on unique identifiers for each document.

Also, when caching, you should pay attention to the `Cache-Control` and `Pragma` headers. Some documents aren't appropriate for caching, either for security reasons or because they are dynamic documents (e.g., created on the fly by a CGI script). Under HTTP 1.0, the `Pragma` header was used with the value `no-cache` to tell caching proxies and clients not to cache the document. Under HTTP 1.1, the `Cache-Control` header supplants `Pragma`, with several caching directives in addition to `no-cache`. See Appendix A for more information.

### If-Modified-Since, et al.

To accommodate client-side caching of documents, the client can use the `If-Modified-Since` header with the GET method. When using this option, the client requests the server to send the requested information associated with the URL only if it has been modified since a client-specified time.

---

* On the other hand, sometimes it takes longer to pick up everyone in a carpool than it would take to drive to work alone. This sometimes happens with caching proxy servers, where it takes longer to go through the cache than it takes to fetch a new copy of the document. Your mileage will vary.

If the document was modified, the server will give a status code of 200 and will send the document in the entity-body of its reply. If the document was not modified, the server will give a response code of 304 (Not Modified).

An example `If-Modified-Since` header might read:

```
If-Modified-Since: Fri, 02-Jun-95 02:42:43 GMT
```

The same formats accepted for the `Date` header (listed in Appendix A) are used for the `If-Modified-Since` header.

If the server returns a code of 304, the document has not been modified since the specified time. The client can use the cached version of the document. If the document is newer, the server will send it along with a 200 (OK) code. Servers may also include a `Last-Modified` header with the document, to let the user know when the last change was made to the document.*

Another related client header is `If-Unmodified-Since`, which says to only send the document if it *hasn't* been changed since the specified date. This is useful for ensuring that the data is exactly the way you wanted it to be. For example, if you GET a document from a server, make changes in a publishing tool, and PUT it back to the server, you can use the `If-Unmodified-Since` header to verify that the changes you made are accepted by the server only if the previous one you were looking at is still there.

If the server contains an `Expires` header, the client can take it as an indication that the document will not change before the specified time. Although there are no guarantees, it means that the client does not have to ask the server about the last modified date of the document again until after the expiration date.

### Entity tags

In HTTP 1.1, a new method of cache management is introduced with *entity tags*. The problem solved by entity tags is that there may be several copies of the identical document on the server. The client has no way to know that it's the same document—so even if it already has an equivalent, it will request it again.

Entity tags are unique identifiers that can be associated with all copies of the document. If the document is changed, the entity tag is changed—so a more efficient way of cache management is to check for the entity tag, not for the URL and date.

---

* Not to be confused with the `Age` header. If you make a request to a web server, get a response, and wait 20 seconds, the age of the response is 20 seconds. If you get a document last modified on 02-Jun-95 02:42:43 GMT and has not been modified since, then the last modified date stays the same, even though those 20 seconds go by.

If the server is using entity tags, it sends the document with the ETag header. When the client wants to verify the cache, it uses the If-Match or If-None-Match headers to check against the entity tag for that resource.

## Retrieving Content

The Content-length header specifies the length of the data (in bytes) that is returned by the client-specified URL. Due to the dynamic nature of some requests, the Content-length is sometimes unknown, and this header might be omitted.

There are three common ways that a client can retrieve data from the entity-body of the server's response:

- The first way is to get the size of the document from the Content-length header, and then read in that much data. Using this method, the client knows the size of the document before retrieving it, and can allocate a buffer to fit the exact size.

- In other cases, when the size of the document is too dynamic for a server to predict, the Content-length header is omitted. When this happens, the client reads in the data portion of the server's response until the server disconnects the network connection.* This is the most flexible way to retrieve data, but the client can make no assumptions about the size until the server disconnects the session.

- Another header could indicate when an entity-body ends, like HTTP 1.1's Transfer-Encoding header with the chunked parameter.

When a client is involved in a client-pull/server-push operation, it may be possible that there is no end to the entity-body. For example, a client program may be reading in a continuous feed of news 24 hours a day, or receiving continuous frames of a video broadcast. In practice, this is rarely done, at least not for long periods of time, since it is an expensive consumer of network bandwidth and connect time. In the event that an endless entity-body is undesirable, the client software should have options to configure the maximum time spent (or data received) from a given entity-body.

### Byte ranges

In HTTP 1.1, the client does not have to get the entire entity-body at once, but can get it in pieces, if the server allows it to do so. If the server declares that it supports byte ranges using the Accept-Ranges header:

---

* This only works in HTTP 1.0. In HTTP 1.1, both client and server need a clear understanding of the request/response length, so they can anticipate where the beginning of the next request/response happens.

```
HTTP/1.1 200 OK
[Other headers here]
Accept-Ranges: bytes
```

then the client can request the data in pieces, like so:

```
GET /largefile.html HTTP/1.1
[Other headers here]
Range: 0-65535
```

When the server returns the specified range, it includes a **Content-range** header to indicate which portion of the document is being sent, and also to tell the client how long the file is:

```
HTTP/1.1 200 OK
[Other headers here]
Content-range: 0-65535/83028576
```

The client can use this information to give the user some idea of how long she'll have to wait for the document to be complete.

For caching purposes, a client can use the **If-Range** header along with **Range** to request an updated portion of the document only if the document has been changed. For example:

```
GET /largefile.html HTTP/1.1
[Other headers here]
If-Range: Mon, 02 May 1996 04:51:00 GMT
Range: 0-65535
```

The **If-Range** header can use either a last modified date or an entity tag to verify that the document is still the same.

## Referring Documents

The **Referer** header indicates which document referred to the one currently specified in this request. This helps the server keep track of documents that refer to malformed or missing locations on the server.

For example, if the client opens a connection to *www.ora.com* at port 80 and sends:

```
GET /contact.html HTTP/1.0
Accept: */*
```

the server may respond with:

```
HTTP/1.0 200 OK
Date: Sat, 20-May-95 03:32:38 GMT
MIME-version: 1.0
Content-type: text/html

<h1>Contact Information</h1>
<a href="http://sales.ora.com/sales.html"> Sales Department</a>
```

The user clicks on the hyperlink and the client requests "sales.html" from *sales.ora.com*, specifying that it was sent there from the */contact.html* document on *www.ora.com*:

```
GET /sales.html HTTP/1.0
Accept: */*
Referer: http://www.ora.com/contact.html
```

It is important to design clients that specify only public locations in the **Referer** header to other public documents. The client should never specify a private document (i.e., accessible only through proper authentication) when requesting a public document. Even the name of a sensitive document may be considered a security breach.

## Client and Server Identification

Clients and servers like to know whom they're talking to. Servers know that different clients have different capabilities, and would like to tailor their content for the best effect. For example, sites with JavaScript content would like to know whether you're a JavaScript-capable client, and serve JavaScript-enhanced HTML when possible. There isn't anything in HTTP that describes which languages the browsers understand,* but a server with a properly updated database of browser names could make an informed guess.

Similarly, clients sometimes want to know what kind of server is running. It might know that the latest version of Apache supports byte ranges, or that there's a bug to avoid in a version of some unnamed server. And then there are times when a proxy server would like to block requests from certain browsers—not for the sake of browser-bashing, but usually for the sake of security, when there are known security bugs in a certain version of a browser.

Clients can identify themselves with the **User-Agent** header. The **User-Agent** header specifies the name of the client and other optional components, such as version numbers or subcomponents licensed from other companies. The header may consist of one or more names separated by a space, where each name can contain an optional slash and version number. Optional components of the **User-Agent** might be the type of machine, operating system, or plug-in components of the client program. For example:

```
User-Agent: Mozilla/1.1N (Macintosh; I; 68K)
User-Agent: HTML-checker/1.0
```

Beware that there have been well-documented instances in which clients have lied about who they are—not out of malice (they claim) but because they had

---

* At least not in HTTP 1.0 or 1.1.

implemented all the features of their competitor, and wanted to make sure that they were served HTML that was tailored for that competitor.

Servers identify themselves using the **Server** header. The **Server** header may help clients make inferences about what types of methods and parameters the server can accept, based on the server name and version number.

## Authorization

An **Authorization** header is used to request restricted documents. Upon first requesting a restricted document, the web client requests the document without sending an **Authorization** header. If the server denies access to the document, the server specifies the authorization method for the client to use with the **WWW-Authenticate** header, described later in this chapter. At this point, the client requests the document again, but with an **Authorization** header.

The authorization header is of the general form:

```
Authorization: SCHEME REALM
```

The authorization scheme generally used in HTTP is BASIC, and under the BASIC scheme the credentials follow the format *username:password* encoded in base64. For example, for the username of "webmaster" and a password of "zrqma4v", the authorization header would look like this:

```
Authorization: Basic d2VibWFzdGVyOnpycW1hNHY=
```

When "d2VibWFzdGVyOnpycW1hNHY=" is decoded using base 64, it translates into **webmaster:zrqma4v**.

Here's a verbose example:

When a client requests information that is secure, the server responds with response code 401 (Unauthorized) and an appropriate **WWW-Authenticate** header describing the type of authentication required:

```
GET /sample.html HTTP/1.0
User-Agent: Mozilla/1.1N (Macintosh; I; 68K)
Accept: */*
Accept: image/gif
Accept: image/x-xbitmap
Accept: image/jpeg
```

The server then declares that further authorization is required to access the URL:

```
HTTP/1.0 401 Unauthorized
Date: Sat, 20-May-95 03:32:38 GMT
Server: NCSA/1.3
MIME-version: 1.0
Content-type: text/html
WWW-Authenticate:  BASIC realm="System Administrator"
```

The client now seeks authentication information. Interactive GUI-based browsers might prompt the user for a user name and password in a dialog box. Other clients might just get the information from an online file or a hardware device.

The realm of the BASIC authentication scheme indicates the type of authentication requested. Each realm is defined by the web administrator of the site and indicates a class of users: administrators, CGI programmers, registered users, or anything else that separates one class of authorization from another. In this case, the realm is for system administrators. After encoding the data appropriately for the BASIC authorization method, the client resends the request with proper authorization:

```
GET /sample.html HTTP/1.0
User-Agent: Mozilla/1.1N (Macintosh; I; 68K)
Accept: */*
Accept: image/gif
Accept: image/x-xbitmap
Accept: image/jpeg
Authorization: BASIC d2VibWFzdGVyOnpycW1hNHY=
```

The server checks the authorization, and upon successful authentication, sends the requested data:

```
HTTP/1.0 200 OK
Date: Sat, 20-May-95 03:25:12 GMT
Server: NCSA/1.3
MIME-version: 1.0
Content-type: text/html
Last-modified: Wednesday, 14-Mar-95 18:15:23 GMT
Content-length: 1029

[Entity-body data]
```

In HTTP 1.1, there's also something called `Digest` authentication. See *http://www.w3.org/* for details.

## Cookies

Persistent state, client-side cookies were introduced by Netscape Navigator to enable a server to store client-specific information on the client's machine, and use that information when a server or a particular page is accessed again by the client. The cookie mechanism allows servers to personalize pages for each client, or remember selections the client has made when browsing through various pages of a site. Cookies are not part of the HTTP specification; however, their use is so entrenched throughout the Web today that all HTTP programmers should be aware of the `Set-Cookie` and `Cookie` headers, even if they choose not to honor them.

Cookies work in the following way: When a server (or CGI program running on a server) identifies a new user, it adds the `Set-Cookie` header to its response, containing an identifier for that user and other information that the server may glean from the client's input. The client is expected to store the information from the `Set-Cookie` header on disk, associated with the URL that assigned that cookie. In subsequent requests to that URL, the client should include the cookie information using the `Cookie` header. The server or CGI program uses this information to return a document tailored to that specific client. The cookies should be stored on the client user's system, so the information remains even when the client has been terminated and restarted.

For example, the client may fill in a form opening a new account. The request might read:

```
POST /www.whosis.com/order.pl HTTP/1.0
[Client headers here]

type=new&firstname=Linda&lastname=Mui
```

The server stores this information along with a new account ID, and sends it back in the response:

```
HTTP/1.0 200 OK
[Server headers here]
Set-Cookie: acct=04382374
```

The client saves the cookie information along with the URL. For example, a cookies file might contain the line:

```
www.whosis.com/order.pl acct=04382374
```

Days or months later, when the client returns to the site to place another order, the client should recognize the URL and append the cookie to its headers:

```
GET /www.whosis.com/order.pl
[Client headers here]
Cookie: acct=04382374
```

The server retrieves the cookie, grabs the customer's data from an internal database, and the order form the client receives may already have her ordering information filled in.

# 4

# *The Socket Library*

The socket library is a low-level programmer's interface that allows clients to set up a TCP/IP connection and communicate directly to servers. Servers use sockets to listen for incoming connections, and clients use sockets to initiate transactions on the port that the server is listening on.

Do you really need to know about sockets? Possibly not. In Chapter 5, *The LWP Library*, we cover LWP, a library that includes a simple framework for connecting to and communicating over the Web, making knowledge of the underlying network communication superfluous. If you plan to use LWP you can probably skip this chapter for now (and maybe forever).

Compared to using something like LWP, working with sockets is a tedious undertaking. While it gives you the power to say whatever you want through your network connection, you need to be really careful about what you say; if it's not fully compliant with the HTTP specs, the web server won't understand you! Perhaps your web client works with one web server but not another. Or maybe your web client works most of the time, but not in special cases. Writing a fully compliant application could become a real headache. A programmer's library like LWP will figure out which headers to use, the parameters with each header, and special cases like dealing with HTTP version differences and URL redirections. With the socket library, you do all of this on your own. To some degree, writing a raw client with the socket library is like reinventing the wheel.

However, some people may be forced to use sockets because LWP is unavailable, or because they just prefer to do things by hand (the way some people prefer to make spaghetti sauce from scratch). This chapter covers the socket calls that you can use to establish HTTP connections independently of LWP. At the end of the chapter are some extended examples using sockets that you can model your own programs on.

# A Typical Conversation over Sockets

The basic idea behind sockets (as with all TCP-based client/server services) is that the server sits and waits for connections over the network to the port in question. When a client connects to that port, the server accepts the connection and then converses with the client using whatever protocol they agree on (e.g., HTTP, NNTP, SMTP, etc.).

Initially, the server uses the *socket()* system call to create the socket, and the *bind()* call to assign the socket to a particular port on the host. The server then uses the *listen()* and *accept()* routines to establish communication on that port.

On the other end, the client also uses the *socket()* system call to create a socket, and then the *connect()* call to initiate a connection associated with that socket on a specified remote host and port.

The server uses the *accept()* call to intercept the incoming connection and initiate communication with the client. Now the client and server can each use *sysread()* and *syswrite()* calls to speak HTTP, until the transaction is over.

Instead of using *sysread()* and *syswrite()*, you can also just read from and write to the socket as you would any other file handle (e.g., *print <FH>;*).

Finally, either the client or server uses the *close()* or *shutdown()* routine to end the connection.

Figure 4-1 shows the flow of a sockets transaction.

# Using the Socket Calls

The socket library is part of the standard Perl distribution. Include the socket module like this:

```
use Socket;
```

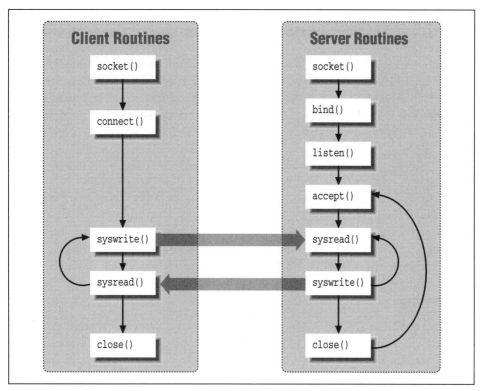

*Figure 4-1. Socket calls*

Table 4-1 lists the socket calls available using the socket library in Perl.

*Table 4-1. Socket Calls*

| Function | Usage | Purpose |
|----------|-------|---------|
| *socket()* | Both client and server | Create a generic I/O buffer in the operating system |
| *connect()* | Client only | Establish a network connection and associate it with the I/O buffer created by *socket()* |
| *sysread()* | Both client and server | Read data from the network connection |
| *syswrite()* | Both client and server | Write data to the network connection |
| *close()* | Both client and server | Terminate communication |
| *bind()* | Server only | Associate a socket buffer with a port on the machine |
| *listen()* | Server only | Wait for incoming connection from a client |
| *accept()* | Server only | Accept the incoming connection from client |

Conceptually, think of a socket as a "pipe" between the client and server. Data written to one end of the pipe appears on the other end of the pipe. To create a pipe, call *socket()*. To write data into one end of the pipe, call *syswrite()*. To read on the other end of the pipe, call *sysread()*. Finally, to dispose of the pipe and cease communication between the client and server, call *close()*.

Since this book is primarily about client programming, we'll talk about the socket calls used by clients first, followed by the calls that are only used on the server end. Although we're only writing client programs, we cover both client and server functions, for the sake of showing how the library fits together.

## Initializing the Socket

Both the client and server use the *socket()* function to create a generic "pipe" or I/O buffer in the operating system. The *socket()* call takes several arguments, specifying which file handle to associate with the socket, what the network protocol is, and whether the socket should be stream-oriented or record-oriented. For HTTP transactions, sockets are stream-oriented connections running TCP over IP, so HTTP-based applications must associate these characteristics with a newly created socket.

For example, in the following line, the SH file handle is associated with the newly created socket. *PF_INET* indicates the Internet Protocol while *getproto-byname('tcp')* indicates that the Transmission Control Protocol (TCP) runs on top of IP. Finally, *SOCK_STREAM* indicates that the socket is stream-oriented, as opposed to record-oriented:

```
socket(SH, PF_INET, SOCK_STREAM, (getprotobyname('tcp'))[2]) || die $!;
```

If the socket call fails, the program should *die()* using the error message found in $!.

## Establishing a Network Connection

Calling *connect()* attempts to contact a server at a desired host and port. The configuration information is stored in a data structure that is passed to *connect()*.

```
my $sin = sockaddr_in (80,inet_aton('www.ora.com'));
connect(F,$sin) || die $!;
```

The *Socket::sockaddr_in()* routine accepts a port number as the first parameter and a 32-bit IP address as the second number. *Socket::inet_aton()* translates a hostname string or dotted decimal string to a 32-bit IP address. *Socket::sockaddr_in()* returns a data structure that is then passed to *connect()*. From there, *connect()* attempts to establish a network connection to the specified server and port. Upon successful connection, it returns true. Otherwise, it returns false upon error and assigns $! with an error message.

After defining the data structure, *connect()* associates its information with the socket and attempts to contact the server at the specified host and port. Upon error, programs should terminate with an error code:

```
connect(SH, $dest) || die $!;
```

## Writing Data to a Network Connection

To write to the file handle associated with the open socket connection, use the *syswrite()* routine. The first parameter is the file handle to write the data to. The data to write is specified as the second parameter. Finally, the third parameter is the length of the data to write. Like this:

```
$buffer="hello world!";
syswrite(FH, $buffer, length($buffer));
```

An easier way to communicate is with *print.* When used with an autoflushed file handle, the result is the same as calling *syswrite().* The *print* command is more flexible than *syswrite()* because the programmer can specify more complex string expressions that are difficult to specify in *syswrite().* Using *print,* the previous example looks like this:

```
select(FH);
$|=1;                  # set $| to non-zero to make selection autoflushed
print FH "hello world!";
```

## Reading Data From a Network Connection

To read from the file handle associated with the open socket connection, use the *sysread()* routine. In the first parameter, a file handle is given to specify the connection to read from. The second parameter specifies a scalar variable to store the data that was read. Finally, the third parameter specifies the maximum number of bytes you want to read from the connection. The *sysread()* routine returns the number of bytes actually read:

```
sysread(FH, $buffer, 200);  # read at most 200 bytes from FH
```

If you want to read a line at a time from the file handle, you can also use the angle operator on it, like so:

```
$buffer = <FH>;
```

## Closing the Connection

After the network transaction is complete, *close()* disconnects the network connection.

```
close(FH);
```

# Server Socket Calls

The following functions set the socket in server mode and map a client's incoming request to a file handle. After a client request has been accepted, all subsequent communication with the client is referenced through the file handle with *sysread()* and *syswrite()*, as described earlier.

## Binding to the Port

A sockets-based server application first creates the socket as follows:

```
my $proto = getprotobyname('tcp');
socket(F, PF_INET, SOCK_STREAM, $proto) || die $!;
```

Next, the program calls *bind()* to associate the socket with a port number on the machine. If another program is already using the port, *bind()* returns a false (zero) value. Here, we use *sockaddr_in()* to identify the port for *bind()*. (We use port 80, the traditional port for HTTP.)

```
my $sin = sockaddr_in(80,INADDR_ANY);
bind(F,$sin)  || die $!;
```

## Waiting for a Connection

The *listen()* function tells the operating system that the server is ready to accept incoming network connections on the port. The first parameter is the file handle of the socket to listen to. In the event that multiple client programs are connecting to the port at the same time, a queue of network connections is maintained by the operating system. The queue length is specified in the second parameter:

```
listen(F, $length) || die $!;
```

## Accepting a Connection

The *accept()* function waits for an incoming request to the server. For parameters, *accept()* uses two file handles. The one we've been dealing with so far is a generic file handle associated with the socket. In the above example code, we've called it F. This is passed in as the second parameter. The first parameter is a file handle that *accept()* will associate with a specific network connection.

```
accept(FH,F)  || die $!;
```

So when a client connects to the server, *accept()* associates the client's connection with the file handle passed in as the first parameter. The second parameter, F, still refers to a generic socket that is connected to the designated port and is not specifically connected to any clients.

You can now read and write to the filehandle to communicate with the client. In this example, the filehandle is **FH**. For example:

```
print FH "HTTP/1.0 404 Not Found\n";
```

# Client Connection Code

The following Perl function encapsulates all the necessary code needed to establish a network connection to a server. As input, *open_TCP()* requires a file handle as a first parameter, a hostname or dotted decimal IP address as the second parameter, and a port number as the third parameter. Upon successfully connecting to the server, *open_TCP()* returns 1. Otherwise, it returns **undef** upon error.

```perl
############
# open_TCP #
############
#
# Given ($file_handle, $dest, $port) return 1 if successful, undef when
# unsuccessful.
#
# Input: $fileHandle is the name of the filehandle to use
#         $dest is the name of the destination computer,
#                 either IP address or hostname
#         $port is the port number
#
# Output: successful network connection in file handle
#

use Socket;

sub open_TCP
{
  # get parameters
  my ($FS, $dest, $port) = @_;

  my $proto = getprotobyname('tcp');
  socket($FS, PF_INET, SOCK_STREAM, $proto);
  my $sin = sockaddr_in($port,inet_aton($dest));
  connect($FS,$sin) || return undef;

  my $old_fh = select($FS);
  $| = 1;          # don't buffer output
  select($old_fh);
  1;
}
1;
```

## Using the open_TCP() Function

Let's try out the function. In the following code, you will need to include the *open_TCP()* function. You can include it in the same file or put it in another file and use the *require* directive to include it. If you put it in a separate file and *require* it, remember to put a "1;" as the last line of the file that is being required. In the following example, we've placed the *open_TCP()* routine into another file (*tcp.pl*, for lack of imagination), and *required* it along with the socket library itself:

```
#!/usr/local/bin/perl
use Socket;
require "tcp.pl";
```

Once the socket library and *open_TCP()* routine are included, the example below uses *open_TCP()* to establish a connection to port 13 on the local machine:

```
# connect to daytime server on the machine this client is running on
if (open_TCP(F, "localhost", 13) == undef) {
  print "Error connecting to server\n";
  exit(-1);
}
```

If the local machine is running the *daytime* server, which most UNIX systems and some NT systems run, *open_TCP()* returns successfully. Then, output from the *daytime* server is printed:

```
# if there is any input, echo it
print $_ while (<F>);
```

Then we close the connection.

```
close(F);
```

After running the program, you should see the local time, for example:

```
Tue Jun 14 00:03:12 1996
```

This can also be done by using *telnet* to connect to port 13:

```
(intense) /homes/apm> telnet localhost 13
Trying 127.0.0.1...
Connected to localhost.
Escape character is '^'.
Tue Jun 14 00:03:12 1996
Connection closed by foreign host.
```

# Your First Web Client

Let's modify the previous code to work with a web server instead of the *daytime* server. Also, instead of embedding the machine name of the server into the source code, let's modify the code to accept a hostname from the user on the command line. Since port 80 is the standard port that web servers use, we'll use port 80 in the code instead of the daytime server's port:

```
# contact the server
if (open_TCP(F, $ARGV[0], 80) == undef) {
  print "Error connecting to server at $ARGV[0]\n";
  exit(-1);
}
```

In the interest of making the program a little more user-friendly, let's add some help text:

```
# If no parameters were given, print out help text
if ($#ARGV) {
  print "Usage: $0 Ipaddress\n";
  print "\n Returns the HTTP result code from a server.\n\n";
  exit(-1);
}
```

Instead of connecting to the port and listening for data, the client needs to send a request before data can be retrieved from the server:

```
print F "GET / HTTP/1.0\n\n";
```

Then the response code is retrieved and printed out:

```
$ReturnStatus=<F>;
print "The server had a response line of: $ReturnStatus\n";
```

After all the modifications, the new code looks like this:

```
#!/usr/local/bin/perl

use Socket;
require "tcp.pl";

# If no parameters were given, print out help text
if ($#ARGV) {
  print "Usage: $0 Ipaddress\n";
  print "\n Returns the HTTP result code from a web server.\n\n";
  exit(-1);
}

# contact the server
if (open_TCP(F, $ARGV[0], 80) == undef) {
  print "Error connecting to server at $ARGV[0]\n";
  exit(-1);
}

# send the GET method with / as a parameter
print F "GET / HTTP/1.0\n\n";

# get the response
$return_line=<F>;
```

```
# print out the response
print "The server had a response line of: $return_line";
close(F);
```

Let's run the program and see the result:

```
The server had a response line of: HTTP/1.0 200 OK
```

# *Parsing a URL*

At the core of every good web client program is the ability to parse a URL into its components. Let's start by defining such a function. (If you plan to use LWP, there's something like this in the URI::URL class, and you can skip the example.)

```
# Given a full URL, return the scheme, hostname, port, and path
# into ($scheme, $hostname, $port, $path).  We'll only deal with
# HTTP URLs.

sub parse_URL {

  # put URL into variable
  my ($URL) = @_;

  # attempt to parse.  Return undef if it didn't parse.
  (my @parsed =$URL =~ m@(\w+)://([^/:]+)(:\d*)?([^#]*)@) || return undef;

  # remove colon from port number, even if it wasn't specified in the URL
  if (defined $parsed[2]) {
    $parsed[2]=~ s/^://;
  }

  # the path is "/" if one wasn't specified
  $parsed[3]='/' if ($parsed[0]=~/http/i && (length $parsed[3])==0);

  # if port number was specified, we're done
  return @parsed if (defined $parsed[2]);

  # otherwise, assume port 80, and then we're done.
  $parsed[2] = 80;

  @parsed;
}


# grab_urls($html_content, %tags) returns an array of links that are
# referenced from within html.


sub grab_urls {

  my($data, %tags) = @_;
  my @urls;

  # while there are HTML tags
```

```
  skip_others: while ($data =~ s/<([^>]*)>//)  {

    my $in_brackets=$1;
    my $key;

    foreach $key (keys %tags) {

      if ($in_brackets =~ /^\s*$key\s+/i) {      # if tag matches, try parms
        if ($in_brackets =~ /\s+$tags{$key}\s*=\s*"([^"]*)"/i) {
          my $link=$1;
          $link =~ s/[\n\r]//g;  # kill newlines,returns anywhere in url
          push (@urls, $link);
          next skip_others;
        }
        # handle case when url isn't in quotes (ie: <a href=thing>)
        elsif ($in_brackets =~ /\s+$tags{$key}\s*=\s*([^\s]+)/i) {
          my $link=$1;
          $link =~ s/[\n\r]//g;  # kill newlines,returns anywhere in url
          push (@urls, $link);
          next skip_others;
        }
      }          # if tag matches
    }            # foreach tag
  }              # while there are brackets
  @urls;
}


1;
```

Given a full URL, *parse_URL()* will break it up into smaller components. The real work is done with:

```
# attempt to parse.  Return undef if it didn't parse.
(my @parsed =$URL =~ m@(\w+)://([^/:]+)(:\d*)?([^#]*)@)  || return undef;
```

After this initial parse some of the components need to be cleaned up:

1. If an optional port was given, remove the colon from *$parsed*[2].

2. If no document path was given, it becomes "/". For example, "http://www.ora.com" becomes "http://www.ora.com/".

The function returns an array of the different URL components: (*$scheme, $host-name, $port, $path*). Or **undef** upon error.

Let's try *parse_URL()* with "http://www.ora.com/index.html" as input:

```
parse_URL("http://www.ora.com/index.html");
```

The *parse_URL()* routine would return the following array: ('http', 'www.ora.com', 80, '/index.html'). We've saved this routine in a file called *web.pl*, and we'll use it in examples (with a *require 'web.pl'*) in this chapter.

# *Hypertext UNIX cat*

Now that we have a function that parses URLs, let's use it to create a hypertext version of the UNIX *cat* command, called *hcat*. (There's an LWP version of this in Chapter 6, *Example LWP Programs*.)

Basically speaking, this program looks at its command-line arguments for URLs. It prints out the full response for the given URL, including the response code, headers, and entity-body. If the user only wants the response code, he can use the *-r* option. Similarly, the *-H* option specifies that only headers are wanted. A *-d* option prints out only the entity body. One can mix these options, too. For example, if the user only wants the response code and headers, she could use *-rH*. If no arguments are used, or if the *-h* option is specified, help text is printed out.

Let's go over the command-line parsing:

```
# parse command line arguments
getopts('hHrd');

# print out usage if needed
if (defined $opt_h || $#ARGV<0) { help(); }

# if it wasn't an option, it was a URL
while($_ = shift @ARGV) {
  hcat($_, $opt_r, $opt_H, $opt_d);
}
```

The call to *Getopts()* indicates that we're interested in the *-h*, *-H*, *-r*, and *-d* command-line options. When *Getopts()* finds these switches, it sets $*opt_\** (where * is the switch that was specified), and leaves any "foreign" text back on *@ARGV*. If the user didn't enter any valid options or a URL, help text is printed. Finally, for any remaining command-line parameters, treat them as URLs and pass them to the *hcat()* routine.

Examples:

Print out response line only:

```
% hcat -r http://www.ora.com
```

Print out response line and entity-body, but not the headers:

```
% hcat -rd http://www.ora.com
```

Use multiple URLs:

```
% hcat http://www.ora.com http://www.ibm.com
```

Back to the program. Inside of the *hcat()* function, we do some basic URL processing:

```
# if the URL isn't a full URL, assume that it is a http request
```

```
$full_url="http://$full_url" if ($full_url !~
                    m/(\w+):\/\/([^\/:]+)(:\d*)?([^#]*)/);
```

```
# break up URL into meaningful parts
my @the_url = &parse_URL($full_url);
```

Then we send an HTTP request to the server.

```
# connect to server specified in 1st parameter
if (!defined open_TCP('F', $the_url[1], $the_url[2])) {
  print "Error connecting to web server: $the_url[1]\n";
  exit(-1);
}

# request the path of the document to get
  print F "GET $the_url[3] HTTP/1.0\n";
  print F "Accept: */*\n";
  print F "User-Agent: hcat/1.0\n\n";
```

Now we wait for a response from the server. We read in the response and selectively echo it out, where we look at the *$response*, *$header*, and *$data* variables to see if the user is interested in looking at each part of the reply:

```
# get the HTTP response line
my $the_response=<F>;
print $the_response if ($all || defined $response);

# get the header data
while(<F>=~ m/^(\S+):\s+(.+)/) {
  print "$1: $2\n" if ($all || defined $header);
}

# get the entity body
if ($all || defined $data) {
  print while (<F>);
}
```

The full source code looks like this:

```
#!/usr/local/bin/perl -w

# socket based hypertext version of UNIX cat


use strict;
use Socket;                  # include Socket module
require 'tcp.pl';            # file with Open_TCP routine
require 'web.pl';            # file with parseURL routine
use vars qw($opt_h $opt_H $opt_r $opt_d);
use Getopt::Std;


# parse command line arguments
getopts('hHrd');
```

```perl
# print out usage if needed
if (defined $opt_h || $#ARGV<0) { help(); }

# if it wasn't an option, it was a URL
while($_ = shift @ARGV) {
  hcat($_, $opt_r, $opt_H, $opt_d);
}

# Subroutine to print out usage information


sub usage {
  print "usage: $0 -rhHd URL(s)\n";
  print "        -h           help\n";
  print "        -r           print out response\n";
  print "        -H           print out header\n";
  print "        -d           print out data\n\n";
  exit(-1);
}


# Subroutine to print out help text along with usage information


sub help {
  print "Hypertext cat help\n\n";
  print "This program prints out documents on a remote web server.\n";
  print "By default, the response code, header, and data are
printed\n";
  print "but can be selectively printed with the -r, -H, and -d
options.\n\n";

  usage();
}


# Given a URL, print out the data there


sub hcat {

  # grab paramaters
  my ($full_url, $response, $header, $data)=@_;

  # assume that response, header, and data will be printed
  my $all = !($response || $header || $data);

  # if the URL isn't a full URL, assume that it is a http request
  $full_url="http://$full_url" if ($full_url !~
                            m/(\w+):\/\/([^\/:]+)(:\d*)?([^#]*)/);

  # break up URL into meaningful parts
  my @the_url = parse_URL($full_url);
  if (!defined @the_url) {
```

```
   print "Please use fully qualified valid URL\n";
   exit(-1);
}

# we're only interested in HTTP URL's
return if ($the_url[0] !~ m/http/i);

# connect to server specified in 1st parameter
if (!defined open_TCP('F', $the_url[1], $the_url[2])) {
  print "Error connecting to web server: $the_url[1]\n";
  exit(-1);
}

# request the path of the document to get
  print F "GET $the_url[3] HTTP/1.0\n";
  print F "Accept: */*\n";
  print F "User-Agent: hcat/1.0\n\n";

# print out server's response.

# get the HTTP response line
my $the_response=<F>;
print $the_response if ($all || defined $response);

# get the header data
while(<F>=~ m/^(\S+):\s+(.+)/) {
  print "$1: $2\n" if ($all || defined $header);
}

# get the entity body
if ($all || defined $data) {
  print while (<F>);
}

# close the network connection
close(F);

}
```

# Shell Hypertext cat

With *hcat*, one can easily retrieve documents from remote web servers. But there are times when a client request needs to be more complex than *hcat* is willing to allow. To give the user more flexibility in sending client requests, we'll change *hcat* into *shcat*, a shell utility that accepts methods, headers, and entity-body data from standard input. With this program, you can write shell scripts that specify different methods, custom headers, and submit form data.

All of this can be done by changing a few lines around. In *hcat*, where you see this:

```
# request the path of the document to get
  print F "GET $the_url[3] HTTP/1.0\n";
```

```
print F "Accept: */*\n";
print F "User-Agent: hcat/1.0\n\n";
```

Replace it with this:

```
# copy STDIN to network connection
while (<STDIN>) {print F;}
```

and save it as *shcat*. Now you can say whatever you want on *shcat*'s STDIN, and
it will forward it on to the web server you specify. This allows you to do things
like HTML form postings with POST, or a file upload with PUT, and selectively
look at the results. At this point, it's really all up to you what you want to say, as
long as it's HTTP compliant.

Here's a UNIX shell script example that calls *shcat* to do a file upload:

```
#!/bin/ksh
echo "PUT /~apm/hi.txt HTTP/1.0
User-Agent: shcat/1.0
Accept: */*
Content-type: text/plain
Content-length: 2

hi" | shcat http://publish.ora.com/
```

# *Grep out URL References*

When you need to quickly get a list of all the references in an HTML page, here's
a utility you can use to fetch an HTML page from a server and print out the URLs
referenced within the page. We've taken the *hcat* code and modified it a little.
There's also another function that we added to parse out URLs from the HTML.
Let's go over that first:

```
sub grab_urls {

  my($data, %tags) = @_;
  my @urls;

  # while there are HTML tags
  skip_others: while ($data =~ s/<([^>]*)>//)   {

    my $in_brackets=$1;
    my $key;

    foreach $key (keys %tags) {

      if ($in_brackets =~ /^\s*$key\s+/i) {      # if tag matches, try parms
        if ($in_brackets =~ /\s+$tags{$key}\s*=\s*"([^"]*)"/i) {
          my $link=$1;
          $link =~ s/[\n\r]//g;  # kill newlines,returns anywhere in url
          push (@urls, $link);
          next skip_others;
        }
```

```
        # handle case when url isn't in quotes (ie: <a href=thing>)
        elsif ($in_brackets =~ /\s+$tags{$key}\s*=\s*([^\s]+)/i) {
          my $link=$1;
          $link =~ s/[\n\r]//g;   # kill newlines,returns anywhere in url
          push (@urls, $link);
          next skip_others;
        }
      }              # if tag matches
    }                # foreach tag
  }                  # while there are brackets
  @urls;
}
```

The *grab_urls()* function has two parameters. The first argument is a scalar containing the HTML data to go through. The second argument is a hash of tags and parameters that we're looking for. After going through the HTML, *grab_urls()* returns an array of links that matched the regular expression of the form: *<tag parameter="...">*. The outer *if* statement looks for HTML tags, like <A>, <IMG>, <BODY>, <FRAME>. The inner *if* statement looks for parameters to the tags, like SRC and HREF, followed by text. Upon finding a match, the referenced URL is pushed into an array, which is returned at the end of the function. We've saved this in *web.pl*, and will include it in the *hgrepurl* program with a *require 'web.pl'*.

The second major change from *hcat* to *hgrepurl* is the addition of:

```
my $data='';
# get the entity body
while (<F>) {$data.=$_};

# close the network connection
close(F);


# fetch images and hyperlinks into arrays, print them out

if (defined $images || $all) {
  @links=grab_urls($data, ('img', 'src', 'body', 'background'));
}
if (defined $hyperlinks || $all) {
  @links2= grab_urls($data, ('a', 'href'));
}

my $link;
for $link (@links, @links2) { print "$link\n"; }
```

This appends the entity-body into the scalar of *$data*. From there, we call *grab_urls()* twice. The first time looks for image references by recognizing <img src="..."> and <body background="..."> in the HTML. The second time looks for hyperlinks by searching for instances of <a href="...">. Each call to *grab_urls()* returns an array of URLs, stored in *@links* and *@links2*, respectively. Finally, we print the results out.

Other than that, there are some smaller changes. For example, we look at the response code. If it isn't 200 (OK), we skip it.

```
# if not an "OK" response of 200, skip it
   if ($the_response !~ m@^HTTP/\d+\.\d+\s+200\s@) {return;}
```

We've retrofitted the reading of the response line, headers, and entity-body to not echo to STDOUT. This isn't needed anymore in the context of this program. Also, instead of parsing the *-r*, *-H*, and *-d* command-line arguments, we look for *-i* for displaying image links only, and *-l* for displaying only hyperlinks.

So, to see just the image references at *www.ora.com*, one would do this:

```
% hgrepurl -i http://www.ora.com
```

Or just the hyperlinks at *www.ora.com*:

```
% hgrepurl -i http://www.ora.com
```

Or both images and hyperlinks at *www.ora.com*:

```
% hgrepurl http://www.ora.com
```

The complete source code looks like this:

```
#!/usr/local/bin/perl -w


# socket based hypertext grep URLs.  Given a URL, this
# prints out URLs of hyperlinks and images.

use strict;
use Socket;                     # include Socket module
require 'tcp.pl';               # file with Open_TCP routine
require 'web.pl';               # file with parseURL routine
use vars qw($opt_h $opt_i $opt_l);
use Getopt::Std;

# parse command line arguments
getopts('hil');

# print out usage if needed
if (defined $opt_h || $#ARGV<0) { help(); }

# if it wasn't an option, it was a URL
while($_ = shift @ARGV) {
  hgu($_, $opt_i, $opt_l);
}


# Subroutine to print out usage information


sub usage {
  print "usage: $0 -hil URL(s)\n";
```

```perl
    print "        -h          help\n";
    print "        -i          print out image URLs\n";
    print "        -l          print out hyperlink URLs\n";
    exit(-1);
}


# Subroutine to print out help text along with usage information


sub help {
  print "Hypertext grep URL help\n\n";
  print "This program prints out hyperlink and image links that\n";
  print "are referenced by a user supplied URL on a web server.\n\n";

  usage();
}


# hypertext grep url


sub hgu {

  # grab parameters
  my($full_url, $images, $hyperlinks)=@_;
  my $all = !($images || $hyperlinks);
  my @links;
  my @links2;

  # if the URL isn't a full URL, assume that it is a http request
  $full_url="http://$full_url" if ($full_url !~
                        m/(\w+):\/\/([^\/:]+)(:\d*)?([^#]*)/);

  # break up URL into meaningful parts
  my @the_url = parse_URL($full_url);

  if (!defined @the_url) {
    print "Please use fully qualified valid URL\n";
    exit(-1);
  }

  # we're only interested in HTTP URL's
  return if ($the_url[0] !~ m/http/i);

  # connect to server specified in 1st parameter
  if (!defined open_TCP('F', $the_url[1], $the_url[2])) {
    print "Error connecting to web server: $the_url[1]\n";
    exit(-1);
  }

  # request the path of the document to get
    print F "GET $the_url[3] HTTP/1.0\n";
    print F "Accept: */*\n";
```

```perl
    print F "User-Agent: hgrepurl/1.0\n\n";

# print out server's response.

# get the HTTP response line
my $the_response=<F>;

# if not an "OK" response of 200, skip it
if ($the_response !~ m@^HTTP/\d+\.\d+\s+200\s@) {return;}

# get the header data
while(<F>=~ m/^(\S+):\s+(.+)/) {
  # skip over the headers
}

my $data='';
# get the entity body
while (<F>) {$data.=$_};

# close the network connection
close(F);


# fetch images and hyperlinks into arrays, print them out

if (defined $images || $all) {
  @links=grab_urls($data, ('img', 'src', 'body', 'background'));
}
if (defined $hyperlinks || $all) {
  @links2= grab_urls($data, ('a', 'href'));
}

my $link;
for $link (@links, @links2) { print "$link\n"; }

}
```

# *Client Design Considerations*

Now that we've done a few examples, let's address some issues that arise when
developing, testing, and using web client software. Most of these issues are automatically handled by LWP, but when programming directly with sockets, you
have to take care of them yourself.

*How does your client handle tag parameters?*

The decision to process or ignore extra tag parameters depends on the application of the web client. Some tag parameters change the tag's appearance by
adjusting colors or sizes. Other tags are informational, like variable names and
hidden variable declarations in HTML forms. Your client may need to pay
close attention to these tags. For example, if your client sends form data, it

may want to check all the parameters. Otherwise, your client may send data that is inconsistent with what the HTML specified—e.g., an HTML form might specify that a variable's value may not exceed a length of 20 characters. If the client ignored this parameter, it might send data over 20 characters. As the HTML standard evolves, your client may require some updating.

*What does your client do when the server's expected HTML format changes?*

Examine the data coming back from the server. After your client can handle the current data, think about possible changes that may occur in the data. Some changes won't affect your client's functionality. For example, textual descriptions in a file listing may be updated. But other changes, like the general format of the HTML, may cause your current client to interpret important values incorrectly. Changes in data may be unpredictable. When your client doesn't understand the data, it is safer for the client not to assume anything, to abort its current operation, and to notify someone to look into it. The client may need to be updated to handle the changes at the server.

*Does the client analyze the response line and headers?*

It is not advisable to write clients that skip over the HTTP response line and headers. While it may be easier to do so, it often comes back to haunt you later. For example, if the URL used by the client becomes obsolete or is changed, the client may interpret the entity-body incorrectly. Media types for the URL may change, and could be noticed in the HTTP headers returned by the server. In general, the client should be equipped to handle variations in metadata as they occur.

*Does your client handle URL redirection? Does it need to?*

Perhaps the desired data still exists, but not at the location specified by your client. In the event of a redirection, will your client handle it? Does it examine the `Location` header? The answers to these questions depend on the purpose of the client.

*Does the client send authorization information when it shouldn't?*

Two or more separate organizations may have CGI programs on the same server. It is important for your client not to send authorization information unless it is requested. Otherwise, the client may expose its authentication to an outside organization. This opens up the user's account to outsiders.

*What does your client do when the server is down?*

When the server is down, there are several options. The most obvious option is for the client to attempt the HTTP request at a later time. Other options are to try an alternate server or abort the transaction. The programmer should give the user some configuration options about the client's actions.

*What does your client do when the server response time is long?*

For simple applications, it may be better to allow the user to interrupt the application. For user-friendly or unattended batch applications, it is desirable to time out the connection and notify the user.

*What does your client do when the server has a higher version of HTTP?*

And what happens when the client doesn't understand the response? The most logical thing is to attempt to talk on a common denominator. Chances are that just about anything will understand HTTP/1.0, if that's what you feel comfortable using. In most cases, if the client doesn't understand the response, it would be nice to tell the user—or at least let the user know to get the latest version of HTTP for the client!

5

# The LWP Library

As we showed in Chapter 1, the Web works over TCP/IP, in which the client and server establish a connection and then exchange necessary information over that connection. Chapters 2 and 3 concentrated on HTTP, the protocol spoken between web clients and servers. Now we'll fill in the rest of the puzzle: how your program establishes and manages the connection required for speaking HTTP.

In writing web clients and servers in Perl, there are two approaches. You can establish a connection manually using sockets, and then use raw HTTP; or you can use the library modules for WWW access in Perl, otherwise known as LWP. LWP is a set of modules for Perl 5 that encapsulate common functions for a web client or server. Since LWP is much faster and cleaner than using sockets, this book uses it for all the examples in Chapters 6 and 7. If LWP is not available on your platform, see Chapter 4, which gives more detailed descriptions of the socket calls and examples of simple web programs using sockets.

The LWP library is available at all CPAN archives. CPAN is a collection of Perl libraries and utilities, freely available to all. There are many CPAN mirror sites; you should use the one closest to you, or just go to *http://www.perl.com/CPAN/* to have one chosen for you at random. LWP was developed by a cast of thousands (well, maybe a dozen), but its primary driving force is Gisle Aas. It is based on the *libwww* library developed for Perl 4 by Roy Fielding.

Detailed discussion of each of the routines within LWP is beyond the scope of this book. However, we'll show you how LWP can be used, and give you a taste of it to get you started. This chapter is divided into three sections:

- First, we'll show you some very simple LWP examples, to give you an idea of what it makes possible.

- Next, we'll list most of the useful routines within the LWP library.

- At the end of the chapter, we'll present some examples that glue together the different components of LWP.

# Some Simple Examples

LWP is distributed with a very helpful—but very short—"cookbook" tutorial, designed to get you started. This section serves much the same function: to show you some simpler applications using LWP.

## Retrieving a File

In Chapter 4, we showed how a web client can be written by manually opening a socket to the server and using I/O routines to send a request and intercept the result. With LWP, however, you can bypass much of the dirty work. To give you an idea of how simple LWP can make things, here's a program that retrieves the URL in the command line and prints it to standard output:

```
#!/bin/perl
use LWP::Simple;

print (get $ARGV[0]);
```

The first line, starting with #!, is the standard line that calls the Perl interpreter. If you want to try this example on your own system, it's likely you'll have to change this line to match the location of the Perl 5 interpreter on your system.

The second line, starting with *use*, declares that the program will use the LWP::Simple class. This class of routines defines the most basic HTTP commands, such as *get*.

The third line uses the *get()* routine from LWP::Simple on the first argument from the command line, and applies the result to the *print()* routine.

Can it get much easier than this? Actually, yes. There's also a *getprint()* routine in LWP::Simple for getting and printing a document in one fell swoop. The third line of the program could also read:

```
getprint($ARGV[0]);
```

That's it. Obviously there's some error checking that you could do, but if you just want to get your feet wet with a simple web client, this example will do. You can call the program *geturl* and make it executable; for example, on UNIX:

```
% chmod +x geturl
```

Windows NT users can use the *pl2bat* program, included with the Perl distribution, to make the *geturl.pl* executable from the command line:

```
C:\your\path\here> pl2bat geturl
```

You can then call the program to retrieve any URL from the Web:

```
% geturl http://www.ora.com/
<HTML>
<HEAD>
<LINK REV=MADE HREF="mailto:webmaster@ora.com">
<TITLE>O'Reilly &amp; Associates</TITLE>
</HEAD>
<BODY bgcolor=#ffffff>
...
```

## *Parsing HTML*

Since HTML is hard to read in text format, instead of printing the raw HTML, you could strip it of HTML codes for easier reading. You could try to do it manually:

```
#!/bin/perl

use LWP::Simple;

foreach (get $ARGV[0]) {
    s/<[^>]*>//g;
    print;
}
```

But this only does a little bit of the job. Why reinvent the wheel? There's something in the LWP library that does this for you. To parse the HTML, you can use the HTML module:

```
#!/bin/perl

use LWP::Simple;
use HTML::Parse;

print parse_html(get ($ARGV[0]))->format;
```

In addition to LWP::Simple, we include the HTML::Parse class. We call the *parse_html()* routine on the result of the *get()*, and then format it for printing.

You can save this version of the program under the name *showurl*, make it executable, and see what happens:

```
% showurl http://www.ora.com/
O'Reilly & Associates

    About O'Reilly -- Feedback -- Writing for O'Reilly

    What's New -- Here's a sampling of our most recent postings...
```

```
* This Week in Web Review: Tracking Ads
  Are you running your Web site like a business? These tools can help.

* Traveling with your dog? Enter the latest Travelers' Tales
  writing contest and send us a tale.


New and Upcoming Releases
...
```

## Extracting Links

To find out which hyperlinks are referenced inside an HTML page, you could go
to the trouble of writing a program to search for text within angle brackets (< . . . >
), parse the enclosed text for the <A> or <IMG> tag, and extract the hyperlink
that appears after the HREF or SRC parameter. LWP simplifies this process down
to two function calls. Let's take the *geturl* program from before and modify it:

```perl
#!/usr/local/bin/perl
use LWP::Simple;
use HTML::Parse;
use HTML::Element;

$html        = get $ARGV[0];
$parsed_html = HTML::Parse::parse_html($html);

for (@{ $parsed_html->extract_links() }) {
  $link = $_->[0];
  print "$link\n";
}
```

The first change to notice is that in addition to LWP::Simple and HTML::Parse, we
added the HTML::Element class.

Then we get the document and pass it to *HTML::Parse::parse_html()*. Given
HTML data, the *parse_html()* function parses the document into an internal representation used by LWP.

```perl
$parsed_html = HTML::Parse::parse_html($html);
```

Here, the *parse_html()* function returns an instance of the HTML::TreeBuilder
class that contains the parsed HTML data. Since the HTML::TreeBuilder class
inherits the HTML::Element class, we make use of *HTML::Element::extract_links()*
to find all the hyperlinks mentioned in the HTML data:

```perl
for (@{ $parsed_html->extract_links() }) {
```

*extract_links()* returns a list of array references, where each array in the list
contains a hyperlink mentioned in the HTML. Before we can access the hyperlink
returned by *extract_links()*, we dereference the list in the *for* loop:

```perl
for (@{ $parsed_html->extract_links() }) {
```

and dereference the array within the list with:

```
$link = $_->[0];
```

After the deferencing, we have direct access to the hyperlink's location, and we print it out:

```
print "$link\n";
```

Save this program into a file called *showlink* and run it:

```
% showlink http://www.ora.com/
```

You'll see something like this:

```
graphics/texture.black.gif
/maps/homepage.map
/graphics/headers/homepage-anim.gif
http://www.oreilly.de/o/comsec/satan/index.html
/ads/international/satan.gif
http://www.ora.com/catalog/pperl2
...
```

## Expanding Relative URLs

From the previous example, the links from *showlink* printed out the hyperlinks exactly as they appear within the HTML. But in some cases, you want to see the link as an absolute URL, with the full glory of a URL's scheme, hostname, and path. Let's modify *showlink* to print out absolute URLs all the time:

```
#!/usr/local/bin/perl
use LWP::Simple;
use HTML::Parse;
use HTML::Element;
use URI::URL;

$html        = get $ARGV[0];
$parsed_html = HTML::Parse::parse_html($html);

for (@{ $parsed_html->extract_links() }) {
  $link=$_->[0];
  $url       = new URI::URL $link;
  $full_url = $url->abs($ARGV[0]);
  print "$full_url\n";
}
```

In this example, we've added URI::URL to our ever-expanding list of classes. To expand each hyperlink, we first define each hyperlink in terms of the URL class:

```
$url = new URI::URL $link;
```

Then we use a method in the URL class to expand the hyperlink's URL, with respect to the location of the page it was referenced from:

```
$full_url = $url->abs($ARGV[0]);
```

Save the program in a file called *fulllink*, make it executable, and run it:

```
% fulllink http://www.ora.com/
```

You should see something like this:

```
http://www.ora.com/graphics/texture.black.gif
http://www.ora.com/maps/homepage.map
http://www.ora.com/graphics/headers/homepage-anim.gif
http://www.oreilly.de/o/comsec/satan/index.html
http://www.ora.com/ads/international/satan.gif
http://www.ora.com/catalog/pperl2
...
```

You should now have an idea of how easy LWP can be. There are more examples at the end of this chapter, and the examples in Chapters and 7 all use LWP. Right now, let's talk a little more about the more interesting modules, so you know what's possible under LWP and how everything ties together.

## *Listing of LWP Modules*

There are eight main modules in LWP: File, Font, HTML, HTTP, LWP, MIME, URI, and WWW. Figure 5-1 sketches out the top-level hierarchy within LWP.

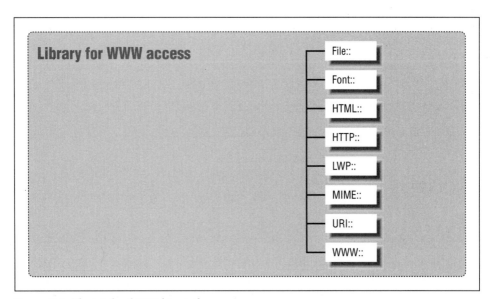

*Figure 5-1. The top-level LWP hierarchy*

- The File module parses directory listings.

- The Font module handles Adobe Font Metrics.

- In the HTML module, HTML syntax trees can be constructed in a variety of ways. These trees are used in rendering functions that translate HTML to PostScript or plain text.

- The HTTP module describes client requests, server responses, and dates, and computes a client/server negotiation.

- The LWP module is the core of all web client programs. It allows the client to communicate over the network with the server.

- The MIME module converts to/from base 64 and quoted printable text.

- In the URI module, one can escape a URI or specify or translate relative URLs to absolute URLs.

- Finally, in the WWW module, the client can determine if a server's resource is accessible via the Robot Exclusion Standard.

In the context of web clients, some modules in LWP are more useful than others. In this book, we cover LWP, HTML, HTTP, and URI. HTTP describes what we're looking for, LWP requests what we're looking for, and the HTML module is useful for interpreting HTML and converting it to some other form, such as PostScript or plain text. The URI module is useful for dissecting fully constructed URLs, specifying a URL for the HTTP or LWP module, or performing operations on URLs, such as escaping or expanding.

In this section, we'll give you an overview of the some of the more useful functions and methods in the LWP, HTML, HTTP, and URI modules. The other methods, functions, and modules are, as the phrase goes, beyond the scope of this book. So, let's go over the core modules that are useful for client programming.

## *The LWP Module*

The LWP module, in the context of web clients, performs client requests over the network. There are 10 classes in all within the LWP module, as shown in Figure 5-2, but we're mainly interested in the Simple, UserAgent, and RobotUA classes, described below.

### *LWP::Simple*

When you want to quickly design a web client, but robustness and complex behavior are of secondary importance, the LWP::Simple class comes in handy. Within it, there are seven functions:

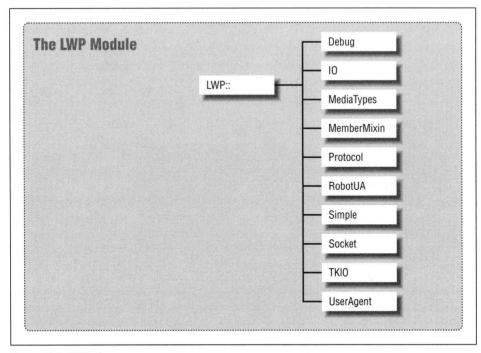

The LWP Module

LWP::

- Debug
- IO
- MediaTypes
- MemberMixin
- Protocol
- RobotUA
- Simple
- Socket
- TKIO
- UserAgent

*Figure 5-2. LWP classes*

*get($url)*

> Returns the contents of the URL specified by *$url*. Upon failure, *get()* returns undef. Other than returning undef, there is no way of accessing the HTTP status code or headers returned by the server.

*head($url)*

> Returns header information about the URL specified by *$url* in the form of: (*$content_type, $document_length, $modified_time, $expires, $server*). Upon failure, *head()* returns an empty list.

*getprint($url)*

> Prints the contents of the URL on standard output, where the URL is specified by *$url*. The HTTP status code given by the server is returned by *getprint()*.

*getstore($url, $file)*

> Stores the contents of the URL specified by *$url* into a file named by *$file*. The HTTP status code is returned by *getstore()*.

*mirror($url, $file)*

> Copies the contents of the URL specified by *$url* into a file named by *$file*, when the modification time or length of the online version is different from that of the file.

*is_success($rc)*

Given a status code from *getprint()*, *getstore()*, or *mirror()*, returns true if the request was successful.

*is_error($rc)*

Given a status code from *getprint()*, *getstore()*, or *mirror()*, returns true if the request was not successful.

### LWP::UserAgent

Requests over the network are performed with the LWP::UserAgent module. To create an LWP::UserAgent object, you would do:

```
$ua = new LWP::UserAgent;
```

The most useful method in this module is *request()*, which contacts a server and returns the result of your query. Other methods in this module change the way *request()* behaves. You can change the timeout value, customize the value of the User-Agent header, or use a proxy server. Here's an overview of most of the useful methods:

*$ua->request($request [, $subroutine [, $size]])*

Performs a request for the resource specified by *$request*, which is an HTTP::Request object. Normally, doing a *$result=$ua->request($request)* is enough. On the other hand, if you want to request data as it becomes available, you can specify a reference to a subroutine as the second argument, and *request()* will call the subroutine whenever there are data to be processed. In that case, you can specify an optional third argument that specifies the desired size of the data to be processed. The subroutine should expect chunks of the entity-body data as a scalar as the first parameter, a reference to an HTTP::Response object as the second argument, and a reference to an LWP::Protocol object as the third argument.

*$ua->request($request, $file_path)*

When invoked with a file path as the second parameter, this method writes the entity-body of the response to the file, instead of the HTTP::Response object that is returned. However, the HTTP::Response object can still be queried for its response code.

*$ua->credentials($netloc, $realm, $uname, $pass)*

Use the supplied username and password for the given network location and realm. To use the username "webmaster" and password of "yourguess" with the "admin" realm at *www.ora.com*, you would do this:

```
$ua->credentials('www.ora.com', 'admin', 'webmaster', 'yourguess').
```

*$ua->get_basic_credentials($realm, $url)*

> Returns (*$uname, $pass*) for the given realm and URL. *get_basic_credentials()* is usually called by *request()*. This method becomes useful when creating a subclass of LWP::UserAgent with its own version of *get_basic_credentials()*. From there, you can rewrite *get_basic_credentials()* to do more flexible things, like asking the user for the account information, or referring to authentication information in a file, or whatever. All you need to do is return a list, where the first element is a username and the second element is a password.

*$ua->agent([$product_id])*

> When invoked with no arguments, this method returns the current value of the identifier used in the User-Agent HTTP header. If invoked with an argument, the User-Agent header will use that identifier in the future. (As described in Chapter 3, the User-Agent header tells a web server what kind of client software is performing the request.)

*$ua->from([$email_address])*

> When invoked with no arguments, this method returns the current value of the email address used in the From HTTP header. If invoked with an argument, the From header will use that email address in the future. (The From header tells the web server the email address of the person running the client software.)

*$ua->timeout([$secs])*

> When invoked with no arguments, the *timeout()* method returns the timeout value of a request. By default, this value is three minutes. So if the client software doesn't hear back from the server within three minutes, it will stop the transaction and indicate that a timeout occurred in the HTTP response code. If invoked with an argument, the timeout value is redefined to be that value.

*$ua->use_alarm([$boolean])*

> Retrieves or defines the ability to use *alarm()* for timeouts. By default, timeouts with *alarm()* are enabled. If you plan on using *alarm()* for your own purposes, or *alarm()* isn't supported on your system, it is recommended that you disable *alarm()* by calling this method with a value of 0 (zero).

*$ua->is_protocol_supported($scheme)*

> Given a scheme, this method returns a true or false (nonzero or zero) value. A true value means that LWP knows how to handle a URL with the specified scheme. If it returns a false value, LWP does not know how to handle the URL.

*$ua->mirror($url, $file)*

> Given a URL and file path, this method copies the contents of *$url* into the file when the length or modification date headers are different. If the file does

not exist, it is created. This method returns an HTTP::Response object, where the response code indicates what happened.

*$ua->proxy( (@scheme | $scheme), $proxy_url)*

Defines a URL to use with the specified schemes. The first parameter can be an array of scheme names or a scalar that defines a single scheme. The second argument defines the proxy's URL to use with the scheme.

*$ua->env_proxy()*

Defines a scheme/proxy URL mapping by looking at environment variables. For example, to define the HTTP proxy, one would define the *http_proxy* environment variable with the proxy's URL. To define a domain to avoid the proxy, one would define the *no_proxy* environment variable with the domain that doesn't need a proxy.

*$ua->no_proxy($domain,...)*

Do not use a proxy server for the domains given as parameters.

### LWP::RobotUA

The Robot User Agent (LWP::RobotUA) is a subclass of LWP::UserAgent. User agent applications directly reflect the actions of the user. For example, in a user agent application, when a user clicks on a hyperlink, he expects to see the data associated with the hyperlink. On the other hand, a robot application requests resources in an automated fashion. Robot applications cover such activities as searching, mirroring, and surveying. Some robots collect statistics, while others wander the Web and summarize their findings for a search engine. For this type of application, a robot application should use LWP::RobotUA instead of LWP::User-Agent. The LWP::RobotUA module observes the Robot Exclusion Standards, which web server administrators can define on their web site to keep robots away from certain (or all) areas of the web site.* To create a new LWP::RobotUA object, one could do:

```
$ua = LWP::RobotUA->new($agent_name, $from, [$rules])
```

where the first parameter is the identifier that defines the value of the **User-Agent** header in the request, the second parameter is the email address of the person using the robot, and the optional third parameter is a reference to a WWW::RobotRules object. If you omit the third parameter, the LWP::RobotUA module requests the *robots.txt* file from every server it contacts, and generates its own WWW::RobotRules object.

---

\* The Robot Exclusion Standard is currently available as an informational draft by Martijn Koster at *http:/ /info.webcrawler.com/mak/projects/robots/norobots-rfc.txt*. Also see Appendix C for more information.

Since LWP::RobotUA is a subclass of LWP::UserAgent, the LWP::UserAgent methods are also available in LWP::RobotUA. In addition, LWP::RobotUA has the following robot-related methods:

*$ua->delay([$minutes])*

>   Returns the number of minutes to wait between requests. If a parameter is given, the time to wait is redefined to be the time given by the parameter. Upon default, this value is 1 (one). It is generally not very nice to set a time of zero.

*$ua->rules([$rules])*

>   Returns or defines a the WWW:RobotRules object to be used when determining if the module is allowed access to a particular resource.

*$ua->no_visits($netloc)*

>   Returns the number of visits to a given server. *$netloc* is of the form: *user:password@host:port*. The user, password, and port are optional.

*$ua->host_wait($netloc)*

>   Returns the number of seconds the robot must wait before it can request another resource from the server. *$netloc* is of the form of: *user:password@host:port*. The user, password, and port are optional.

*$ua->as_string()*

>   Returns a human-readable string that describes the robot's status.

## *The HTTP Module*

The HTTP module specifies HTTP requests and responses, plus some helper functions to interpret or convert data related to HTTP requests and responses. There are eight classes within the HTTP module, as shown in Figure 5-3, but we're mainly interested in the Request, Response, Header, and Status classes.

The two main modules that you'll use in the HTTP module are HTTP::Request and HTTP::Response. HTTP::Request allows one to specify a request method, URL, headers, and entity-body. HTTP::Response specifies a HTTP response code, headers, and entity-body. Both HTTP::Request and HTTP::Response are subclasses of HTTP::Message and inherit HTTP::Message's facility to handle headers and an entity-body.

For both HTTP::Request and HTTP::Response, you might want to define the headers in your request or look at the headers in the response. In this case, you can use HTTP::Headers to poke around with your HTTP::Request or HTTP::Response object.

In addition to HTTP::Headers for looking at HTTP::Response headers, HTTP::Status includes functions to classify response codes into the categories of

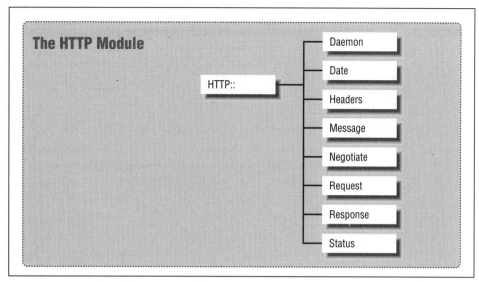

*Figure 5-3. Structure of the HTTP module*

informational, successful, redirection, error, client error, or server error. It also exports symbolic aliases of HTTP response codes; one could refer to the status code of 200 as RC_OK, and refer to 404 as RC_NOT_FOUND.

The HTTP::Date module converts date strings from and to machine time.

### HTTP::Request

This module summarizes a web client's request. For a simple GET or HEAD request, you could define the GET method and a URL to apply it to, and the headers would be filled in by LWP. For a POST or PUT, you might want to specify a custom HTTP::Headers object at the third parameter, or the *$content* parameter for an entity-body. Since HTTP::Request inherits everything in HTTP::Message, you can use the header and entity-body manipulation methods from HTTP::Message in HTTP::Request objects.

*$r = new HTTP::Request $method, $url, [$header, [$content]]*
> The first parameter, *$method*, expects an HTTP method, like GET, HEAD, POST, PUT, etc. The second parameter, *$url*, is the URL to apply the method to. This can be a string, like "www.ora.com", or a reference to a URI::URL object. To specify your own headers, you can specify an optional third parameter as a reference to an HTTP::Headers object. The fourth parameter, also optional, is a scalar that specifies the HTTP entity-body of the request. If omitted, the entity-body is empty.

*$r->method([$val])*

> To see what the HTTP::Request object has as its HTTP method, call the object's *method()* method without any parameters, and it will return the object's current HTTP method. To define a new HTTP method for the HTTP::Request object, call the object's *method()* method with your new HTTP method.*

*$r->url([$val])*

> To see what the HTTP::Request object has as its request URL, call the object's *url()* method without any parameters, and it will return the object's current URL. To define a new URL, call *url()* with your new URL as a parameter, like *$myobject->url('www.ora.com')*.

*$r->header($field [=> $val],...)*

> When called with just an HTTP header as a parameter, this method returns the current value for the header. For example, *$myobject->('content-type')* would return the value for the object's `Content-type` header. To define a new header value, invoke *header()* with an associative array with *header =>* *value* pairs, where the value is a scalar or reference to an array. For example, to define the `Content-type` header, you would do this:
>
> ```
> $r->header('Content-type' => 'text/plain')
> ```
>
> By the way, since HTTP::Request inherits HTTP::Message, and HTTP::Message contains all the methods of HTTP::Headers, you can use all the HTTP::Headers methods within an HTTP::Request object. See "HTTP::Headers" later in this section.

*$r->content([$content])*

> To get the entity-body of the request, call the *content()* method without any parameters, and it will return the object's current entity-body. To define the entity-body, invoke *content()* with a scalar as its first parameter. This method, by the way, is inherited from HTTP::Message.

*$r->add_content($data)*

> Appends *$data* to the end of the object's current entity-body.

*$r->as_string()*

> This returns a text version of the request, useful for debugging purposes. For example:
>
> ```
> use HTTP::Request;
>
> $request = new HTTP::Request 'PUT', 'http://www.ora.com/example/
> hi.text';
> ```

---

* Where *method()* is in the object-oriented sense, like `$myobject->method('GET')`, and the other method is an HTTP method, like GET or HEAD.

```
$request->header('content-length' => 2);
$request->header('content-type' => 'text/plain');
$request->content('hi');
print $request->as_string();
```

would look like this:

```
--- HTTP::Request=HASH(0x68148) ---
PUT http://www.ora.com/example/hi.text
Content-Length: 2
Content-Type: text/plain

hi
-----------------------------------
```

### HTTP::Response

Responses from a web server are described by HTTP::Response objects. If LWP has problems fulfilling your request, it internally generates an HTTP::Response object and fills in an appropriate response code. In the context of web client programming, you'll usually get an HTTP::Response object from LWP::UserAgent and LWP::RobotUA. If you plan to write extensions to LWP or a web server or proxy server, you might use HTTP::Response to generate your own responses.

*$r = new HTTP::Response ($rc, [$msg, [$header, [$content]]])*

In its simplest form, an HTTP::Response object can contain just a response code. If you would like to specify a more detailed message than "OK" or "Not found," you can specify a human-readable description of the response code as the second parameter. As a third parameter, you can pass a reference to an HTTP::Headers object to specify the response headers. Finally, you can also include an entity-body in the fourth parameter as a scalar.

*$r->code([$code])*

When invoked without any parameters, the *code()* method returns the object's response code. When invoked with a status code as the first parameter, *code()* defines the object's response to that value.

*$r->is_info()*

Returns true when the response code is 100 through 199.

*$r->is_success()*

Returns true when the response code is 200 through 299.

*$r->is_redirect()*

Returns true when the response code is 300 through 399.

*$r->is_error()*

Returns true when the response code is 400 through 599. When an error occurs, you might want to use *error_as_HTML()* to generate an HTML explanation of the error.

*$r->message([$message])*

Not to be confused with the entity-body of the response. This is the human-readable text that a user would usually see in the first line of an HTTP response from a server. With a response code of 200 (RC_OK), a common response would be a message of "OK" or "Document follows." When invoked without any parameters, the *message()* method returns the object's HTTP message. When invoked with a scalar parameter as the first parameter, *message()* defines the object's message to the scalar value.

*$r->header($field [=> $val],...)*

When called with just an HTTP header as a parameter, this method returns the current value for the header. For example, `$myobject->('content-type')` would return the value for the object's **Content-type** header. To define a new header value, invoke *header()* with an associative array of *header => value* pairs, where *value* is a scalar or reference to an array. For example, to define the `Content-type` header, one would do this:

```
$r->header('content-type' => 'text/plain')
```

By the way, since HTTP::Request inherits HTTP::Message, and HTTP::Message contains all the methods of HTTP::Headers, you can use all the HTTP::Headers methods within an HTTP::Request object. See "HTTP::Headers" later in this section.

*$r->content([$content])*

To get the entity-body of the request, call the *content()* method without any parameters, and it will return the object's current entity-body. To define the entity-body, invoke *content()* with a scalar as its first parameter. This method, by the way, is inherited from HTTP::Message.

*$r->add_content($data)*

Appends *$data* to the end of the object's current entity-body.

*$r->error_as_HTML()*

When *is_error()* is true, this method returns an HTML explanation of what happened. LWP usually returns a plain text explanation.

*$r->base()*

Returns the base of the request. If the response was hypertext, any links from the hypertext should be relative to the location specified by this method. LWP looks for the **BASE** tag in HTML and **Content-base/Content-location**

HTTP headers for a base specification. If a base was not explicitly defined by the server, LWP uses the requesting URL as the base.

*$r->as_string()*

This returns a text version of the response. Useful for debugging purposes. For example,

```
use HTTP::Response;
use HTTP::Status;

$response = new HTTP::Response(RC_OK, 'all is fine');
$response->header('content-length' => 2);
$response->header('content-type' => 'text/plain');
$response->content('hi');
print $response->as_string();
```

would look like this:

```
--- HTTP::Response=HASH(0xc8548) ---
RC: 200 (OK)
Message: all is fine

Content-Length: 2
Content-Type: text/plain

hi
----------------------------------
```

*$r->current_age*

Returns the numbers of seconds since the response was generated by the original server. This is the *current_age* value as described in section 13.2.3 of the HTTP 1.1 spec 07 draft.

*$r->freshness_lifetime*

Returns the number of seconds until the response expires. If expiration was not specified by the server, LWP will make an informed guess based on the Last-modified header of the response.

*$r->is_fresh*

Returns true if the response has not yet expired. Returns true when *(freshness_ lifetime > current_age)*.

*$r->fresh_until*

Returns the time when the response expires. The time is based on the number of seconds since January 1, 1970, UTC.

### HTTP::Headers

This module deals with HTTP header definition and manipulation. You can use these methods within HTTP::Request and HTTP::Response.

*$h = new HTTP::Headers([$field => $val],...)*

Defines a new HTTP::Headers object. You can pass in an optional associative array of *header => value* pairs.

*$h->header($field [=> $val],...)*

When called with just an HTTP header as a parameter, this method returns the current value for the header. For example, *$myobject->('content-type')* would return the value for the object's Content-type header. To define a new header value, invoke *header()* with an associative array of *header => value* pairs, where the value is a scalar or reference to an array. For example, to define the Content-type header, one would do this:

```
$h->header('content-type' => 'text/plain')
```

*$h->push_header($field, $val)*

Appends the second parameter to the header specified by the first parameter. A subsequent call to *header()* would return an array. For example:

```
$h->push_header(Accept => 'image/jpeg');
```

*$h->remove_header($field,...)*

Removes the header specified in the parameter(s) and the header's associated value.

### HTTP::Status

This module provides functions to determine the type of a response code. It also exports a list of mnemonics that can be used by the programmer to refer to a status code.

*is_info()*

Returns true when the response code is 100 through 199.

*is_success()*

Returns true when the response code is 200 through 299.

*is_redirect()*

Returns true when the response code is 300 through 399.

*is_client_error()*

Returns true when the response code is 400 through 499.

*is_server_error()*

Returns true when the response code is 500 through 599.

*is_error()*

Returns true when the response code is 400 through 599. When an error occurs, you might want to use *error_as_HTML()* to generate an HTML explanation of the error.

There are some mnemonics exported by this module. You can use them in your programs. For example, you could do something like:

```
if ($rc = RC_OK) {....}
```

Here are the mnemonics:

RC_CONTINUE (100)

RC_SWITCHING_PROTOCOLS (101)

RC_OK (200)

RC_CREATED (201)

RC_ACCEPTED (202)

RC_NON_AUTHORITATIVE_INFORMA-TION (203)

RC_NO_CONTENT (204)

RC_RESET_CONTENT (205)

RC_PARTIAL_CONTENT (206)

RC_MULTIPLE_CHOICES (300)

RC_MOVED_PERMANENTLY (301)

RC_MOVED_TEMPORARILY (302)

RC_SEE_OTHER (303)

RC_NOT_MODIFIED (304)

RC_USE_PROXY (305)

RC_BAD_REQUEST (400)

RC_UNAUTHORIZED (401)

RC_PAYMENT_REQUIRED (402)

RC_FORBIDDEN (403)

RC_NOT_FOUND (404)

RC_METHOD_NOT_ALLOWED (405)

RC_NOT_ACCEPTABLE (406)

RC_PROXY_AUTHENTICATION_REQUIRED (407)

RC_REQUEST_TIMEOUT (408)

RC_CONFLICT (409)

RC_GONE (410)

RC_LENGTH_REQUIRED (411)

RC_PRECONDITION_FAILED (412)

RC_REQUEST_ENTITY_TOO_LARGE (413)

RC_REQUEST_URI_TOO_LARGE (414)

RC_UNSUPPORTED_MEDIA_TYPE (415)

RC_INTERNAL_SERVER_ERROR (500)

RC_NOT_IMPLEMENTED (501)

RC_BAD_GATEWAY (502)

RC_SERVICE_UNAVAILABLE (503)

RC_GATEWAY_TIMEOUT (504)

RC_HTTP_VERSION_NOT_SUPPORTED (505)

See the section "Server Response Codes" in Chapter 3 for more information.

### HTTP::Date

The HTTP::Date module is useful when you want to process a date string.

### time2str([$time])

Given the number of seconds since machine epoch,[*] this function generates the equivalent time as specified in RFC 1123, which is the recommended time format used in HTTP. When invoked with no parameter, the current time is used.

---

* Which is January 1, 1970, UTC on UNIX systems.

*str2time($str [, $zone])*

Converts the time specified as a string in the first parameter into the number of seconds since epoch. This function recognizes a wide variety of formats, including RFC 1123 (standard HTTP), RFC 850, ANSI C *asctime()*, common log file format, UNIX "ls -l", and Windows "dir", among others. When a time zone is not implicit in the first parameter, this function will use an optional time zone specified as the second parameter, such as "-0800" or "+0500" or "GMT". If the second parameter is omitted and the time zone is ambiguous, the local time zone is used.

## *The HTML Module*

The HTML module provides an interface to parse HTML into an HTML parse tree, traverse the tree, and convert HTML to other formats. There are eleven classes in the HTML module, as shown in Figure 5-4.

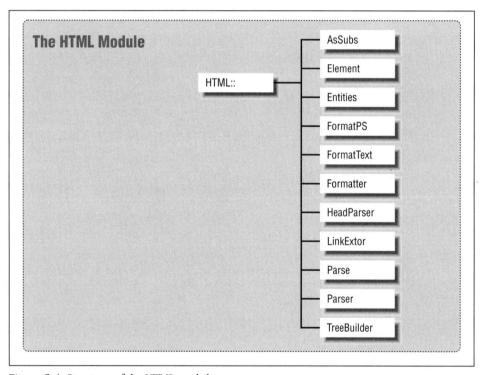

*Figure 5-4. Structure of the HTML module*

Within the scope of this book, we're mostly interested in parsing the HTML into an HTML syntax tree, extracting links, and converting the HTML into text or PostScript. As a warning, chances are that you will need to explicitly do garbage collection when you're done with an HTML parse tree.[*]

### HTML::Parse

*parse_html($html, [$obj])*

> Given a scalar variable containing HTML as a first parameter, this function generates an HTML syntax tree and returns a reference to an object of type HTML::TreeBuilder. When invoked with an optional second parameter of type HTML::TreeBuilder,[†] the syntax tree is constructed with that object, instead of a new object. Since HTML::TreeBuilder inherits HTML::Parser and HTML::Element, methods from those classes can be used with the returned HTML::TreeBuilder object.

*parse_htmlfile($file, [$obj])*

> Same as *parse_html()*, except that the first parameter is a scalar containing the location of a file containing HTML.

With both *parse_html()* and *parse_htmlfile()*, you can customize some of the parsing behavior with some flags:

*$HTML::Parse::IMPLICIT_TAGS*

> Assumes certain elements and end tags when not explicitly mentioned in the HTML. This flag is on by default.

*$HTML::Parse::IGNORE_UNKNOWN*

> Ignores unknown tags. On by default.

*$HTML::Parse::IGNORE_TEXT*

> Ignores the text content of any element. Off by default.

*$HTML::Parse::WARN*

> Calls *warn()* when there's a syntax error. Off by default.

### HTML::Element

The HTML::Element module provides methods for dealing with nodes in an HTML syntax tree. You can get or set the contents of each node, traverse the tree, and delete a node. We'll cover *delete()* and *extract_links()*.

---

[*] Since HTML syntax trees use circular references, the Perl garbage collector does not currently dispose of the memory used by the tree. You'll have to call the *delete()* method for the root node in an HTML syntax tree to manually deallocate memory used by the tree. Future versions of Perl or LWP may handle this automatically. See online documentation at *www.perl.com* for up-to-date information.

[†] Or a subclass of HTML::Parser, which HTML::TreeBuilder happens to be.

*$h->delete()*

Deallocates any memory used by this HTML element and any children of this element.

*$h->extract_links([@wantedTypes])*

Returns a list of hyperlinks as a reference to an array, where each element in the array is another array. The second array contains the hyperlink text and a reference to the HTML::Element that specifies the hyperlink. If invoked with no parameters, *extract_links()* will extract any hyperlink it can find. To specify certain types of hyperlinks, one can pass in an array of scalars, where the scalars are: body, base, a, img, form, input, link, frame, applet, and area.

For example:

```
use HTML::Parse;

$html='<img src="dot.gif"> <img src="dot2.gif">';
$tree=HTML::Parse::parse_html($html);

$link_ref = $tree->extract_links();
@link   = @$link_ref;   # dereference the array reference

for ($i=0; $i <= $#link; $i++) {
  print "$link[$i][0]\n";
}
```

prints out:

```
dot.gif
dot2.gif
```

### HTML::FormatText

The HTML::FormatText module converts an HTML parse tree into text.

*$formatter = new HTML::FormatText*

Creates a new HTML::FormatText object.

*$formatter->format($html)*

Given an HTML parse tree, as returned by *HTML::Parse::parse_html()*, this method returns a text version of the HTML.

### HTML::FormatPS

The HTML::FormatPS module converts an HTML parse tree into PostScript.

*$formatter = new HTML::FormatPS(parameter, ...)*

Creates a new HTML::FormatPS object with parameters of PostScript attributes. Each attribute is an associative array. One can define the following attributes:

*PaperSize*

Possible values of 3, A4, A5, B4, B5, Letter, Legal, Executive, Tabloid, Statement, Folio, 10x14, and Quarto. The default is A4.*

*PaperWidth*

Width of the paper in points.

*PaperHeight*

Height of the paper in points.

*LeftMargin*

Left margin in points.

*RightMargin*

Right margin in points.

*HorizontalMargin*

Left and right margin. Default is 4 cm.

*TopMargin*

Top margin in points.

*BottomMargin*

Bottom margin in points.

*VerticalMargin*

Top and bottom margin. Default is 2 cm.

*PageNo*

Boolean value to display page numbers. Default is 0 (off).

*FontFamily*

Font family to use on the page. Possible values are Courier, Helvetica and Times. Default is Times.

*FontScale*

Scale factor for the font.

*Leading*

Space between lines, as a factor of the font size. Default is 0.1.

For example, you could do:

```
$formatter = new HTML::FormatPS('papersize' => 'Letter');
```

*$formatter->format($html);*

Given an HTML syntax tree, returns the HTML representation as a scalar with PostScript content.

---

* A4 is the standard paper size in Europe. Americans will probably want to change this to Letter.

## *The URI Module*

The URI module contains functions and modules to specify and convert URIs. (URLs are a type of URI.) There are only two classes within the URI module, as shown in Figure 5-5.

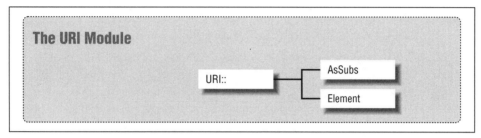

*Figure 5-5. Structure of the URI module*

We'll talk about escaping and unescaping URIs, as well as specifying URLs in the URI::URL module.

### *URI::Escape*

#### *uri_escape($uri, [$escape])*

Given a URI as the first parameter, returns the equivalent URI with certain characters replaced with % followed by two hexadecimal digits. The first parameter can be a text string, like "http://www.ora.com", or an object of type URI::URL. When invoked without a second parameter, *uri_escape()* escapes characters specified by RFC 1738. Otherwise, one can pass in a regular expression (in the context of [ ]) of characters to escape as the second parameter. For example:

```
$escaped_uri = uri_escape($uri, 'aeiou')
```

escapes all lowercase vowels in *$uri* and returns the escaped version. You might wonder why one would want to escape certain characters in a URI. Here's an example: If a file on the server happens to contain a question mark, you would want to use this function to escape the question mark in the URI before sending the request to the server. Otherwise, the question mark would be interpreted by the server to be a query string separator.

#### *uri_unescape($uri)*

Substitutes any instance of % followed by two hexadecimal digits back into its original form and returns the entire URI in unescaped form.

### URI::URL

*new URI::URL($url_string [, $base_url])*

Creates a new URI::URL object with the URL given as the first parameter. An optional base URL can be specified as the second parameter and is useful for generating an absolute URL from a relative URL.

*URI::URL::strict($bool)*

When set, the URI::URL module calls *croak()* upon encountering an error. When disabled, the URI::URL module may behave more gracefully. The function returns the previous value of *strict()*.

*$url->base ([$base])*

Gets or sets the base URL associated with the URL in this URI::URL object. The base URL is useful for converting a relative URL into an absolute URL.

*$url->abs([$base, [$allow_scheme_in_relative_urls]])*

Returns the absolute URL, given a base. If invoked with no parameters, any previous definition of the base is used. The second parameter is a Boolean that modifies *abs()*'s behavior. When the second parameter is nonzero, *abs()* will accept a relative URL with a scheme but no host, like "http:index.html". By default, this is off.

*$url->rel($base)*

Given a base as a first parameter or a previous definition of the base, returns the current object's URL relative to the base URL.

*$url->crack()*

Returns an array with the following data:

(*scheme, user, password, host, port, epath, eparams, equery, frag*)

*$url->scheme([$scheme])*

When invoked with no parameters, this returns the scheme in the URL defined in the object. When invoked with a parameter, the object's scheme is assigned to that value.

*$url->netloc()*

When invoked with no parameters, this returns the network location for the URL defined in the object. The network location is a string composed of "user:password@host:port", where user, password, and port may be omitted when not defined. When *netloc()* is invoked with a parameter, the object's network location is defined to that value. Changes to the network location are reflected in the *user()*, *password()*, *host()*, and *port()* method.

*$url->user()*

When invoked with no parameters, this returns the user for the URL defined in the object. When invoked with a parameter, the object's user is assigned to that value.

*$url->password()*

When invoked with no parameters, this returns the password in the URL defined in the object. When invoked with a parameter, the object's password is assigned to that value.

*$url->host()*

When invoked with no parameters, this returns the hostname in the URL defined in the object. When invoked with a parameter, the object's hostname is assigned to that value.

*$url->port()*

When invoked with no parameters, this returns the port for the URL defined in the object. If a port wasn't explicitly defined in the URL, a default port is assumed. When invoked with a parameter, the object's port is assigned to that value.

*$url->default_port()*

When invoked with no parameters, this returns the default port for the URL defined in the object. The default port is based on the scheme used. Even if the port for the URL is explicitly changed by the user with the *port()* method, the default port is always the same.

*$url->epath()*

When invoked with no parameters, this returns the escaped path of the URL defined in the object. When invoked with a parameter, the object's escaped path is assigned to that value.

*$url->path()*

Same as *epath()* except that the path that is set/returned is not escaped.

*$url->eparams()*

When invoked with no arguments, this returns the escaped parameter of the URL defined in the object. When invoked with an argument, the object's escaped parameter is assigned to that value.

*$url->params()*

Same as *eparams()* except that the parameter that is set/returned is not escaped.

*$url->equery()*

When invoked with no arguments, this returns the escaped query string of the URL defined in the object. When invoked with an argument, the object's escaped query string is assigned to that value.

*$url->query()*

> Same as *equery()* except that the parameter that is set/returned is not escaped.

*$url->frag()*

> When invoked with no arguments, this returns the fragment of the URL defined in the object. When invoked with an argument, the object's fragment is assigned to that value.

*$url->full_path()*

> Returns a string consisting of the escaped path, escaped parameters, and escaped query string.

*$url->eq($other_url)*

> Returns true when the object's URL is equal to the URL specified by the first parameter.

*$url->as_string()*

> Returns the URL as a scalar string. All defined components of the URL are included in the string.

# *Using LWP*

Let's try out some LWP examples and glue a few functions together to produce something useful. First, let's revisit a program from the beginning of the chapter:

```
#!/usr/local/bin/perl
use LWP::Simple;

print (get ($ARGV[0]));
```

Because this is a short and simple example, there isn't a whole lot of flexibility here. For example, when *LWP::Simple::get()* fails, it doesn't give us a status code to use to figure out what went wrong. The program doesn't identify itself with the `User-Agent` header, and it doesn't support proxy servers. Let's change a few things.

## *Using LWP::UserAgent*

LWP::UserAgent has its advantages when compared to LWP::Simple. With only a few more lines of code, one can follow HTTP redirections, authenticate requests, use the `User-Agent` and `From` headers, set a timeout, and use a proxy server. For the remainder of this chapter, we'll experiment with various aspects of LWP::UserAgent to show you how everything fits together.

First, let's convert our LWP::Simple program into something that uses LWP::UserAgent:

```
use LWP::UserAgent;
use HTTP::Request;
```

```
use HTTP::Response;

my $ua = new LWP::UserAgent;

my $request = new HTTP::Request('GET', $ARGV[0]);
my $response = $ua->request($request);
if ($response->is_success) {
    print $response->content;
} else {
    print $response->error_as_HTML;
}
```

Let's try it out:

```
% hcat_plain http://www.ora.com/
```

By converting to LWP::UserAgent, we've instantly gained the ability to report error messages and follow a URL redirection. Let's go through the code line by line, just to make sure you see how the different objects interact.

First, we include the modules that we plan to use in our program:

```
use LWP::UserAgent;
use HTTP::Request;
use HTTP::Response;
```

Then we create a new LWP::UserAgent object:

```
my $ua = new LWP::UserAgent;
```

We construct an HTTP request by creating a new HTTP::Request object. Within the constructor, we define the HTTP GET method and use the first argument (*$ARGV[0]*) as the URL to get:

```
my $request = new HTTP::Request('GET', $ARGV[0]);
```

We pass the HTTP::Request object to *$ua*'s *request()* method. In other words, we're passing an HTTP::Request object to the *LWP::UserAgent->request()* method, where *$ua* is an instance of LWP::UserAgent. LWP::UserAgent performs the request and fetches the resource specified by *$ARGV[0]*. It returns a newly created HTTP::Response object, which we store in *$response:*

```
my $response = $ua->request($request);
```

We examine the HTTP response code with *HTTP::Response->is_success()* by calling the *is_success()* method from the *$response* object. If the request was successful, we use *HTTP::Response::content()* by invoking *$response*'s *content()* method to retrieve the entity-body of the response and print it out. Upon error, we use *HTTP::Response::error_as_HTML* by invoking *$response*'s *error_as_HTML()* method to print out an error message as HTML.

In a nutshell, we create a request with an HTTP::Request object. We pass that request to LWP::UserAgent's request method, which does the actual request. It returns an HTTP::Response object, and we use methods in HTTP::Response to determine the response code and print out the results.

## Adding Proxy Server Support

Let's add some more functionality to the previous example. In this case, we'll add support for a proxy server. A proxy server is usually used in firewall environments, where the HTTP request is sent to the proxy server, and the proxy server forwards the request to the real web server. If your network doesn't have a firewall, and you don't plan to have proxy support in your programs, then you can safely skip over this part now and come back when you eventually need it.

To show how flexible the LWP library is, we've added only two lines of code to the previous example, and now the web client knows that it should use the proxy at *proxy.ora.com* at port 8080 for HTTP requests, but to avoid using the proxy if the request is for a web server in the *ora.com* domain:

```
use LWP::UserAgent;
use HTTP::Request;
use HTTP::Response;

my $ua = new LWP::UserAgent;

$ua->proxy('http', 'http://proxy.ora.com:8080/');
$ua->no_proxy('ora.com');

my $request = new HTTP::Request('GET', $ARGV[0]);
my $response = $ua->request($request);
if ($response->is_success) {
    print $response->content;
} else {
    print $response->error_as_HTML;
}
```

The invocation of this program is exactly the same as the previous example. If you downloaded this program from the O'Reilly web site, you could then use it like this:

```
% hcat_proxy  http://www.ora.com/
```

## Adding Robot Exclusion Standard Support

Let's do one more example. This time, let's add support for the Robot Exclusion Standard. As discussed in the LWP::RobotUA section, the Robot Exclusion Standard gives webmasters the ability to block off certain areas of the web site from the automated "robot" type of web clients. It is arguable that the programs we've gone through so far aren't really robots; chances are that the user invoked the program by hand and is waiting for a reply. But for the sake of example, and to show how easy it is, let's add support for the Robot Exclusion Standard to our previous example.

```perl
use LWP::RobotUA;
use HTTP::Request;
use HTTP::Response;

my $ua = new LWP::RobotUA('hcat_RobotUA', 'examples@ora.com');

$ua->proxy('http', 'http://proxy.ora.com:8080/');
$ua->no_proxy('ora.com');

my $request = new HTTP::Request('GET', $ARGV[0]);
my $response = $ua->request($request);
if ($response->is_success) {
    print $response->content;
} else {
    print $response->error_as_HTML;
}
```

Since LWP::RobotUA is a subclass of LWP::UserAgent, LWP::RobotUA contains all the methods as LWP::UserAgent. So we replaced the *use LWP::UserAgent* line with *use LWP::RobotUA*. Instead of declaring a new LWP::UserAgent object, we declare a new LWP::RobotUA object.

LWP::RobotUA's constructor is a little different, though. Since we're programming a web robot, the name of the robot and the email address of the user are mandatory. So, we pass that information to the LWP::RobotUA object through the constructor. In practice, one would determine the email address of the client user in advance. The "examples@ora.com" is provided for illustration purposes only.

See Appendix C for more details about the Robot Exclusion Standard.

6

# *Example LWP Programs*

This chapter presents LWP programs that are more robust and feature-rich than the examples shown in previous chapters. While Chapter 5, *The LWP Library*, focused on teaching LWP and explained how LWP objects fit together, this chapter shows you some sample LWP programs with more user-friendly options and features.

We present three broad categories of web client programs:

- *Simple* clients—programs that perform actions for users in real time, usually with a finite list of URLs to act upon. In this section, we present LWP versions of the *hcat* and *hgrepurl* programs that were presented in Chapter 4, *The Socket Library*.

- *Periodic* clients—robots that perform a request repeatedly, with some delay between each request. Periodic clients typically request the same resource over and over, or a different resource in a predictable manner. For example, a client may request *0100.gif* at 1 a.m., *0200.gif* at 2 a.m, etc. A periodic client might check some data and perform action when a condition is met. In this section, we present a program that periodically checks the status of a Federal Express document.

- *Recursive* clients—robots that follow hyperlinks or other references on an HTML page. In this section, we present a program that looks for bad links in a web site.

The boundaries between these categories are not set in stone. It is possible to write a periodic client that also happens to be a recursive client. Or a simple client might become periodic if the document indicates that the page should be refreshed every 15 minutes. We're not trying to classify all programs into one category or another; these categories are given as a way to identify distinct behaviors that a client may exhibit.

The examples in this chapter all use a simple command-line interface. In Chapter 7, *Graphical Examples with Perl/Tk*, we have some additional examples with a graphical interface using the Tk extension to Perl.

# Simple Clients

Simple clients are programs that perform actions for users in real time, usually with a finite list of URLs to act upon. In this section, we'll show LWP versions of the socket-based *hcat* and *hgrepurl* programs that were presented in Chapter 4.

## Hypertext UNIX cat Revisited

As you might recall, the sockets version of *hcat* used the *open_TCP()* function to establish a connection to a web server, and then issued an HTTP request, like "GET / HTTP/1.0". In LWP, many of the details are hidden from the programmer. Instead of this:

```
open_TCP(F, $the_url[1], $the_url[2])
print F "GET $the_url[3] HTTP/1.0\n";
print F "Accept: */*\n";
print F "User-Agent: hcat/1.0\n\n";
```

in LWP, it can be written like this:

```
my $ua = new LWP::UserAgent;
$ua->agent("hcat/1.0");
my $request = new HTTP::Request("GET", $path);
my $response = $ua->request($request);
```

They both do the same thing; they request a document from a user-specified web server and identify themselves in the User-Agent header. But one looks a lot cleaner than the other. Instead of using the nitty-gritty socket code that talks directly to the web server, you merely describe to LWP what the action should be. LWP handles it for you. Many things, like handling URL redirection or handling HTTP version differences, will be handled automatically by LWP.

Also, the following lines in the sockets version of *hcat* can be replaced:

```
# print out server's response.

  # get the HTTP response line
  $the_response=<F>;
  print $the_response if ($all || $response);

  # get the header data
```

```
   while(<F>=~ m/^(\S+):\s+(.+)/) {
     print "$1: $2\n" if ($all || $header);
   }

   # get the entity body
   if ($all || $data) {
     print while (<F>);
   }
```

In LWP, these lines can be written as:

```
   my $code=$response->code;
   my $desc = HTTP::Status::status_message($code);
   my $headers=$response->headers_as_string;
   my $body =  $response->content;

   if ($opt_r || $all) { print "HTTP/1.0 $code $desc\n"; }
   if ($opt_H || $all) { print "$headers\n";             }
   if ($opt_d || $all) { print $body;                    }
```

In addition, we've added proxy support, since it's trivial in LWP:

```
   my $ua = new LWP::UserAgent;
   $ua->agent("hcat/1.0");

   # If proxy server specified, define it in the User Agent object
     if (defined $proxy) {
       my $url = new URI::URL $path;
       my $scheme = $url->scheme;
       $ua->proxy($scheme, $proxy);
     }
```

The source in its entirety looks like this:

```
   #!/usr/local/bin/perl -w

   use strict;
   use HTTP::Status;
   use HTTP::Response;
   use LWP::UserAgent;
   use URI::URL;
   use vars qw($opt_h $opt_r $opt_H $opt_d $opt_p);
   use Getopt::Std;

   my $url;
   my $goterr;
```

After calling all the necessary Perl modules and declaring variables, we process command-line arguments:

```
   getopts('hrHdp:');
   my $all = !($opt_r || $opt_H || $opt_d);    # all=1 when -r -H -d not set

   if ($opt_h || $#ARGV==-1) {  # print help text when -h or no args
     print_help();
     exit(0);
   }
```

Then, for any string that remains as a command-like parameter, we treat it as a URL, process it, and print out the result:

```
my $goterr = 0;  # make sure we clear the error flag

while ($url = shift @ARGV) {

  my ($code, $desc, $headers, $body)=simple_get('GET', $url, $opt_p);
  if ($opt_r || $all) { print "HTTP/1.0 $code $desc\n"; }
  if ($opt_H || $all) { print "$headers\n";             }
  if ($opt_d || $all) { print $body;                    }

  $goterr |= HTTP::Status::is_error($code);
}

exit($goterr);
```

The *print-help()* routine just prints out a range line and a list of command-line options:

```
sub print_help {
  print <<"HELP";
usage: $0 [-hrmbp] [proxy URL] URLs

 -h help
 -r response line only
 -H HTTP header data only
 -d data from entity body
 -p use this proxy server

Example:  $0 -p http://proxy:8080/ http://www.ora.com

HELP
}
```

The actual processing is done in a separate function, called *simple_get()*:

```
sub simple_get() {

  my ($method, $path, $proxy) = @_;

# Create a User Agent object
  my $ua = new LWP::UserAgent;
  $ua->agent("hcat/1.0");

# If proxy server specified, define it in the User Agent object
  if (defined $proxy) {
    my $url = new URI::URL $path;
    my $scheme = $url->scheme;
    $ua->proxy($scheme, $proxy);
  }

# Ask the User Agent object to request a URL.
# Results go into the response object (HTTP::Reponse).
```

```
    my $request = new HTTP::Request($method, $path);
    my $response = $ua->request($request);

  # Parse/convert the response object for "easier reading"

    my $code=$response->code;
    my $desc = HTTP::Status::status_message($code);
    my $headers=$response->headers_as_string;

    my $body =  $response->content;
    $body =  $response->error_as_HTML if ($response->is_error);

    return ($code, $desc, $headers, $body);
  }
```

Within *simple_get()*, an LWP::UserAgent object is created, and a proxy server is defined for the object if one was specified to *simple_get()*. A new HTTP::Request object is created with the HTTP method and path that are passed to *simple_get()*. The request is given to UserAgent's *request()* method, and an HTTP::Response object is returned. From there, *HTTP::Response::code()*, *HTTP::Response::headers_as_string()*, and *HTTP::Response::content()* are used to extract the response information from the HTTP::Response object.

## Hypertext Grep URLs Revisited

The code that does the HTTP request of *hgrepurl* looks very much like *hcat*'s. Instead of repeating that information, let's center on another chunk of code that changed from the sockets version of *hgrepurl*.

In Chapter 4, the raw sockets version checked the response code and then skipped over the HTTP headers:

```
# if not an "OK" response of 200, skip it
if ($the_response !~ m@^HTTP/\d+\.\d+\s+200\s@) {return;}

# get the header data
while(<F>=~ m/^(\S+):\s+(.+)/) {
  # skip over the headers
}
```

In LWP, this can more easily be said with something like this:

```
    if ($response->code!= RC_OK) { return; }
    if ($response->content_type !~ m@text/html@) { return; }
```

In the process of finding URLs without the help of LWP, one would have to do something like this:

```
$data =~ s/<([^>]*)>//;
$in_brackets=$1;
$key='a';
$tag='href';
```

```
  if ($in_brackets =~ /^\s*$key\s+/i) {      # if tag matches, try parms
    if ($in_brackets =~ /\s+$tag\s*=\s*"([^"]*)"/i) {
      $link=$1;
      $link =~ s/[\n\r]//g;  # kill newlines,returns anywhere in url
      # process the URL here
    }
  }
```

But in LWP, this simplifies to something like this:

```
my $parsed_html=HTML::Parse::parse_html($data);
for (@{ $parsed_html->extract_links(qw (body img)) }) {
  my ($link) = @$_;
  # process the URL here
}
```

As you can see, LWP simplified a lot of the code. Let's go over *hgrepurl* in a little more detail:

```
#!/usr/local/bin/perl -w

use strict;
use HTTP::Status;
use HTTP::Response;
use LWP::UserAgent;
use URI::URL;
use HTML::Parse;
use vars qw($opt_h $opt_i $opt_l $opt_p);
use Getopt::Std;

my $url;
```

After calling all the necessary modules and declaring variables, there's the usual command-line processing with *getopts()*:

```
getopts('hilp:');
my $all = !($opt_i || $opt_l);        # $all=1 when -i -l not set

if ($opt_h || $#ARGV==-1) { # print help text when -h or no args
  print_help();
  exit(0);
}
```

Any remaining command-line arguments are treated as URLs and passed to *get_html()*:

```
while ($url = shift @ARGV) {

  my ($code, $type, $data)  = get_html($url, $opt_p, $opt_i, $opt_l);
  if (not_good($code, $type)) { next; }
  if ($opt_i || $all) { print_images($data, $url); }
  if ($opt_l || $all) { print_hyperlinks($data, $url); }

} # while there are URLs on the command line
```

As in *hcat,* *print_help()* displays a help message:

```
sub print_help {
  print << "HELP";
usage: $0 [-hilp] [proxy URL] URLs

 -h help
 -i grep out images references only
 -l grep out hyperlink references only
 -p use this proxy server

Example:  $0 -p http://proxy:8080/ http://www.ora.com

HELP
}
```

The *get_html()* routine is defined next. The response of *get_html()* is the response code, content type, and entity-body of the reply.

```
sub get_html () {
  my($url, $proxy, $want_image, $want_link) = @_;

# Create a User Agent object
  my $ua = new LWP::UserAgent;
  $ua->agent("hgrepurl/1.0");

# If proxy server specified, define it in the User Agent object
  if (defined $proxy) {
    my $proxy_url = new URI::URL $url;
    $ua->proxy($proxy_url->scheme, $proxy);
  }

# Ask the User Agent object to request a URL.
# Results go into the response object (HTTP::Reponse).

  my $request = new HTTP::Request('GET', $url);
  my $response = $ua->request($request);

  return ($response->code, $response->content_type,
      $response->content);
}
```

The *not_good()* routine tells us if the document that was returned was HTML, since the program doesn't really make sense otherwise:

```
# returns 1 if the request was not OK or HTML, else 0

sub not_good {
  my ($code, $type) = @_;

  if ($code != RC_OK) {
    warn("$url had response code of $code");
    return 1;
```

```
    }

    if ($type !~ m@text/html@) {
      warn("$url is not HTML.");
      return 1;
    }
    return 0;
}
```

The *print-images()* and *print-hyperlinks()* routines display any links found in the document:

```
sub print_images {

  my ($data, $model) = @_;

  my $parsed_html=HTML::Parse::parse_html($data);
  for (@{ $parsed_html->extract_links(qw (body img)) }) {
    my ($link) = @$_;
    my ($absolute_link) = globalize_url($link, $model);
    print "$absolute_link\n";
  }
  $parsed_html->delete(); # manually do garbage collection
}

sub print_hyperlinks {

  my ($data, $model) = @_;

  my $parsed_html=HTML::Parse::parse_html($data);
  for (@{ $parsed_html->extract_links(qw (a)) }) {
    my ($link) = @$_;
    my ($absolute_link) = globalize_url($link, $model);
    print "$absolute_link\n";
  }
  $parsed_html->delete(); # manually do garbage collection
}
```

Finally, the *globalize_url()* function returns the absolute URL version of a relative URL.

```
sub globalize_url() {

  my ($partial, $model) = @_;
  my $url = new URI::URL($partial, $model);
  my $globalized = $url->abs->as_string;

  return $globalized;
}
```

# *Periodic Clients*

The Federal Express checker program, or *FedEx*, is very much like the previous program, *hgrepurl*. They're similar because they both look at the entity-body and attempt to find some useful information in it. While *hgrepurl* merely prints out any URLs that it finds, the *FedEx* program looks for a certain phrase followed by a colon (:) followed by more text. After shipping out a few documents and watching the HTML that corresponds to each, we've noticed the following pattern:

1. When a document is delivered, the text "Delivered To : " shows up in the entity-body and is followed by the name of the recipient of the document.

2. For some reason, when the document is delivered, the "Delivered To : " is sometimes blank, but the "Delivery Time : " field is filled in.

3. If the tracking information isn't ready, or if the requested information doesn't exist, there isn't a "Delivered To : " field at all. In this case, there's a descriptive error message between the `<!-- BEGIN TRACKING INFORMATION -->` and `<!-- END TRACKING INFORMATION -->` tags in the response.

4. If "Delivered To : " shows up in the reply (with or without text after the colon), the query was successful but the document is not at the destination yet.

5. Otherwise, the request resulted in an error.

Given all this, we wrote a *FedEx* package that connects to the Federal Express web site and does a query on a periodic basis. The package is implemented as a class, so you can easily transport this to another program, if you want. In Chapter 7, we'll show a graphical interface to this package.

For now, let's dissect the FedEx class. First, we have a constructor that accepts three parameters from the programmer: the URL of the CGI program to use, the email address of the person using the program, and an optional third parameter that specifies a proxy server to use. These settings are stored internally in the newly created FedEx object as a URI::URL object and LWP::RobotUA object:

```perl
package FedEx;
sub new {

    my($class, $cgi_url, $email, $proxy) = @_;
    my $user_agent_name = 'ORA-Check-FedEx/1.0';

    my $self  = {};
    bless $self, $class;

    $self->{'url'} = new URI::URL $cgi_url;

    $self->{'robot'} = new LWP::RobotUA $user_agent_name, $email;
```

```
$self->{'robot'}->delay(0);    # we'll delay requests by hand

if ($proxy) {
  $self->{'robot'}->proxy('http', $proxy);
}

$self;
}
```

The *check()* method accepts a tracking number, country string, and date as parameters. From there, a properly encoded query string is added to the URI::URL object with a call to *$self->{'url'}query()*. A new HTTP::Request() object is made with the URI::URL object as a parameter. The request is issued with the call to *$self->{'robot'}->request()* and a HTTP::Response object is returned:

```
sub check {

  my ($self, $track_num, $country, $date) = @_;

  $self->{'url'}->query("trk_num=$track_num&dest_cntry=" .
    "$country&ship_date=$date");
  my $request = new HTTP::Request 'GET', $self->{'url'};

  my $response = $self->{'robot'}->request($request);
  $self->{'status'} = $response->code();
```

If the HTTP request was a success, then we can analyze the response. If the FedEx document was delivered, the "Delivered To : " field is filled out. When this happens, the FedEx package sets a few internal values to reflect this:

```
if ($response->content =~ /Delivered To : (\w.*)/) {

  # package delivered
  $self->{'who_got_it'} = $1;
  $self->{'delivered'} = 1;
}
```

As noted before, sometimes when the document is delivered, the "Delivered To : " field is blank, but the "Delivery Time : " field is set:

```
elsif ($response->content =~ /Delivery Time : \w.*/) {

  # package delivered
  $self->{'who_got_it'} = 'left blank by FedEx computer';
  $self->{'delivered'} = 1;
}
```

If "Delivered To : " shows up in the reply, the query was successful but the document didn't arrive. But if it didn't show up, there's something wrong with the request. A descriptive error message should show up between the <!-- BEGIN TRACKING INFORMATION --> and <!-- END TRACKING INFORMATION --> tags:

```
if ($response->content !~ /Delivered To : /) {
```

```
        $self->{'status'} = RC_BAD_REQUEST;

        # get explanation from HTML response
        my $START = '<!-- BEGIN TRACKING INFORMATION -->';
        my $END   = '<!-- END TRACKING INFORMATION -->';

        if   ($response->content =~ /$START(.*?)$END/s) {
          $self->{'error_as_HTML'} = $1;
        }
        else {
          # couldn't get explanation, use generic one
          $self->{'error_as_HTML'} = 'Unexpected HTML response from FedEx';
    } # couldn't get error explanation
```

And then there are cases when the HTTP response didn't result in a status code of 200 (OK):

```
        $self->{'error_as_HTML'} = $response->error_as_HTML;
```

That just about wraps up the FedEx package.

For the sake of being a good Object-Oriented citizen, a public interface to the FedEx object's settings are available. The *retrieve_okay()* method returns true when the HTTP response code was 200. The *delivered()* method returns true if the document was delivered. The *who_got_it()* method returns the name of the recipient of a delivered package. Finally, the *error_info()* method prints out an HTML error message.

Now that we've reviewed the important parts of the FedEx package, let's take a look at the complete example. Note how one creates a FedEx object and calls it. We'll come back to this example and redo it as a graphical client in Chapter 7:

```
    #!/usr/local/bin/perl -w
    use strict;

    use HTML::FormatText;
    use HTML::Parse;
    use vars qw($opt_h $opt_a $opt_e $opt_d $opt_c $opt_p);
    use Getopt::Std;

    # URL that handles our FedEx query
    my $cgi = 'http://www.fedex.com/cgi-bin/track_it';

    getopts('ha:e:d:c:p:');

    # print help upon request or when arguments are missing
    if ($opt_h  || !($opt_a && $opt_e && $opt_d && $opt_c )) {
      print_help();
      exit(0);
    }

    #
```

```
my $tracker = new FedEx $cgi, $opt_e, $opt_p;

my $keep_checking = 1;
```

First, we declare local variables, call all necessary modules, get command-line options, etc.

The body of the program is just a loop that keeps checking the FedEx site until the package is delivered or an error is found:

```
while ($keep_checking) {
  $tracker->check($opt_a, $opt_c, $opt_d);

  if ($tracker->retrieve_okay) {

    if ($tracker->delivered) {
      print "Tracking number $opt_a was delivered to: ",
            $tracker->who_got_it, "\n";
      $keep_checking = 0;

    }
    else {

      # request was okay, but not delivered.  Let's wait
      sleep (60 * 30);  # sleep 30 minutes
    }

  }
  else {

    # request not successful
    my $html_error_message = $tracker->error_info;

    my $parsed    = parse_html($html_error_message);
    my $converter = new HTML::FormatText;
    print $converter->format($parsed);

    $keep_checking = 0;
  }
}
```

The *print_help()* routine prints a help message, as always:

```
sub  print_help {

  print <<HELP
This program prints a notification when a FedEx shipment is delivered.
fedex -a 1234 -e user\@host.com -d 120396 -c U.S.A. [ -p http://
host:port/ ]

h - this help text
a - airbill number
e - your email address
d - date in MMDDYY format that document was sent
```

```
c - country of recipient
p - use this proxy server [optional]
HELP
}
```

Now the code we showed you previously, defining the FedEx package:

```
package FedEx;

use HTTP::Request;
use HTTP::Response;
use LWP::RobotUA;
use HTTP::Status;

sub new {

  my($class, $cgi_url, $email, $proxy) = @_;
  my $user_agent_name = 'ORA-Check-FedEx/1.0';

  my $self  = {};
  bless $self, $class;

  $self->{'url'} = new URI::URL $cgi_url;

  $self->{'robot'} = new LWP::RobotUA $user_agent_name, $email;
  $self->{'robot'}->delay(0);    # we'll delay requests by hand

  if ($proxy) {
    $self->{'robot'}->proxy('http', $proxy);
  }

  $self;
}

sub check {

  my ($self, $track_num, $country, $date) = @_;

  $self->{'url'}->query("trk_num=$track_num&dest_cntry=" .
    "$country&ship_date=$date");
  my $request = new HTTP::Request 'GET', $self->{'url'};

  my $response = $self->{'robot'}->request($request);
  $self->{'status'} = $response->code();

  if ($response->code == RC_OK) {

    if ($response->content =~ /Delivered To : (\w.*)/) {

      # package delivered
      $self->{'who_got_it'} = $1;
      $self->{'delivered'} = 1;
    }

    # Odd cases when package is delivered but "Delivered To" is blank.
```

```perl
      # Check for delivery time instead.

      elsif ($response->content =~ /Delivery Time : \w.*/) {

        # package delivered
        $self->{'who_got_it'} = 'left blank by FedEx computer';
        $self->{'delivered'} = 1;
      }
      else {

        # package wasn't delivered
        $self->{'delivered'} = 0;

        # if there isn't a "Delivered To : " field, something's wrong.
        # error messages seen between HTML comments

        if ($response->content !~ /Delivered To : /) {
          $self->{'status'} = RC_BAD_REQUEST;

          # get explanation from HTML response
    my $START = '<!-- BEGIN TRACKING INFORMATION -->';
    my $END = '<!-- END TRACKING INFORMATION -->';

          if   ($response->content =~ /$START(.*?)$END/s) {

        $self->{'error_as_HTML'} = $1;

          }
          else {
            # couldn't get explanation, use generic one
            $self->{'error_as_HTML'} = 'Unexpected HTML response from
              FedEx';

          }      # couldn't get error explanation
        }        # unexpected reply
      }          # not delivered yet
    }            # if HTTP response of RC_OK (200)
    else {
      $self->{'error_as_HTML'} = $response->error_as_HTML;
    }

}

sub retrieve_okay {

  my $self = shift;
  if ($self->{'status'} != RC_OK) {return 0;}
  1;
}

sub delivered {

  my $self = shift;
  $self->{'delivered'};
}
```

```
sub who_got_it {

  my $self = shift;
  $self->{'who_got_it'};
}

sub error_info {

  my $self = shift;
  $self->{'error_as_HTML'};
}
```

# *Recursive Clients*

Recursive clients are robots that follow hyperlinks or other references on an HTML page. In this section, we present a program that looks for bad links in a web site. I've created a package called *CheckSite* that follows links within HTML and reports various properties of each page. The constructor accepts the email address, delay time between requests, maximum number of requests, verbose flag, and optional proxy URL as parameters. As in the FedEx example, this creates an LWP::RobotUA object inside the CheckSite package.

```
package CheckSite;
sub new {

  my ($class, $email, $delay, $max, $verbose, $proxy) = @_;
  my $self = {};
  bless $self, $class;


  # Create a User Agent object, give it a name, set delay between requests
  $self->{'ua'} = new LWP::RobotUA 'ORA_checksite/1.0', $email;
  if (defined $delay) {$self->{'ua'}->delay($delay);}

  # If proxy server specified, define it in the User Agent object
  if (defined $proxy) {
    $self->{'ua'}->proxy('http', $proxy);
  }

  $self->{'max'} = $max;
  $self->{'verbose'} = $verbose;

  $self;
}
```

Then the *scan()* method does all the real work. The *scan()* method accepts a URL as a parameter. In a nutshell, here's what happens:

The *scan()* method pushes the first URL into a queue. For any URL pulled from the queue, any links on that page are extracted from that page and pushed on the queue. To keep track of which URLs have already been visited (and not to push them back onto the queue), we use an associative array called *%touched* and associate any URL that has been visited with a value of 1. There are other useful variables that are also used, to track which document points to what, the content-type of the document, which links are bad, which links are local, which links are remote, etc.

For a more detailed look at how this works, let's step through it.

First, the initial URL is pushed onto a queue:

```
push (@urls , $root_url);
```

The URL is then checked with a HEAD method. If we can determine that the URL is not an HTML document, we can skip it. Otherwise, we follow that with a GET method to get the HTML:

```
my $request  = new HTTP::Request('HEAD', $url);
my $response = $self->{'ua'}->request($request);

# if not HTML, don't bother to search it for URLs
next if ($response->header('Content-Type') !~ m@text/html@ );


# it is text/html, get the entity-body this time
$request->method('GET');
$response = $self->{'ua'}->request($request);
```

Then we extract the links from the HTML page. Here, we use our own function to extract the links. There is a similar function in the LWP library that extracts links, but we opted not to use it, since it is less prone to find links in slightly malformed HTML:

```
my @rel_urls = grab_urls($data);

foreach $verbose_link (@rel_urls) {
...
}
```

With each iteration of the *foreach* loop, we process one link. If we haven't seen it before, we add it to the queue:

```
foreach $verbose_link (@rel_urls) {

  if (! defined $self->{'touched'}{$full_child}) {
    push (@urls, $full_child);
  }

  # remember which url we just pushed, to avoid repushing
  $self->{'touched'}{$full_child} = 1;
}
```

While all of this is going on, we keep track of which documents don't exist, what their content types are, which ones are local to the web server, which are not local, and which are not HTTP-based. After *scan()* finishes, all of the information is available from CheckSite's public interface. The *bad()* method returns an associative array of any URLs that encountered errors. Within the associative array, one uses the URL as a key, and the key value is a \n delimited error message. For the *not_web()*, *local()*, and *remote()* methods, a similar associative array is returned, where the URL is a key in the array and denotes that the URL is not HTTP-based, is local to the web server, or is not local to the web server, in that order. The *type()* method returns an associate array of URLs, where the value of each URL hash contains the content-type for the URL. And finally, the *ref()* method is an associative array of URLs with values of referring URLs, delimited by \n. So if the URL hash of "www.ora.com" has a value of "a.ora.com" and "b.ora.com", that means "a.ora.com" and "b.ora.com" both point to "www.ora.com".

Here's the complete source of the CheckSite package, with some sample code around it to read in command-line arguments and print out the results:

```perl
#!/usr/local/bin/perl -w
use strict;

use vars qw($opt_a $opt_v $opt_l $opt_r $opt_R $opt_n $opt_b
            $opt_h $opt_m $opt_p $opt_e $opt_d);
use Getopt::Std;


# Important variables
#----------------------------
# @lookat       queue of URLs to look at
# %local        $local{$URL}=1  (local URLs in associative array)
# %remote       $remote{$URL}=1 (remote URLs in associative array)
# %ref          $ref{$URL}="URL\nURL\n" (list of URLs separated by \n)
# %touched      $touched{$URL}=1 (URLs that have been visited)
# %notweb       $notweb{$URL}=1 if URL is non-HTTP
# %badlist      $badlist{$URL}="reason" (URLs that failed. Separated with \n)

getopts('avlrRnbhm:p:e:d:');

# Display help upon -q, no args, or no e-mail address

if ($opt_h || $#ARGV == -1 || (! $opt_e) ) {
  print_help();
  exit(-1);
}

# set maximum number of URLs to visit to be unlimited

my ($print_local, $print_remote, $print_ref, $print_not_web,
    $print_bad,   $verbose,      $max,        $proxy,
    $email,       $delay,        $url);
```

```
$max=0;

if ($opt_l) {$print_local=1;}
if ($opt_r) {$print_remote=1;}
if ($opt_R) {$print_ref=1;}
if ($opt_n) {$print_not_web=1;}
if ($opt_b) {$print_bad=1;}
if ($opt_v) {$verbose=1;}
if (defined $opt_m) {$max=$opt_m;}
if ($opt_p) {$proxy=$opt_p;}
if ($opt_e) {$email=$opt_e;}
if (defined $opt_d) {$delay=$opt_d;}
if ($opt_a) {
  $print_local=$print_remote=$print_ref=$print_not_web=$print_bad = 1;
}

my $root_url=shift @ARGV;

# if there's no URL to start with, tell the user
unless ($root_url) {
  print "Error: need URL to start with\n";
  exit(-1);
}

# if no "output" options are selected, make "print_bad" the default
if (!($print_local || $print_remote || $print_ref ||
  $print_not_web || $print_bad)) {
  $print_bad=1;
}

# create CheckSite object and tell it to scan the site
my $site = new CheckSite($email, $delay, $max, $verbose, $proxy);
$site->scan($root_url);

# done with checking URLs.  Report results


# print out references to local machine
if ($print_local) {
  my %local = $site->local;

  print "\nList of referenced local URLs:\n";
  foreach $url (keys %local) {
    print "local: $url\n";
  }
}


# print out references to remote machines
if ($print_remote) {
  my %remote = $site->remote;

  print "\nList of referenced remote URLs:\n";
  foreach $url (keys %remote) {
```

```
      print "remote: $url\n";
   }
}


# print non-HTTP references
if ($print_not_web) {
  my %notweb = $site->not_web;

  print "\nReferenced non-HTTP links:\n";
  foreach $url (keys %notweb) {
    print "notweb: $url\n";
  }
}

# print reference list (what URL points to what)
if ($print_ref) {
  my $refer_by;
  my %ref = $site->ref;

  print "\nReference information:\n";
  while (($url,$refer_by) = each %ref) {
    print "\nref: $url is referenced by:\n";
    $refer_by =~ s/\n/\n  /g;  # insert two spaces after each \n
    print "  $refer_by";
  }
}

# print out bad URLs, the server response line, and the Referer
if ($print_bad) {
  my $reason;
  my $refer_by;
  my %bad = $site->bad;
  my %ref = $site->ref;

  print "\nThe following links are bad:\n";
  while (($url,$reason) = each %bad) {
    print "\nbad: $url  Reason: $reason";
    print "Referenced by:\n";
     $refer_by = $ref{$url};
     $refer_by =~ s/\n/\n  /g;  # insert two spaces after each \n
     print "  $refer_by";
  } # while there's a bad link
} # if bad links are to be reported


sub print_help() {
  print <<"USAGETEXT";
Usage:  $0 URL\n
Options:
  -l          Display local URLs
  -r          Display remote URLs
  -R          Display which HTML pages refers to what
  -n          Display non-HTML links
```

```
  -b          Display bad URLs (default)
  -a          Display all of the above
  -v          Print out URLs when they are examined
  -e email    Mandatory: Specify email address to include
        in HTTP request.
  -m #        Examine at most # URLs\n
  -p url    Use this proxy server
  -d #        Delay # minutes between requests.  (default=1)
        Warning: setting # to 0 is not very nice.
  -h          This help text

Example: $0 -e me\@host.com -p http://proxy/ http://site_to_check/
USAGETEXT
  }



package CheckSite;

use HTTP::Status;
use HTTP::Request;
use HTTP::Response;
use LWP::RobotUA;
use URI::URL;

sub new {

  my ($class, $email, $delay, $max, $verbose, $proxy) = @_;
  my $self = {};
  bless $self, $class;


  # Create a User Agent object, give it a name, set delay between requests
  $self->{'ua'} = new LWP::RobotUA 'ORA_checksite/1.0', $email;
  if (defined $delay) {$self->{'ua'}->delay($delay);}

  # If proxy server specified, define it in the User Agent object
  if (defined $proxy) {
    $self->{'ua'}->proxy('http', $proxy);
  }

  $self->{'max'} = $max;
  $self->{'verbose'} = $verbose;

  $self;
}

sub scan {

  my ($self, $root_url)   = @_;
  my $verbose_link;
  my $num_visited = 0;
  my @urls;
```

```
# clear out variables from any previous call to scan()
undef %{ $self->{'bad'} };
undef %{ $self->{'not_web'} };
undef %{ $self->{'local'} };
undef %{ $self->{'remote'} };
undef %{ $self->{'type'} };
undef %{ $self->{'ref'} };
undef %{ $self->{'touched'} };

my $url_strict_state = URI::URL::strict();   # to restore state later
URI::URL::strict(1);


my $parsed_root_url = eval { new URI::URL $root_url; };
push (@urls , $root_url);
$self->{'ref'}{$root_url} = "Root URL\n";


while (@urls) {              # while URL queue not empty
  my $url=shift @urls;        # pop URL from queue & parse it

  # increment number of URLs visited and check if maximum is reached
  $num_visited++;
  last if (  ($self->{'max'}) && ($num_visited > $self->{'max'}) );

  # handle verbose information
  print STDERR "Looking at $url\n" if ($self->{'verbose'});

  my $parsed_url = eval { new URI::URL $url; };

  # if malformed URL (error in eval) , skip it
  if ($@) {
    $self->add_bad($url, "parse error: $@");
    next;
  }

  # if not HTTP, skip it
  if ($parsed_url->scheme !~ /http/i) {
    $self->{'not_web'}{$url}=1;
    next;
  }

  # skip urls that are not on same server as root url
  if (same_server($parsed_url, $parsed_root_url)) {
    $self->{'local'}{$url}=1;
  } else {                                # remote site
    $self->{'remote'}{$url}=1;
    next;               # only interested in local references
  }

  # Ask the User Agent object to get headers for the url
  # Results go into the response object (HTTP::Response).


  my $request  = new HTTP::Request('HEAD', $url);
```

```perl
my $response = $self->{'ua'}->request($request);

# if response wasn't RC_OK (200), skip it
if ($response->code != RC_OK) {
  my $desc = status_message($response->code);
  $self->add_bad($url, "${desc}\n");
  next;
}

# keep track of every url's content-type
$self->{'type'}{$url} = $response->header('Content-Type');

# if not HTML, don't bother to search it for URLs
next if ($response->header('Content-Type') !~ m@text/html@ );


# it is text/html, get the entity-body this time
$request->method('GET');
$response = $self->{'ua'}->request($request);

# if not OK or text/html... weird, it was a second ago.  skip it.
next if ($response->code != RC_OK);
next if ($response->header('Content-Type') !~ m@text/html@ );

my $data     = $response->content;
my @rel_urls = grab_urls($data);

foreach $verbose_link (@rel_urls) {

  my $full_child =  eval {
    (new URI::URL $verbose_link, $response->base)->
    abs($response->base,1);
  };

  # if LWP doesn't recognize the child url, treat it as malformed
  if ($@) {

# update list of bad urls, remember where it happened
$self->add_bad($verbose_link, "unrecognized format: $@");
    $self->add_ref($verbose_link, $url);

    next;
  }
  else {

    # remove fragment in http urls
    if ( ($full_child->scheme() =~ /http/i) ) {
      $full_child->frag(''));
    }

    # handle reference list and push unvisited links onto queue
    $self->add_ref($full_child, $url);
    if (! defined $self->{'touched'}{$full_child}) {
      push (@urls, $full_child);
```

```
      }

          # remember which url we just pushed, to avoid repushing
          $self->{'touched'}{$full_child} = 1;

      }     # process valid links on page
    }         # foreach url in this page
  }           # while url(s) in queue

  URI::URL::strict($url_strict_state);  # restore state before exiting

} # scan

sub same_server {
  my ($host1, $host2) = @_;

  my $host2_name = $host2->host;

  if ($host1->host !~ /^$host2_name$/i) {return 0;}
  if ($host1->port != $host2->port) {return 0;}

  1;
}


# grab_urls($html_content) returns an array of links that are referenced
# from within the html.  Covers <body background>, <img src>, and <a href>.
# This includes a little more functionality than the
# HTML::Element::extract_links() method.
#BACK
sub grab_urls {

  my ($data) = @_;
  my @urls;
  my $key;
  my $link;


  my %tags = (
    'body' => 'background',
    'img'  => 'src',
    'a'    => 'href'
  );

  # while there are HTML tags
  skip_others: while ($data =~ s/<([^>]*)>//)   {

    my $in_brackets=$1;

    foreach $key (keys %tags) {

      if ($in_brackets =~ /^\s*$key\s+/i) {      # if tag matches, try parms
        if ($in_brackets =~ /\s+$tags{$key}\s*=\s*["']([^"']*)["']/i) {
          $link=$1;
          $link =~ s/[\n\r]//g;  # kill newlines,returns anywhere in url
```

```
          push @urls, $link;
       next skip_others;
          }
     # handle case when url isn't in quotes (ie: <a href=thing>)
         elsif ($in_brackets =~ /\s+$tags{$key}\s*=\s*([^\s]+)/i) {
            $link=$1;
            $link =~ s/[\n\r]//g;   # kill newlines,returns anywhere in url
            push @urls, $link;
       next skip_others;
          }
       }          # if tag matches
     }            # foreach <a|img|body>
   }              # while there are brackets
   @urls;
}


# public interface to class's internal variables

# return associative array of bad urls and their error messages
sub bad {
  my $self = shift;
  %{ $self->{'bad'} };
}


# return associative array of encountered urls that are not http based
sub not_web {
  my $self = shift;
  %{ $self->{'not_web'} };
}


# return associative array of encountered urls that are local to the
# web server that was queried in the latest call to scan()

sub local {
  my $self = shift;
  %{ $self->{'local'} };
}


# return associative array of encountered urls that are not local to the
# web server that was queried in the latest call to scan()

sub remote {
  my $self = shift;
  %{ $self->{'remote'} };
}


# return associative array of encountered urls and their content-type
sub type {
  my $self = shift;
  %{ $self->{'type'} };
}


# return associative array of encountered urls and their parent urls,
# where parent urls are separated by newlines in one big string
```

```
sub ref {
  my $self = shift;
  %{ $self->{'ref'} };
}

# return associative array of encountered urls.  If we didn't push it
# into the queue of urls to visit, it isn't here.

sub touched {
  my $self = shift;
  %{ $self->{'touched'} };
}

# add_bad($child, $parent)
#   This keeps an associative array of urls, where the associated value
#   of each url is an error message that was encountered when
#   parsing or accessing the url.  If error messages already exist for
#   the url, any additional error messages are concatenated to existing
#   messages.

sub add_bad {
  my ($self, $url, $msg) = @_;

  if (! defined $self->{'bad'}{$url} ) {
    $self->{'bad'}{$url}  = $msg;
  }
  else {
    $self->{'bad'}{$url}  .= $msg;
  }
}

# add_ref($child, $parent)
#   This keeps an associative array of urls, where the associated value
#   of each url is a string of urls that refer to it.  So if
#   url 'a' and 'b' refer to url 'c', then $self->{'ref'}{'c'}
#   would have a value of 'a\nb\n'.  The newline separates parent urls.

sub add_ref {

  my ($self, $child, $parent) = @_;

  if (! defined  $self->{'ref'}{$child} ) {
    $self->{'ref'}{$child} = "$parent\n";
  }
  elsif ($self->{'ref'}{$child} !~ /$parent\n/) {
    $self->{'ref'}{$child} .= "$parent\n";
  }fo

    }
```

In the following chapter, we'll do a few more examples, this time graphical examples using the Tk extension to Perl.

# 7

# *Graphical Examples with Perl/Tk*

The Tk extension to Perl can be used to create a Graphical User Interface (GUI) to your Perl programs on UNIX. Why would you want to do this? Several reasons, such as ease of use, or to be able to display HTML nicely. Instead of just writing a "cool script," you could go as far as writing your own custom browser.

In this chapter, we show a few examples of Tk-based web clients, which go beyond the command-line interface that we've been using so far in this book:*

- *xword*, a dictionary client

- *track*, a graphical version of the FedEx example shown in Chapter 6.

- *webping*, an at-a-glance display of the status of multiple web servers

One caveat about Tk, and it's a serious one. At this writing, the Tk module to Perl (also known as *pTk*) only runs on UNIX machines with the X Window System. While the Tk extension to the Tcl language has been successfully ported to Microsoft Windows, the Perl port is still pending, although it is rumored to be in the works.

Still, even with its limited availability, we think the ability to give your programs an easy-to-use graphical interface is important enough to devote a chapter to it. And who knows—by the time you're reading this, the pTk port to Windows might already be completed, and this whole paragraph may be moot.

---

* I say "we," but I really mean "she"—this chapter was written by Nancy Walsh, who combined her knowledge of Tk with my knowledge of LWP.

# *A Brief Introduction to Tk*

Tk was originally developed by John Ousterhout as an extension to his Tcl language, for providing a graphical user interface for the X Window System. It was ported to Perl soon afterwards; Nick Ing-Simmons did most of the work to make it functional as a module with Perl. You can get Tk from any CPAN archive (*http://www.perl.com/CPAN/*).

The Tk extension provides an easy way to draw a window, put widgets into it (such as buttons, check boxes, entry fields, menus, etc.), and have them perform certain actions based on user input. A simple "Hello World" program would look like this:

```
1    #!/usr/bin/perl -w
2    use Tk;
3    my $mw = MainWindow->new;
4    $mw->Button(-text => "Hello World!", -command =>sub{exit})->pack;
5    MainLoop;
```

(The line numbers are not part of the actual code; they are just included for ease in reference.)

When you run it, it would look like Figure 7-1.

*Figure 7-1. A simple Tk widget*

Pushing the "Hello World" button will exit the program, and your window will then go away. Line 1 tells the shell to invoke Perl to interpret the rest of the file, and Line 2 then tells Perl that we need to use the Tk module. Line 3 tells the system that you want it to build you a generic, standard window. Line 4 creates a button, displays it (using the *pack* method), and gives the button something to do when pushed.

Line 5 tells the program to "go do it." *MainLoop* kicks off the event handler for the graphical interface. The most important concept to understand with Perl/Tk is that the program won't do a single thing until it hits the *MainLoop* statement. You won't see any graphical output at all until then. We prepare it by telling it what we want to draw, and what should happen when certain events happen, such as a mouse click on our button in our "Hello World" program. The more complex the things you want the GUI to do, the more complex the code looks for setting it up.

Since the purpose of this chapter is to show some examples using Tk and to interact with the WWW, we won't be going into much more detail about what Tk does and why. Some places you might look for help are the newsgroup *comp.lang.perl.tk* for Perk/Tk-specific questions, or the Perl/Tk FAQ at *http:// w4.lns.cornell.edu/~pvhp/ptk/ptkFAQ.html*. Any search site will point you to at least 30 web sites as well. And of course the Tk source includes "pod" documentation: run *pod2text* on *Tk.pm* to get started.

Before we continue, there a few odd  things you need to know about Perl/Tk:

- => is functionally the same as a comma (,). Using => makes it easier to detect "pairs" of items in a list.

- Widgets are always built referencing another part of the GUI, if not the main window (in our examples, *$mw*), then another widget or frame. This builds the parent/child hierarchy and allows the packer to know what to pack where.

- The *pack()* method essentially displays the widget on the screen, according to any parameters sent to it. Alternately, it could un-display it as well. If you don't *pack()* a widget, it won't show up.

Now on to some examples.

# *A Dictionary Client: xword*

For our first example, we want to build a simple application that has only a few types of widgets in it. The *xword* program will prompt the user for a word, then use an online dictionary to define it, and return the formatted results.

When you need a quick word definition, instead of running a web browser (which can often have a lengthy startup time with all those fancy plug-ins), surfing to the site via a bookmark, and then entering the word to get your answer, you can use this simple program that will just prompt for the word and go look it up without all that extra hassle. Anyone familiar with the *xwebster* client for the X Window System will find *xword* to be vaguely familiar, but our version doesn't require a local licensed dictionary server; we use one already existing on the Web. Since the program is so simple, you can probably just iconify it, and then bring it back up whenever you're stumped for the spelling or meaning of another word.

So in designing our window, we want a place to enter the word, and a place to display the results. We also need to be able to exit the program (always a must). It seems pretty simple, until we remember that the definition information sent back to us is going to come back in HTML. I really don't want to have to visually dig through a bunch of HTML codes to find out the answer I'm looking for, so I want my program to handle that as well when it displays the answer. We have two options: ignore the HTML codes completely or find a simple way to parse them and make the output look a little nicer.

Luckily, the HTML module distributed with LWP will do most of the work for us. As described in Chapter 5, *The LWP Library*, the HTML package contains a function called *parse_html()*, which takes a string containing HTML as its argument, and returns a pointer to a data structure with all the HTML tags and text parsed out and remembered in order. Now we can use another function called *traverse()*, which operates on this data structure and lets us specify what function to call for each piece of information it contains.

Keeping all this in mind, let's look at our program:

```
#!/usr/bin/perl

use Tk;
require LWP::UserAgent;
use HTML::Parse;
```

We first use the #! notation to tell the kernel we'll be using Perl. We need the Tk package for the GUI interface, the LWP::UserAgent to connect to the web site, and HTML::Parse to help us parse the results:

```
%html_action =
  (
   "</TITLE>",  \&end_title,
   "<H1>",       \&start_heading,
   "</H1>",      \&end_heading,
   "<H2>",       \&start_heading,
   "</H2>",      \&end_heading,
   "<H3>",       \&start_heading,
   "</H3>",      \&end_heading,
   "<H4>",       \&start_heading,
   "</H4>",      \&end_heading,
   "<H5>",       \&start_heading,
   "</H5>",      \&end_heading,
   "<H6>",       \&start_heading,
   "</H6>",      \&end_heading,
   "<P>",        \&paragraph,
   "<BR>",       \&line_break,
   "<HR>",       \&draw_line,
   "<A>",        \&flush_text,
   "</A>",       \&end_link,
   "</BODY>",    \&line_break,
  );
```

In order for us not to rethink the HTML each time, we build an associative array whose key is the HTML tag we want to take action on, and the value is a function reference. We'll cover what the functions take as arguments later on. Now, while we are traversing the document, we can ignore any tags that aren't in our array, and perform actions on ones that are:

```
$ua = new LWP::UserAgent;
$dictionary_url = "http://work.ucsd.edu:5141/cgi-bin/http_webster";
```

We need to set up a few basic globals, the UserAgent object being one of them. We'll use the dictionary server at UC San Diego as the default. While other dictionary servers would probably work, slight modifications to the code might be necessary. Now we can get on with building the actual interface:

```
$mw = MainWindow->new;
$mw->title("xword");
$mw->CmdLine;
```

So we create our window. *$mw->CmdLine* allows parsing of any *-geometry* or *-iconic* command line arguments automatically:

```
$frame1 = $mw->Frame(-borderwidth => 2,
            -relief => 'ridge');
$frame1->pack(-side => 'top',
        -expand => 'n',
        -fill => "x");
$frame2 = $mw->Frame;
$frame2->pack(-side => 'top', -expand => 'yes', -fill => 'both');
$frame3 = $mw->Frame;
$frame3->pack(-side => 'top', -expand => 'no', -fill => 'x');
```

We create three frames,* which essentially divide our window in thirds. The top frame, *$frame1*, will contain the place to type a word and the Lookup button. The middle frame, *$frame2*, will contain the text widget and its associated scrollbar. *$frame3* will contain a text informational display and the exit button. *$frame2* is the only one that will expand itself into any available space, making it the largest section of the window. Now, let's actually create the stuff to go in our empty frames:

```
$frame1->Label(-text => "Enter Word: ")->pack(-side => "left",
                        -anchor => "w");
$entry = $frame1->Entry(-textvariable => \$word,
            -width => 40);
$entry->pack(-side => "left",
        -anchor => "w",
        -fill => "x",
        -expand => "y");

$bttn = $frame1->Button(-text => "Lookup",
            -command => sub { &do_search(); });
$bttn->pack(-side => "left",
```

---

* Frames are just invisible containers for other widgets. They group things together so the window will look the way you want it to. You can make them visible by specifying *-borderwidth* and *-relief* options.

```
           -anchor => "w");

     $entry->bind('<Return>', sub { &do_search(); } );
```

We create a Label so we know what to type in the entry area. We then create the
Entry widget where the typing of the word will take place. We want lots of room
to type, so we set it up with a default width of 40. Also note that we are storing
anything that's been entered with the Entry widget in a global variable called
*$word*.

The last item is our Lookup button. We configure it to call the function *do_search*
when the button is clicked. One last refinement: we want to be able to just hit
return after typing in our word, so we bind the key sequence Return to also call
the *do_search()* function.*

```
     $scroll = $frame2->Scrollbar;
     $text = $frame2->Text(-yscrollcommand => ['set', $scroll],
                    -wrap => 'word',
                    -font => 'lucidasans-12',
                    -state => 'disabled');
     $scroll->configure(-command => ['yview', $text]);
     $scroll->pack(-side => 'right', -expand => 'no', -fill => 'y');
     $text->pack(-side => 'left', -anchor => 'w',
             -expand => 'yes', -fill => 'both');
```

Next we set up the middle area of our window to hold a text widget and a
scrollbar. I'm making lucidasans-12† the default font for the text, but you can
change this to any font you prefer. We also want our text to wrap around automatically at word boundaries (as opposed to character boundaries). Also note that
we "disable" the text widget. This is done because the standard behavior of the
text widget is to allow the user to type things into it. We want to use it for display
purposes only, so we disable it. Most of the other stuff is setting the scrollbar to
scroll up and down and assigning it to the text widget.

```
     $frame3->Label(-textvariable => \$INFORMATION,
              -justify => 'left')->pack(-side => 'left',
                          -expand => 'no',
                          -fill => 'x');
     $frame3->Button(-text => "Exit",
              -command => sub{exit} )->pack(-side => 'right',
                              -anchor => 'e');
```

The third portion of our window is just going to contain an information label, and
the exit button. We don't have anything to save when we quit, so we just map it
directly to *sub{exit}*.

---

* You'll note that it looks like a lot of extra effort to declare *sub { do_search() }*. Doing it this way prevents
any parameters from being sent to our function when it is called.

† To check to make sure you have this font family on your system, use *xlsfonts*. If you don't have it, just
pick another font you do have.

```
$text->tag('configure', '</H1>', -font => 'lucidasans-bold-24');
$text->tag('configure', '</H2>', -font => 'lucidasans-bold-18');
$text->tag('configure', '</H3>', -font => 'lucidasans-bold-14');
$text->tag('configure', '</H4>', -font => 'lucidasans-bold-12');
$text->tag('configure', '</H5>', -font => 'lucidasans-bold-12');
$text->tag('configure', '</H6>', -font => 'lucidasans-bold-12');
```

Our window is basically set up—but our text widget isn't completely set up yet. We need to create some "tags" (identifiers that distinguish different portions of the text widget) to change the font when we find certain HTML tags. In this case, they are all HTML end tags for headers. We don't want to make this too complicated, so we won't handle many more complicated HTML tags. Note that our tag names are the same as the HTML tag names—this makes it easy to switch back and forth later on.

```
$entry->focus;
MainLoop;
```

Finally, we set our focus on the entry widget so we can start typing a word when the application comes up. Then we call *MainLoop* to start the event handler. The rest of the code gets called as certain events happen. (Remember how we told the Lookup button to call *do_search()* when pressed?) So let's look at the specifics of what happens in our window. Let's say we typed in the word "example" and hit Return. The global *$word* will contain the string "example", and the *do_search()* function will be called:

```
sub do_search {
    my ($url) = @_;

    return if ($word =~ /^\s*$/);

    $url = "$dictionary_url?$word" if (! defined $url);
```

The *do_search()* function will take an optional *$url* argument, to give it an alternative place to connect to. Otherwise it expects *$word* to contain something. We just hit Return from the entry widget, so *$word* contains the string "example", and *$url* is undefined. If we accidentally hit Return before typing anything, we don't want to search for a nonstring, so we return from the subroutine if that's the case:

```
$INFORMATION = "Connect: $url";

$text->configure(-cursor=> 'watch');
$mw->idletasks;
```

We give the user some feedback by placing along the bottom of the application a "Connect..." string, and we also change the cursor to a watch. *$mw->idletasks* just tells the window to do anything it was waiting to do, so that we can actually see the watch and information string:

```
my $request = new HTTP::Request('GET', $url);
```

```
my $response = $ua->request($request);
if ($response->is_error) {
$INFORMATION = "ERROR: Could not retrieve $url";
} elsif ($response->is_success) {
my $html = parse_html($response->content);

## Clear out text item
$text->configure(-state => "normal");

$text->delete('1.0', 'end');
$html->traverse(\&display_html);
$text->configure(-state => "disabled");
$html_text = "";
$INFORMATION = "Done";
}

$text->configure(-cursor => 'top_left_arrow');
}
```

Next we try to connect to the *$url*. If we fail, the program should display a simple error message in the information area. If we succeed, then we want to get the actual document out and parse it. *$html* will contain the HTML tree object. We reconfigure the text object to "normal" so that we can place text in it,* delete anything that might have been there previously, and then call *traverse* for the HTML object (telling *traverse* to call *display_html* for each item). After the entire document has been traversed (we'll see what that does in a minute), we re-disable the text widget, and declare ourselves done for that particular word lookup.

Our function, *display_html*, gets called with three arguments: a *$node* pointer, a *$startflag* flag, and the *$depth* we are into the tree. We only care about the first two arguments, since they will help us decide what action to perform.

```
sub display_html {
    my ($node, $startflag, $depth) = @_;
    my ($tag, $type, $coderef);  ## This tag is the HTML tag...

    if (!ref $node) {
        $html_text .= $node;
    } else {
    if ($startflag) {
    $tag = $node->starttag;
} else {
        $tag = $node->endtag;
}

    ## Gets rid of any 'extra' stuff in the tag, and saves it
```

---

* One of the annoying things about a text widget is that when you disable it for the user, you also disable it for yourself. If you want to do anything to it other than destroy it, you need to configure it back to normal.

```
if ($tag =~ /^(<\w+)\s(.*)>/) {
        $tag = "$1>";
        $extra = $2;
}

if (exists $html_action{$tag}) {
$html_text =~ s/\s+/ /g;
        &{ $html_action{$tag} }($tag, $html_text);
        $html_text = "";
}
    }
    1;
}
```

That's the entire function, but it does quite a bit. The *$node* could either be an object or a simple text string. For the simple case, when it's just text, we append it to any prior text (remember, we could be ignoring HTML tags, along the way, that had text before them) and save it for future use. If *$node* is an object pointer, then we have to determine what kind it is, and decide if we care about the HTML tag it's telling us about.

HTML tags usually come in pairs, so *$startflag* tells us when we found the first of a pair. We want to know what that tag was, so we call the *starttag* method. Certain tags have other information associated with them (i.e., the <A> tag), and we want to save that for future use in *$extra*. Remember that we are trying to get just the plain simple tag to use in our lookup array.

We do a few more things to clean up, and then we can do our lookup. If we care about this *$tag*, then we compress all spaces in the current text string (makes the display a little bit nicer) and call the function specified in our lookup array, passing it *$tag* and *$html_text*. We left *$extra* as a global because most of our functions won't use it.

All that work was just to figure out what function to call. We could have done a big huge if..then..else statement instead of utilizing a lookup hash, but that would have been large and unwieldy, and would also have made it more difficult to add new tag handling functions. The following are those tag handling functions, and most of them are pretty short:

```
sub end_title {
    $mw->title("xword: ". $_[1]);
}
```

When we find the end title tag, we change our window title to reflect it (a lot like a standard web browser).

```
sub start_heading {
    &flush_text(@_);
    $text->insert('end', "\n\n");
}
```

When we start a heading, we need to delimit it from the prior text (which we insert into our text widget with the *flush_text()* function) with a few returns. Note that *flush_text()* takes the same arguments as any of our tag handlers. This allows us to specify it explicitly in the lookup hash if we want to:

```
sub end_heading {
    $text->insert('end', $_[1], $_[0]);
    $text->insert('end', "\n");
}
```

At the end of the heading, we insert the heading text and another return character. The third argument to the insert function is our actual HTML tag. (In this case it could be </H1> or </H2> and so on.) This tells the text widget to use that tag to format the text. For our headings, we set up that text tag to be a font-changing tag:

```
sub paragraph {
    &flush_text(@_);
    $text->insert('end', "\n\n");
}
```

A paragraph marker, <P>, just means insert a few returns. We also have to flush out any text prior to it:

```
sub line_break {
    &flush_text(@_);
    $text->insert('end', "\n");
}
```

Similar to <P>, the <BR> also just inserts a return:

```
sub draw_line {
    &flush_text(@_);
    $text->insert('end', "\n--------------------------------------\n");
}
```

The <HR> tag inserts a much nicer looking line in our normal web browser, but for our purposes, this set of dashes will accomplish pretty much the same thing:

```
sub flush_text {
    $text->insert('end', $_[1]);
}
```

This function just inserts the text it's handed, as is:

```
sub end_link {
  ## Don't want to add links to mailto refs.
  if ($extra =~ /HREF\s*=\s*"(.+)"/ && $extra !~ /mailto/) {
  my $site = $1;

    ## The tags must have unique names to allow for a different
    ## binding to each one. (Otherwise we'd just be changing that same
    ## tag binding over and over again.)
```

```
        my $newtag = "LINK". $cnt++;

        $text->tag('configure', $newtag, -underline => 'true',
                -foreground => 'blue');
        $text->tag('bind', $newtag, '<Enter>',
                sub { $text->configure(-cursor => 'hand2');
                    $INFORMATION = $site; });
        $text->tag('bind', $newtag, '<Leave>',
                sub { $text->configure(-cursor => 'top_left_arrow');
                    $INFORMATION = "";});

        $text->tag('bind', $newtag, '<ButtonPress>',
                sub { &do_search($site); });

        $text->insert('end', $_[1], $newtag);
        } else {
        &flush_text(@_);
        }


    }
```

Our *end_link()* function is the most complicated, simply because we want to handle links. If you look at the output from our dictionary server on your normal web browser, you'll notice that almost every single piece of text it returns is a link to look up another word. I thought it would be easier to just click on those words and do the lookup than to type in the word again and possibly spell it wrong. We accomplish this by utilizing the text widget tags. If you want the specific word to do something different when you click on it, you have to create a new tag—so we are creating tags on-the-fly (unlike our heading tags, which remained the same no matter where they were in the document, or what text they surrounded).

We use a regexp to extract the URL from our *$extra* variable. We create a new name for our tag. (We never have to know what the name is again, so it's merely a place holder for the text widget.) We create our tag to change the text to be underlined and blue, much as a link would look in a full-blown web browser. We also bind that tag to change the cursor into a little hand when we enter the tag, and to change it back to the standard pointer when we leave that section of text. This gives the users some good feedback on the fact that they can do something with it. We also do one other simple thing: we display the URL in our information area so that users will know what will happen when they click.

The last bind we perform is one that tells the application to call our function, *do_search()*, with the URL we extracted from the HTML tag. Then we insert the text for the link into the text widget, and associate it with the tag we just built.

There are a few other things that could be added to *xword* to make it even nicer. A Back button would be useful, so that after you looked up 10 or so words, you could click on Back to take you backwards through your selections. And how

```
┌──────────────────────────────────────────────────────────────────────┐
│ ● xword: Hypertext Webster Interface -- Definition for "pack"        ▓▓ 卪│
├──────────────────────────────────────────────────────────────────────┤
│ Enter Word: │pack                                              │ │ Lookup ││
├──────────────────────────────────────────────────────────────────────┤
│                                                                    △│
│  Hypertext Webster Interface                                        │
│                                                                     │
│                                                                     │
│  _____                   │
│                                                                     │
│  Webster Definition for "pack"                                      │
│                                                                     │
│   1. pack \'pak\ n [ME, of LG or D origin; akin to MLG & MD pak pack,│
│  MFlem pac] often attrib 1 a: a bundle                              │
│  arranged for convenience in carrying esp. on the back 1 b: a group │
│  or pile of related objects : as 1 b1: a                            │
│  number of separate photographic films packed so as to be inserted  │
│  together into a camera 1 b2: a set of                              │
│  two or three color films or plates for simultaneous exposure 1 b3: │
│  a stack of theatrical flats arranged in                            │
│  sequence 1 c1: PACKET 1 c2: CONTAINER 1 c3: a compact unitized     │
│  assembly to perform a specific function                            │
│  2a: the contents of a bundle 2b: a large amount or number : HEAP   │
│  2c: a full set of playing cards 3a: an act                         │
│  or instance of packing 3b: a method of packing 4a1: a group trained│
│  to hunt or run together 4a2: a group                               │
│  of often predatory animals of the same kind 4a3: a set of persons  │
│  with a common interest : CLIQUE 4b: an                             │
│  organized group of combat craft 5: a concentrated mass 6: wet      │
│  absorbent material for therapeutic                                 │
│  application to the body 7a: a cosmetic paste for the face 7b: an   │
│  application or treatment of oils or creams                         │
│                                                                    ▽│
│                                                         ┌────────┐  │
│                                                         │  Exit  │  │
└──────────────────────────────────────────────────────────────────────┘
```

*Figure 7-2. xword window*

about a list of optional dictionary web servers, in case one is sometimes slow or doesn't respond? These will be left as exercises for the reader.

Some limitations of the HTML parsing: We don't worry about nested HTML tags at all, and we don't worry about fancy things like tables or graphics. Remember, we wanted to keep this simple.

# Check on Package Delivery: Track

Web browsers are great at what they do, but what if we want to query the same page for the same information several times in a row? We could just leave our browser up, and keep hitting "reload" *n* times, but we'd have to remember to do it. A better way would be to write a small application that automatically does our query for us every few minutes.

For this example, we'll interact with the Federal Express tracking page. When you ship a package via FedEx, they keep track of it with a shipping number (also called an airbill number)—and they have been kind enough to make available via the Web a place for us to check up on our packages. If we look at their web page, they have a place to enter the airbill number, a place to select the destination country, and then a place to enter the date. In order to mimic their form, we'll want to have all of these elements in our application.

FedEx has a specific way they want you to specify the country (in all caps, and spelled a particular way), so we just looked at their document source for the list of countries. We will put them all in a listbox, to make it easier to select (instead of trying to guess at the spelling and/or punctuation). The tracking number is fairly easy—it's just a bunch of numbers—so a normal entry widget will do. For the date, another entry widget. Their setup is designed to tell us if we enter an invalid date, so we'll let them handle the error checking on that one.

Now that we know the inputs, we have to decide what to do with them. Basically we want our program to keep looping and re-querying the site. We really don't want our program to loop unless we tell it to, and we also want to be able to stop it from looping at any point. Here's how we accomplish this with Perl/Tk:

```perl
#!/usr/bin/perl -w
use strict;

use HTML::FormatText;
use HTML::Parse;
use Tk;

my $query_interval = 30; # in minutes

my $email = "<your email\@address here>";
my $url = "http://www.fedex.com/cgi-bin/track_it";
```

This is the basic beginning of a Perl/Tk script. We recognize that we want to utilize some of the HTML modules, and of course, the Tk module. We set up some basic globals in our program. The *$query_interval* is in minutes—you can change it to 60 minutes, or 15 minutes. Try not to query too often, though; the status of your package is not likely to change every five minutes. *$email* is your email address. You need to put a "\" in front of the @ sign, so that it won't be interpreted by Perl to be something it's not. This will inform the FedEx web site of who you are. Finally, the *$url* is the destination where we'll be sending our request.

For this program, we are setting the amount of time it waits between loops in a variable. In our next example, we'll show a way to allow the user to change it from the GUI.

```perl
my $mw = MainWindow->new;
$mw->title("Package Tracker");
$mw->CmdLine;
```

We created a window, gave it a title, and allowed the Tk portion to process any command-line options.

```perl
my @destinations =
  ("U.S.A.", "ALBANIA", "ALGERIA", "AMERICAN SAMOA ", "ANDORRA",
    "ANGOLA", "ANGUILLA", "ANTIGUA", "ARGENTINA", "ARMENIA", "ARUBA",
```

```
"AUSTRALIA", "AUSTRIA", "AZERBAIJAN", "BAHAMAS", "BAHRAIN",
"BANGLADESH", "BARBADOS", "BELARUS", "BELGIUM", "BELIZE", "BENIN",
"BERMUDA", "BHUTAN", "BOLIVIA", "BOTSWANA", "BRAZIL",
"BRITISH VIRGIN IS.", "BRUNEI", "BULGARIA", "BURKINO FASO",
"BURUNDI", "CAMBODIA", "CAMEROON", "CANADA", "CAPE VERDE",
"CAYMAN ISLANDS", "CENTRAL AFRICAN REP.", "CHAD", "CHILE",
"CHINA", "COLOMBIA", "CONGO", "COOK ISLANDS", "COSTA RICA",
"COTE D'IVOIRE", "CROATIA", "CYPRUS", "CZECH REPUBLIC", "DENMARK",
"DJIBOUTI", "DOMINICA", "DOMINICAN REPUBLIC", "ECUADOR", "EGYPT",
"EL SALVADOR", "EQUATORIAL GUINEA", "ERITREA", "ESTONIA",
"ETHIOPIA", "FAEROE ISLANDS", "FIJI", "FINLAND", "FRANCE",
"FRENCH GUIANA", "FRENCH POLYNESIA", "GABON", "GAMBIA",
"GEORGIA, REPUBLIC OF", "GERMANY", "GHANA", "GIBRALTAR", "GREECE",
"GREENLAND", "GRENADA", "GUADELOUPE", "GUAM", "GUATEMALA",
"GUINEA", "GUINEA-BISSAU", "GUYANA", "HAITI", "HONDURAS",
"HONG KONG", "HUNGARY", "ICELAND", "INDIA", "INDONESIA",
"IRELAND", "ISRAEL", "ITALY", "JAMAICA", "JAPAN", "JORDAN",
"KAZAKHSTAN", "KENYA", "KUWAIT", "KYRGYZSTAN", "LATVIA",
"LEBANON", "LESOTHO", "LIBERIA", "LIECHTENSTEIN", "LITHUANIA",
"LUXEMBOURG", "MACAU", "MACEDONIA", "MADAGASCAR", "MALAWI",
"MALAYSIA", "MALDIVES", "MALI", "MALTA", "MARSHALL ISLANDS",
"MARTINIQUE", "MAURITANIA", "MAURITIUS", "MEXICO", "MICRONESIA",
"MOLDOVA", "MONACO", "MONGOLIA", "MONTSERRAT", "MOROCCO",
"MOZAMBIQUE", "NAMIBIA", "NEPAL", "NETHERLANDS", "NEW CALEDONIA",
"NEW ZEALAND", "NICARAGUA", "NIGER", "NIGERIA",
"NETHERLANDS ANTILLES", "NORWAY", "OMAN", "PAKISTAN", "PALAU",
"PANAMA", "PAPUA NEW GUINEA", "PARAGUAY", "PERU", "PHILIPPINES",
"POLAND", "PORTUGAL", "QATAR", "REUNION ISLAND", "ROMANIA",
"RUSSIA", "RWANDA", "SAIPAN", "SAN MARINO", "SAUDI ARABIA",
"SENEGAL", "SEYCHELLES", "SIERRA LEONE", "SINGAPORE",
"SLOVAK REPUBLIC", "SLOVENIA", "SOUTH AFRICA", "SOUTH KOREA",
"SPAIN", "SRI LANKA", "ST. KITTS & NEVIS", "ST. LUCIA",
"ST. VINCENT", "SUDAN", "SURINAME", "SWEDEN", "SWAZILAND",
"SWITZERLAND", "SYRIA", "TAIWAN", "TANZANIA", "THAILAND", "TOGO",
"TRINIDAD & TOBAGO", "TUNISIA", "TURKEY",
"TURKMENISTAN, REPUBLIC OF", "TURKS & CAICOS IS.", "U.A.E.",
"UGANDA", "UKRAINE", "UNITED KINGDOM", "URUGUAY",
"U.S. VIRGIN ISLANDS","UZBEKISTAN", "VANUATU", "VATICAN CITY",
"VENEZUELA", "VIETNAM", "WALLIS & FUTUNA ISLANDS", "YEMEN",
"ZAIRE", "ZAMBIA", "ZIMBABWE");
```

Our destinations list is an almost exact copy of the list you'd see on the web page. For ease in using, we placed "U.S.A." as the first item in the list, and we will select it as our default choice when we build the listbox:

```
my $entry_f = $mw->Frame;
$entry_f->pack(-expand => 'n', -fill => 'x');
$entry_f->Label(-text => "Airbill #: ")->pack(-side => 'left',
                       -anchor => 'w',
                       -expand => 'n',
                       -fill => 'none');
my $airbill = "";
my $airbill_entry = $entry_f->Entry(-textvariable => \$airbill,
                     -width => 10);
```

```
$airbill_entry->pack(-side => 'left',
            -anchor => 'w',
            -expand => 'y',
            -fill => 'x');
```

The entry for the airbill requires a label so that the user knows what sort of input is expected. The default for the *$airbill* variable is blank. We save a reference to the entry widget, so that we can set the focus of the application to it right before we enter the *MainLoop*:

```
$entry_f->Label(-text => "Date Shipped: ")->pack(-side => 'left',
                    -anchor => 'w',
                    -expand => 'n',
                    -fill => 'none');

my %months;

my $i = 1;
foreach (qw(Jan Feb Mar Apr May Jun Jul Aug Sep Oct Nov Dec)) {
  $months{$_} = $i++;
}

my $fulltime = localtime;

my ($month, $day, $year) = $fulltime =~
  /\w+\s(\w+)\s(\d+)\s..:..:..\s..(\d\d)$/;

$month = $months{$month};
$month = "0$month" if (length($month) < 2);
$day = "0$day" if (length($day) < 2);

my $date = "$month$day$year";
$entry_f->Entry(-textvariable => \$date,
        -width => 6)->pack(-side => 'left',
                -anchor => 'w',
                -expand => 'n',
                -fill => 'none');
```

We are going to use a default of today for the date field. The FedEx web page expects it in the form of "DayMonthYear", and digits with only one number require a leading zero. The string returned from *localtime()* gives us the correct day, and we strip off the last two digits of the year. For the month we need to translate it to a number value from 01 - 12. We do this using a *%months* hash, where the keys are the string of the month, and the value the number of the month. We add leading zeros to the day and month if necessary.

```
my $lb_f = $mw->Frame;
$lb_f->pack(-anchor => 'n',
        -expand => 'n',
        -fill => 'x');
$lb_f->Label(-text => "Shipped To:")->pack(-side => 'left',
                    -anchor => 'w');
```

We want a label to tell us what the listbox contains, so we create it first:

```
my $scroll = $lb_f->Scrollbar;
my $listbox = $lb_f->Listbox(-selectmode => 'single',
                -height => 1,
                -yscrollcommand => ['set', $scroll],
                -exportselection => 0);
$scroll->configure(-command => ['yview', $listbox]);
$scroll->pack(-side => 'right', -fill => 'y');
$listbox->pack(-side => 'left', -expand => 'yes', -fill => 'both');

$listbox->insert('end', @destinations);
$listbox->selection('set',0);
```

Then we create the scrollbar and the listbox, and put our *@destinations* in the listbox. Remember, we put the entry "U.S.A" first in our list, so when we select the 0th element of the listbox, we get that entry selected. This is a pretty large list, and it takes quite a while to scroll down to Zimbabwe. Although we didn't do it for our example here, you could set up your listbox so that if you typed a letter, it would scroll to the first entry starting with that letter. Or you could put an additional entry, and search for any word starting with those characters:

```
my $response_f = $mw->Frame;
$response_f->pack(-expand => 'y', -fill => 'both');

$response_f->Label(-text => "Response:")->pack(-anchor => 'w',
                    -side => 'left');

my $response_txt = "";
$response_f->Label(-justify => 'left', -borderwidth => 2, -relief =>
'sunken',
            -textvariable => \$response_txt)->pack(-anchor => 'w',
                            -side => 'left',
                            -expand => 'y',
                            -fill => 'x');
```

To show users what happened to their package (or any errors), we build a label that displays any text in the *$response_txt* variable. To change the text, we simply reset *$response_txt* to another text string:

```
my $bttn_f = $mw->Frame;
$bttn_f->pack;

$bttn_f->Button(-text => "Exit", -command => sub{exit})
            ->pack(-side =>'right',  -anchor => 'e');

my $loop_bttn = $bttn_f->Button(-text => "Loop",
        -command => \&loop_query);
$loop_bttn->pack(-side => 'left', -anchor => 'w');

$bttn_f->Button(-text => "Query", -command => \&do_query)->
  pack(-side => 'left',
        -anchor => 'w');
```

The buttons for our track program allow us to exit the program, start the query loop, or manually do a query right now.

```
my $pkg_tracker = new FedEx $url, $email;
my $loop_id;

$airbill_entry->focus;

MainLoop;
```

One last thing before we start the MainLoop to handle the GUI interaction. (Remember, this is different from our query loop.) We have to create a FedEx object and save a reference to it. Now when we do a query, we can utilize this package to do the hard work for us:

```
sub loop_query {
my $bttn_text = $loop_bttn->cget(-text);
if ($bttn_text =~ /^Loop/) {
&do_query;
$loop_bttn->configure(-text => "Stop");
$loop_id = $mw->repeat($query_interval * 60000, \&do_query);
} else {
$loop_bttn->configure(-text => "Loop");
$mw->after('cancel', $loop_id);
}
}
```

The *loop_query()* subroutine gets called when the Loop button is pressed. We query the web site with the information entered, then set up Tk to loop again in *$query_interval* minutes. To let the user know that a loop has been started, we change the text on the button to say "Stop." Note that we check this text to determine whether we are starting or stopping a loop. The *$loop_id* is a global outside of our sub because we need to remember it in order to cancel a loop. For another example of this, look at our next example, *webping*.

```
sub do_query {
    $mw->configure(-cursor => 'watch');
    $mw->idletasks;

    my $dest = $listbox->get($listbox->curselection);

    $pkg_tracker->check($airbill, $dest, $date);

    if ($pkg_tracker->retrieve_okay) {

    if ($pkg_tracker->delivered) {
        $response_txt = "Tracking number $airbill was delivered to: " .
          $pkg_tracker->who_got_it;
    } else {
        $response_txt = "Package not yet delivered";
    }
    } else {
    my $parsed = parse_html($pkg_tracker->error_info);
```

```
    my $converter = new HTML::FormatText;
    $response_txt = $converter->format($parsed);
    chomp($response_txt);
    }

    $response_txt .= "\n[As of " . localtime() . "]";
    $mw->configure(-cursor => 'top_left_arrow');
    $mw->deiconify;
  $mw->bell;
    $mw->update;
}
```

The subroutine *do_query()* actually utilizes the FedEx package that we saw earlier in Chapter 6, and takes the information received and displays it to the user via our *$response_txt*. We set the cursor to a watch to show the user we are actually doing something, and change it back to the default arrow when done. *$mw-> deiconify* will bring the window up if it was iconified during the wait, and the beep will tell the user that she needs to look at the window. We also avoided doing any error checking here. If we get some sort of error message back from the FedEx package, we simply display it, and keep going. It's up to the user to check the response and make adjustments in the entered values, if there was an error.

The rest of the code is repeated from Chapter 6:

```
## Package FedEx Written by Clinton Wong
package FedEx;

use HTTP::Request;
use HTTP::Response;
use LWP::RobotUA;
use HTTP::Status;

sub new {

  my($class, $cgi_url, $email, $proxy) = @_;
  my $user_agent_name = 'ORA-Check-FedEx/1.0';

  my $self  = {};
  bless $self, $class;

  $self->{'url'} = new URI::URL $cgi_url;

  $self->{'robot'} = new LWP::RobotUA $user_agent_name, $email;
  $self->{'robot'}->delay(0);    # we'll delay requests by hand

  if ($proxy) {
    $self->{'robot'}->proxy('http', $proxy);
  }

  $self;
}
```

```perl
sub check {

    my ($self, $track_num, $country, $date) = @_;

    $self->{'url'}->query("trk_num=$track_num&dest_cntry=" .
            "$country&ship_date=$date");
    my $request = new HTTP::Request 'GET', $self->{'url'};

    my $response = $self->{'robot'}->request($request);
    $self->{'status'} = $response->code();

    if ($response->code == RC_OK) {

    if ($response->content =~ /Delivered To : (\w.*)/) {

        # package delivered
        $self->{'who_got_it'} = $1;
        $self->{'delivered'} = 1;
    }

    # Odd cases when package is delivered but "Delivered To" is blank.
    # Check for delivery time instead.

    elsif ($response->content =~ /Delivery Time : \w.*/) {

        # package delivered
        $self->{'who_got_it'} = 'left blank by FedEx computer';
        $self->{'delivered'} = 1;
    }
    else {

        # package wasn't delivered
        $self->{'delivered'} = 0;

        # if there isn't a "Delivered To : " field, something's wrong.
        # error messages seen between HTML comments

        if ($response->content !~ /Delivered To : /) {
        $self->{'status'} = RC_BAD_REQUEST;

        # get explanation from HTML response
        my $START = '<!-- BEGIN TRACKING INFORMATION -->';
        my $END = '<!-- END TRACKING INFORMATION -->';
        if ($response->content =~ /$START(.*?)$END/s) {
            $self->{'error_as_HTML'} = $1;
        }
        else {
            # couldn't get explanation, use generic one
            $self->{'error_as_HTML'} = 'Unexpected HTML response from
FedEx';

        }      # couldn't get error explanation
        }        # unexpected reply
    }            # not delivered yet
    }              # if HTTP response of RC_OK (200)
```

```
        else {
            $self->{'error_as_HTML'} = $response->error_as_HTML;
        }

    }

    sub retrieve_okay {
        my $self = shift;
        return 0 if ($self->{'status'} != RC_OK);
        1;
    }

    sub delivered {
        my $self = shift;
        $self->{'delivered'};
    }

    sub who_got_it {
        my $self = shift;
        $self->{'who_got_it'};
    }

    sub error_info {
        my $self = shift;
        $self->{'error_as_HTML'};
    }
```

The final program ends up looking like Figure 7-3.

*Figure 7-3. Package tracking client*

## *Check if Servers Are up: webping*

For the last example, we'll build a GUI interface that will allow us to check and see if several web sites are running, at pre-specified intervals. Since this action is very similar to the UNIX *ping* command, we call it *webping*. This application would be useful to a web administrator who had to keep track of many different web sites, and wanted to know when one was down or not responding. We'll be utilizing the LWP::Simple module to actually *ping* each site.

The code to check a site's status is as follows, where *$site* is a string containing a standard URL (like *http://www.ora.com*):

```
$content = head($site);
if ($content) {
  ## Site is UP.
} else {
  ## Site is DOWN.
}
```

While that's pretty simple, we have to have some way to set *$site* to a URL. It's not very efficient to have to type a new site on the command line each time we want to verify the status of a site. In order to make our GUI useful, we want to add some basic features to it.

A place to manually enter URLs would be nice, and a display of the sites we have checked and their status would be useful. Having the program automatically perform an update on each of the sites in the list every 30 minutes or so would be extremely useful. In that same vein, specifying the interval would also be easier than editing the source code any time we decide to change how often the *ping* happens. After we build a list of sites, it would be nice for the program to remember them, and bring them up automatically the next time we start the program.

Here's the final code, with most of the mentioned features represented:

```
#!/usr/bin/perl -w
######################################################################
## Webping: A program that will detect and report whether a web site is up.
## usage: webping [ -a ] [ -i <minutes>] [ -f <filename> ] [-- [ -geometry...]]
##    -a : starts prog in "autoping" mode from beginning.
##    -i : Sets the autoping interval to <int>
##    -f : Uses <filename> instead of .webping_sites as site list
##    -- is necessary to separate webping's options from the Window
##    Manager options.  Allows us to utilize GetOptions instead of
##    parsing them manually (ick).
##    The standard wm specs are allowed after the --, -geometry and
##    -iconic being the most useful of them.
######################################################################

use Tk;
use LWP::Simple;
use Getopt::Long;
```

The first section of the code says to use Tk, LWP::Simple, and Getopt::Long. We chose to utilize Getopt::Long so that we wouldn't have to parse any command-line options ourselves. As you can see from our usage statement, we've got quite a few to deal with. Automode is the term we use when the program loops and checks each web site every *n* minutes.

```
## DEFAULT values -- may be changed by specifing cmd line options.
my $site_file = "$ENV{HOME}/.webping_sites";
```

```perl
$ping_interval = 5;
$auto_mode = 0;
@intervals = (5, 10, 15, 20, 25, 30, 35);

sub numerically { $a <=> $b; }
sub antinumerically { $b <=> $a; }

## Parse our specific command line options first
&GetOptions("i=i" => \$ping_interval,
  "f=s" => \$site_file,
            "a" => \$auto_mode);

if (! grep /$ping_interval/, @intervals) {
    push (@intervals, $ping_interval);
}
```

These segments set up stuff the program should know about. There are default values for everything they might set on the command line. We've declared two sorting routines to be used later on. We get the options specified by the user (if any) to put the program in automode, add or set the interval, and determine which file to read our list of web sites from, if not the default file.

Next comes the meat of the GUI: setting up the window, widgets, and callbacks. *webping* does more complicated things than *xword*, so it will take quite a bit more effort to set it all up. No matter what it does, though, it all looks pretty much the same: creating buttons, assigning functions for them to call, and placing the widgets in a sensible order via *pack*. We won't go into too much detail about how this all happens, but here is the code:

```perl
my $mw = MainWindow->new;
$mw->title("Web Ping");
$mw->CmdLine;  ## parse -geometry and etc cmd line options.

$frame1 = $mw->Frame;
$frame1->pack(side => "bottom", -anchor => "n",
        -expand => "n", -fill => "x");

## Create frame for buttons along the bottom of the window
my $button_f = $frame1->Frame(-borderwidth => 2,
                  -relief => "ridge");
$button_f->pack(-side => "top", -anchor => "n",
        -expand => "n",-fill => "x");

$update_bttn = $button_f->Button(-text => "Update",
                  -state => 'disabled',
                  -command => sub { &end_automode;
                            &ping_site });
```

Notice that when we hit the Update button, we end the current automode (if we can). This is so that the program doesn't try to do two things at once.

```perl
$update_bttn->pack(-side => "left", -anchor => "w", -padx => 5);
```

```perl
$del_bttn = $button_f->Button(-text => "Delete",
                  -state => 'disabled',
                  -command => sub { &delete_site });
$del_bttn->pack(-side => "left",
         -anchor => 'w',
         -padx => 10);

$automode_bttn = $button_f->Button(-text => "Start Automode",
                  -command => \&do_automode);
$automode_bttn->pack(-side => 'left');

$button_f->Label(-text => "Interval: ")->pack(-side => "left");

## Create a psuedo pop-up menu using Menubutton
$interval_mb = $button_f->Menubutton(-indicatoron => 1,
               -borderwidth => 2,
               -relief => "raised");
$interval_mb->pack(-side => "left");

$interval_mb->configure(-menu => $interval_mb->Menu(-tearoff => 0),
          -textvariable => \$ping_interval);
map { $interval_mb->radiobutton(-label => $_,
               -variable => \$ping_interval,
               -value => $_,
               -indicatoron => 0) } sort numerically @intervals;
```

Using a menu button like this is often a good way to get a list of items into a very small space:

```perl
$button_f->Button(-text => "Exit",
         -command => \&exit_program)->pack(-side => "right",
                          -anchor => "e");

my $entry_f = $mw->Frame;
$entry_f->pack(-side => 'top', -anchor => 'n', -fill => 'x');

$entry_f->Label(-text => "URL: ")->pack(-side => 'left',
                  -anchor => 'w');
my $entry = $entry_f->Entry(-textvariable => \$url);
$entry->pack(-side => 'left', -anchor => 'w', -expand => 'y',
     -fill => 'x');


$entry_f->Button(-text => "Ping",
         -command => \&add_site)->pack(-side => 'left',
                         -anchor => 'e');
$entry->bind('<Return>', \&add_site);

my $list_f = $mw->Frame;
$list_f->pack(-side => 'top',
          -anchor => 'n',
          -expand => 'yes',
          -fill => 'both');
$history_label = $list_f->Button(-text => "History:",
```

```
                      -borderwidth => 2,
                      -relief => "flat");
    $history_label->pack(-side => 'top', -anchor => 'n', -fill => 'x');

    my $scroll = $list_f->Scrollbar;
    my $list = $list_f->Listbox(-selectmode => 'extended',
                    -yscrollcommand => ['set', $scroll]);
    $scroll->configure(-command => ['yview', $list]);
    $scroll->pack(-side => 'right', -fill => 'y');
    $list->pack(-side => 'left', -expand => 'yes', -fill => 'both');

    ## Bind Listbox so that the "Update" button is enabled whenever a user
    ## has an item selected.
    $list->bind('<Button-1>', sub {
        my @selected = $list->curselection;
        if ($#selected >= 0) {
        $update_bttn->configure(-state => 'normal');
        $del_bttn->configure(-state => 'normal');
        } else {
        $update_bttn->configure(-state => 'disabled');
        $del_bttn->configure(-state => 'disabled');
        }
    } );

    if (open(FH, "$site_file")) {
        while (<FH>) {
        chomp;
        $url = $_;
        &add_site;
        }
        close FH;
    }
    $url = "";
```

Here is where we take advantage of a "remembering" file. When the program exits, we will save the current list of sites to this file. This way, when the program is started the next time, it looks exactly as it did the last time we ran it—except that the program will have updated the list of sites with the current status.

```
    $entry->focus;

    &do_automode if ($auto_mode);

    MainLoop;
```

Off it goes! Now all that's left in our source code are the functions that we've bound to the buttons and various actions in the GUI. Remember, this is where the real work comes in; without these functions the GUI would just be a bunch of flashy buttons and lists.

```
    sub exit_program {
        my @updated = $list->get(0, 'end');
        if (open FH, ">$site_file") {
```

```
     map { print FH "$_\n"; } @updated;
     close FH;
     }
     exit;
}
```

This is how we always save the current state of the site list. The only way to avoid running this function when exiting the application is to use the Window Manager's close/exit/destroy commands:

```
sub ping_site {
   ## get list of indexes in listbox of those selected.
   my $site = "";
   my ($content, @down);
   my @selected = $list->curselection;

   $mw->configure(-cursor => 'watch');
   $mw->idletasks;

   foreach $index (@selected) {
       my $site = $list->get($index);
       $site =~ s/\s.+$//;        ## Strip off last history record (if any)

       $content = head($site);
       if ($content) {
       $site .= " is UP (" . localtime() .")";
       } else {
       $site .= " is DOWN (" . localtime() .")";
       push (@down, $site);
       }
       $list->delete($index);
       $list->insert($index, $site);
   }

   ## Since we've deleted and inserted into the box -- the sites prev
   ## selected now aren't. Luckily we know which ones those were.
   map { $list->selection('set', $_) } @selected;

   ## Set cursor back to the default value
   $mw->configure(-cursor => 'top_left_arrow');

   if ($#down >= 0) {
       $mw->deiconify;
       $mw->update;

       $old_color = $history_label->cget(-background);

       ## Do some stuff to make the user pay attention to us.
       $history_label->configure(-background => "red");
       $history_label->bell;
       $history_label->flash;        $history_label->flash;
       $history_label->configure(-background => $old_color);
   }


}
```

The function *ping_site()* is called when a new site is added to update its status. It is also called when in automode. It checks the sites selected in the listbox. *ping_site()* is where you could put in other things to happen when a site is down. For instance, mail the web administrator, page the administrator with a text message, or whatever you'd like!

```perl
sub add_site {
    return if ($url eq "");                   ## Do nothing, empty string

    ## Validate $url contains correct information (ie a server name)
    $url = "http://$url" if ($url !~ /(\w+):\/\//);

    ## Insert new site name into list, and make sure we can see it.
    $list->insert('end', $url);
    $list->see('end');

    ## Select the item so that ping_site can do all the work
    $list->selection('clear', 0, 'end');
    $list->selection('set', $list->size - 1);

    $url = "";   ## Clear out string for next site

    &ping_site;
}
```

We've set the default behavior of adding a site to automatically *ping* that site. You could comment out that line if you didn't want to wait for the *ping* to happen and you're adding a large number of sites. Remember, this would also affect what happened when the programs started up, since this function is called both at the beginning and during the manual adding of sites.

```perl
sub delete_site {
    my @selected = $list->curselection;

    ## Have to delete items out of list backwards so that indexes
    ## we just retrieved remain valid until we're done.
    map { $list->delete($_) } sort antinumerically @selected;

    $update_bttn->configure(-state => 'disabled');
    $del_bttn->configure(-state => 'disabled');
}
```

The function *delete_site()* will delete any selected items in the listbox. This allows us to remove ou-of-date sites from our list without having to edit the *.webping_sites* file manually.

```perl
sub do_automode {
    ## State if the $automode_bttn will tell us which way we are in.
    my $state = $automode_bttn->cget(-text);

    if ($state =~ /^Start/) {
    $automode_bttn->configure(-text => "End Automode");
```

```
    $mw->iconify if ($auto_mode);

    $interval_mb->configure(-state => 'disabled');

    ## If the user started up from scratch -- then select all (doesn't
    ## make sense to ping _nothing_.
    @selected = $list->curselection;
    $list->selection('set', 0, 'end') if ($#selected < 0);
    $id = $mw->repeat($ping_interval * 60000, \&ping_site);
    } else {
    &end_automode;
    }
 }
 ## end of do_automode ###############################################
```

When starting off in automode, *do_automode()* gets called. It verifies that the list has at least one site selected, and starts the timed loop. The Tk construct to do the "looping" is in the *$mw->repeat()* command. The function *ping_site()* will be called every *$ping_interval* minutes until *end_autmode()* is called.

```
sub end_automode {
my $state = $automode_bttn->cget(-text);
    $interval_mb->configure(-state => 'normal');
    if ($state =~ /^End/) {
$automode_bttn->configure(-text => "Start Automode");
        $mw->after('cancel', $id);
    }
 }
```

And finally, *webping* looks like Figure 7-4.

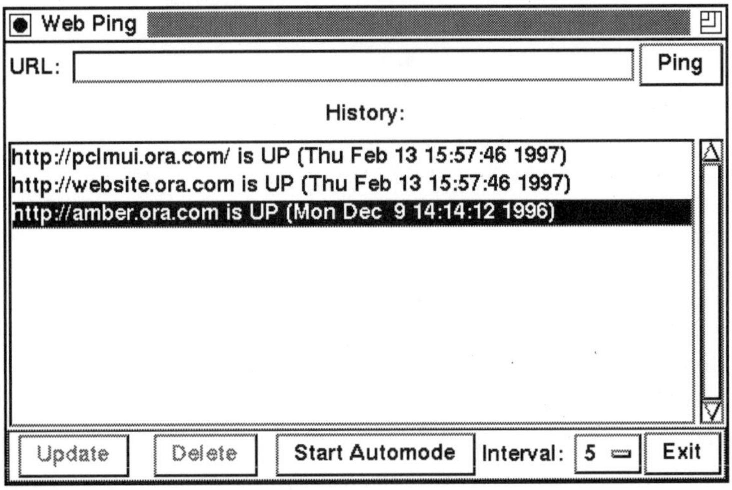

*Figure 7-4. webping client*

# HTTP Headers

HTTP headers are used to transfer all sorts of information between client and server. There are four categories of headers:

| Type | Description |
|---|---|
| General | Information not related to the client, server, or HTTP |
| Request | Preferred document formats and server parameters |
| Response | Information about the server sending the response |
| Entity | Information on the data being sent between the client and server |

General headers and entity headers are the same for both the server and client.

All headers in HTTP messages contain the header name followed by a colon (:), then a space, and the value of the header. Header names are case-insensitive (thus, `Content-Type` is the same as `Content-type`). The value of a header can extend over multiple lines by preceding each extra line with at least one space or tab.

This chapter covers the most recent draft of the HTTP 1.1 specification that was available at publication time (draft 7), as well as some headers that are not in the spec but are in common use regardless.

## General Headers

General headers are used in both client requests and server responses. Some may be more specific to either a client or server message.

## Cache-Control: directives

The `Cache-control` header specifies desired behavior from a caching system, as used in proxy servers. For example:

```
Cache-control: no-cache
```

Both clients and servers can use the `Cache-control` header to specify parameters for the cache or to request certain kinds of documents from the cache. The caching directives are specified in a comma-separated list.

Cache request directives are:

| Directive | Meaning |
|---|---|
| no-cache | Do not cache. The proxy should not send a cached copy of the document and should always request and return the newest copy from the origin-server. The response from the server must not be cached by a proxy. |
| no-store | Remove information promptly after forwarding. The cache should not store anything about the client request or server response. This option prevents the accidental storing of secure or sensitive information in the cache. |
| max-age = *seconds* | Do not send responses older than *seconds*. The cache can send a cached document that has been retrieved within a certain number of seconds from the time it was sent by the origin server. |
| max-stale [ = *seconds* ] | The cache can send a cached document that is older than its expiration date. If *seconds* are given, it must not be expired by more than that time. |
| min-fresh = *seconds* | Send data only if still fresh after the specified number of seconds. The cache can send a cached document only if there are at least a certain number of seconds between now and its expiration time. |
| only-if-cached | Do not retrieve new data. The cache can send a document only if it is in the cache, and should not contact the origin-server to see if a newer copy exists. This option is useful when network connectivity from the cache to origin-server is poor. |

Cache response directives are:

| Directive | Meaning |
|---|---|
| public | The document is cacheable by any cache. |
| private | The document is not cacheable by a shared cache. |
| no-cache | Do not cache the returning document. This prevents caches from returning requested documents when they are stale. |
| no-store | Do not store the returning document. Remove information promptly after forwarding. |

| Directive | Meaning |
|-----------|---------|
| no-transform | Do not convert the entity-body. Useful for applications that require that the message received is exactly what was sent by the server. |
| must-revalidate | The cache must verify the status of stale documents, i.e., the cache cannot blindly use a document that has expired. |
| proxy-revalidate | Client must revalidate data except for private client caches. Public caches must verify the status of stale documents. Like must-revalidate, excluding private caches. |
| max-age= *seconds* | The document should be considered stale in the specified number of seconds from the time of retrieval. |

## *Connection: options*

Specifies options desired for this connection but not for further connections by proxies. For example:

```
Connection: close
```

The `close` option signifies that either the client or server wishes to end the connection (i.e., this is the last transaction). The `keep-alive` option signifies that the client wishes to keep the connection open. The default behavior of web applications differs between HTTP 1.0 and 1.1.

By default, HTTP 1.1 uses persistent connections, where the connection does not automatically close after a transaction. When an HTTP 1.1 web client no longer has any requests, or the server has reached some preprogrammed limit in spending resources on the client, a `Connection: close` header indicates that no more transactions will proceed, and the connection closes after the current one. An HTTP 1.1 client or server that doesn't support persistent connections should always use the `Connection: close` header.

HTTP 1.0, on the other hand, does not have persistent connections by default. If a 1.0 client wishes to use persistent connections, it uses the keep-alive parameter. A `Connection: keep-alive` header is issued by both HTTP 1.0 clients and servers for each transaction under persistent connections. The last transaction does not have a `Connection: keep-alive` header, and behaves like a `Connection: close` header under HTTP 1.1. HTTP 1.0 servers that do not support persistent connections will not have a `Connection: keep-alive` header in their response, and the client should disconnect after the first transaction completes.

Use of the `keep-alive` parameter is known to cause problems with proxy servers that do not understand persistent connections for HTTP 1.0. If a proxy server blindly forwards the `Connection: keep-alive` header, the origin-server and initial client are using persistent connections while the proxy server is not.

The origin server maintains the network connection when the proxy server expects a disconnect; timing problems follow.

See Chapter 3, *Learning HTTP*, for more information on persistent connections.

## Date: dateformat

There are three formats that can be used to express the date. The preferred date format is RFC 1123. For example:

```
Mon, 06 May 1996 04:57:00 GMT
```

The preferred RFC 1123 format specifies all dates in a fixed length string in Greenwich Mean Time (GMT). GMT is always used in HTTP to prevent any misunderstandings among computers communicating in different time zones. The valid days are: Mon, Tue, Wed, Thu, Fri, Sat, and Sun. The months are: Jan, Feb, Mar, Apr, May, Jun, Jul, Aug, Sep, Oct, Nov, and Dec. Leading zeros are padded with whitespace.

For backwards compatibility, the RFC 850 and ANSI C *asctime()* formats are also acceptable:

```
Monday, 06-May-96 04:57:00 GMT
Mon May 6 04:57:00 1996
```

The RFC 1036 format is similar to the one in RFC 1123, except that the string length varies, depending on the day of the week, and the year is specified in two digits instead of four. This makes date parsing more difficult. It is recommended that web clients use the previous format (RFC 1123) instead of this one. The valid days are: Monday, Tuesday, Wednesday, Thursday, Friday, Saturday, Sunday. The months are: Jan, Feb, Mar, Apr, May, Jun, Jul, Aug, Sep, Oct, Nov, and Dec. Leading zeros are padded with whitespace.

ANSI C's *asctime()* format is not encouraged, since there can be misunderstandings about the time zone used by the computer. The valid days are: Mon, Tue, Wed, Thu, Fri, Sat, and Sun. The months are: Jan, Feb, Mar, Apr, May, Jun, Jul, Aug, Sep, Oct, Nov, and Dec. Leading zeros are padded with whitespace.

Despite a heavy preference for RFC 1123's format, current web clients and servers should be able to recognize all three formats. However, when designing web programs, it is desirable to use RFC 1123 when generating dates. Future versions of HTTP may not support the latter two formats.

## MIME-Version: version

The **MIME-Version** header specifies the version of MIME (Multipurpose Internet Mail Extensions) used in the HTTP transaction. This header indicates that the entity-body conforms to a particular version of MIME. If the transaction involves MIME-encoded data, but this header is omitted, the default value is assumed to be 1.0.

Unfortunately, some servers use this header for all transactions, regardless of the entity-body's actual format. For this reason, the HTTP/1.0 protocol suggests that this header should be ignored. If this header is encountered, the entity-body may not have any MIME messages.

Example:

```
MIME-version: 1.0
```

## Pragma: no-cache

The **Pragma** header specifies directives for proxy and gateway systems. Since many proxy systems may exist between a client and server, **Pragma** headers must pass through each proxy. When the **Pragma** header reaches the server, the header may be ignored by the server software.

The only directive defined in HTTP/1.0 is the **no-cache** directive. It is used to tell caching proxies to contact the server for the requested document, instead of using its local cache. This allows the client to request the most up-to-date document from the original web server, without receiving a cached copy from an intermediate proxy server.

The **Pragma** header is an HTTP 1.0 feature, and is maintained in HTTP 1.1 for backward compatibility. No new **Pragma** directives will be defined in the future.

Example:

```
Pragma: no-cache
```

## Transfer-Encoding: encoding_type

The **Transfer-Encoding** header specifies that the message is encoded. This is not the same as content-encoding (an entity-body header, discussed later), since transfer-encodings are a property of the message, not of the entity-body. For example:

```
Transfer-Encoding: chunked
```

In the HTTP 1.1 specification, chunked is the only encoding method supported.

The **chunked** transfer-encoding encodes the message as a series of chunks followed by entity-headers, as shown in Figure A-1. The chunks and entity-headers are in a client's request entity-body or server response entity-body. Each chunk contains a chunk size specified in base 16, followed by CRLF. After that, the chunk body, whose length is specified in the chunk size, is presented, followed by a CRLF. Consecutive chunks are specified one after another, with the last chunk having a length of zero followed by CRLF. Entity-headers follow the chunks, terminated by a CRLF on a line by itself.

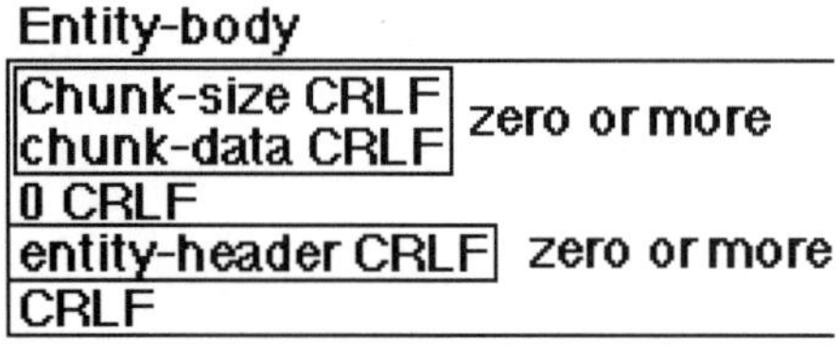

**Entity-body**

| Chunk-size CRLF | zero or more |
| chunk-data CRLF | |
| 0 CRLF | |
| entity-header CRLF | zero or more |
| CRLF | |

*Figure A-1. Chunked transfer encoding*

## Upgrade: protocol/version

Using the `Upgrade` header, the client can specify additional protocols that it understands, and that it would prefer to talk to the server with an alternate protocol. If the server wishes to use the alternate protocol, it returns a response code of 101 and indicates which protocol it is upgrading to, with the `Upgrade` header. After the terminating CRLF in the server's header response, the protocol switches.

Portion of client request:

```
Upgrade: HTTP/1.2
```

Portion of server response:

```
HTTP/1.1 101 Upgrading Protocols
Upgrade: HTTP/1.2
```

## Via: protocol host

The `Via` header is updated by proxy servers as messages pass from client to server and from server to client. Each proxy server appends its protocol and protocol version, hostname, port number, and comment to a comma-separated list on the `Via` header. If the `Via` header does not exist, the first proxy creates it. This information is useful for debugging purposes. If the protocol name is HTTP, it can be omitted. For HTTP, a port number of 80 can be omitted. Comments are optional.

Example:

```
Via: 1.1 proxy.ora.com, 1.0 proxy.internic.gov
```

See the discussion of the TRACE method in Chapter 3 for more information.

# *Client Request Headers*

Client header data communicates the client's configuration and preferred document formats to the server. Request headers are used in a client message to provide information about the client.

## *Accept: type/subtype qvalue*

Specifies media types that the client prefers to accept. For example:

```
Accept: text/*, image/gif
```

Multiple media types can be listed separated by commas. The optional *qvalue* represents, on a scale of 0 to 1, an acceptable quality level for accept types. See Appendix B, *Reference Tables*, for a listing of some commonly-accepted media types. See the section "Media Types" in Chapter 3 for more information.

## *Accept-Charset: character_set qvalue*

Specifies the character sets that the client prefers. Multiple character sets can be listed separated by commas. The optional *qvalue* represents, on a scale of 0 to 1, an acceptable quality level for nonpreferred character sets. If this header is not specified, the server assumes the default of US-ASCII and ISO-8859-1 (a superset of US-ASCII), which are both specified in RFC 1521. For a list of character sets, refer to Appendix B. For example:

```
Accept-charset: ISO-8859-7
```

## *Accept-Encoding: encoding_types*

Through the `Accept-Encoding` header, a client may specify what encoding algorithms it understands. If this header is omitted, the server will send the requested entity-body without any additional encoding. Encoding mechanisms can be used to reduce consumption of scarce resources, at the expense of less expensive resources. For example, large files may be compressed to reduce transmission time over slow network connections.

In the HTTP/1.0 specification, two encoding mechanisms are defined: *x-gzip* and *x-compress*. Multiple encoding schemes can be listed, separated by commas. For reasons of compatibility with historical practice, *gzip* and *compress* should be considered the same as *x-gzip* and *x-compress*.

| Encoding Mechanism | Encoded By |
|---|---|
| x-gzip | Jean-Loup Gailly's GNU zip compression scheme |
| x-compress | Modified Lempel-Ziv compression scheme |

For example:

```
Accept-encoding: x-gzip
```

There is no guarantee that the requested encoding mechanism has been applied to the entity-body returned by the server. If the client specifies an **Accept-encoding** header, it should examine the server's **Content-encoding** header to see if an encoding mechanism was applied. If the **Content-encoding** header has been omitted, no encoding mechanism was applied.

## *Accept-Language: language qvalue*

Specifies the languages that the client prefers. If a client wants to to specify a preference for a particular language, it is done in the **Accept-Language** header. If a server contains the same document in multiple languages, it will send the document in the language of the client's preference, when available. For example:

```
Accept-language: en
```

Multiple languages can be listed separated by commas. The optional *qvalue* represents, on a scale of 0 to 1, an acceptable quality level for nonpreferred languages. Languages are written with their two-letter abbreviations (e.g., *en* for English, *de* for German, *fr* for French, etc.). See Appendix B for a listing of languages.

## *Authorization: scheme credentials*

Provides the client's authorization to access data at a URI. When a requested document requires authorization, the server returns a **WWW-Authenticate** header describing the type of authorization required. The client then repeats the request with the proper authorization information.

The HTTP/1.0 specification defines the BASIC authorization scheme, where the authorization parameter is the string of *username:password* encoded in base 64. For example, for the username of "webmaster" and a password of "zrma4v," the authorization header would look like this:

```
Authorization: BASIC d2VibWFzdGVyOnpycW1hNHY=
```

The value decodes into **webmaster:zrma4v**.

See Chapter 3 for more information on using the **Authorization** header.

## *Cookie: name=value*

Contains a name/value pair of information stored for that URL. For example:

```
Cookie: acct=03847732
```

Multiple cookies can be specified, separated by semicolons. For browsers supporting Netscape persistent cookies—not included in the HTTP standard. See Chapter 3 for more information on cookies.

An issue arises with proxy servers in regard to the headers. Both the `Set-Cookie` and `Cookie` headers should be propagated through the proxy, even if a page is cached or has not been modified (according to the `If-Modified-Since` condition). The `Set-Cookie` header should also never be cached by the proxy.

## *From: email_address*

Gives the email address of the user executing the client. The `From` header helps the server identify the source of malformed requests or excessive resource usage. For example:

```
From: webmaster@www.ora.com
```

This header should be sent when possible, but should not be sent without the user's consent, in the interest of privacy. However, when running clients that use excessive network or server resources, it is advisable to include this header, in the event that an administrator would like to contact the client user.

## *Host: hostname port*

The hostname and port number of the server contacted by the client. Useful for software multihoming. For example:

```
Host: www.ora.com 80
```

Clients must supply this information in HTTP 1.1, so servers with multiple hostnames can easily differentiate between ambiguous URLs.

## *If-Modified-Since: date*

Specifies that the URI data is to be sent only if it has been modified since the date given as the value of this header. This is useful for client-side caching. For example:

```
If-Modified-Since: Mon, 04 May 1996 12:17:34 GMT
```

If the document has not been modified, the server returns a code of 304, indicating that the client should use the local copy. The specified date should follow the format described under the `Date` header. See the "Client Caching" section in Chapter 3 for more information.

## If-Match: entity_tag

A conditional requesting the entity only if it matches the given entity tags (see the `ETag` entity header). An asterisk ( * ) matches any entity, and the transaction continues only if the entity exists. See the "Client Caching" section in Chapter 3 for more information.

## If-None-Match: entity_tag

A conditional requesting the entity only if it does not match any of the given entity tags (see the `ETag` entity header). An asterisk ( * ) matches any entity; if the entity doesn't exist, the transaction continues. See the "Client Caching" section in Chapter 3 for more information.

## If-Range: entity_tag date

A conditional requesting only the portion of the entity that is missing, if it has not been changed, and the entire entity if it has. Used in conjunction with the `Range` header to indicate the entity tag or last modified time of a document on the server. For example:

```
If-Range: Mon, 04 May 1996 12:17:34 GMT
```

If the document has not been modified, the server returns the byte range given by the `Range` header; otherwise, it returns all of the new document. Either an entity tag or a date can be used to identify the partial entity already received; see the `Date` header for information on the format for dates. See the section "Retrieving Content" in Chapter 3 for more information.

## If-Unmodified-Since: date

Specifies that the entity-body should be sent only if the document has been modified since a given date. For example:

```
If-Unmodified-Since: Tue, 05 May 1996 04:03:56 GMT
```

The specified date should follow the format described under the `Date` header. See the "Client Caching" section in Chapter 3 for more information.

## Max-Forwards: n

Limits the number of proxies or gateways that can forward the request. Useful for debugging with the TRACE method, avoiding infinite loops. For example:

```
Max-Forwards: 3
```

A proxy server that receives a `Max-Forwards` value of zero (0) should return the request headers to the client in its response entity-body. See the discussion of the TRACE method in Chapter 3 for more information.

## *Proxy-Authorization: credentials*

Used for a client to identify itself to a proxy requiring authorization.

## *Range: bytes= n-m*

Specifies the partial range(s) requested from the document. For example:

```
Range: 1024-2047,4096-
```

Multiple ranges can be listed, separated by commas. If the first digit in the comma-separated byte range(s) is missing, the range is assumed to count from the end of the document. If the second digit is missing, the range is byte $n$ to the end of the document. The first byte is byte 0. See Chapter 3 for more information.

## *Referer: url*

Gives the URL of the document that refers to the requested URL (i.e., the source document of the link). For example:

```
Referer: http://www.yahoo.com/Internet/
```

See Chapter 3 for more information.

## *User-Agent: string*

Gives identifying information about the client program. For example:

```
User-Agent: Mozilla 3.0b
```

See Chapter 3 for more information.

# *Server Response Headers*

The response headers described here are used in server responses to communicate information about the server and how it may handle requests.

## *Accept-Ranges: bytes|none*

Indicates the acceptance of range requests for a URI, specifying either the range unit (e.g., `bytes`) or `none` if no range requests are accepted. For example:

```
Accept-Ranges: bytes
```

# Age: seconds

Indicates the age of the document in seconds. For example:

```
Age: 3521
```

# Proxy-Authenticate: scheme realm

Indicates the authentication scheme and parameters applicable to the proxy for this URI and the current connection. Used with response 407 (Proxy Authentication Required).

# Public: methods

Indicates methods supported by the server as a comma-separated list. Intended for declaration of nonstandard methods supported at this site. For example:

```
Public: GUNZIP-GET, UNCOMPRESS-GET
```

For methods applicable only to an individual URI, see the **Allow** header.

# Retry-After: date|seconds

Specifies a time when the server can handle requests. Used with response code 503 (Service Unavailable). It contains either an integer number of seconds or a GMT date and time (as described by the **Date** header formats). If the value is an integer, it is interpreted as the number of seconds to wait after the request was issued. For example:

```
Retry-After: 3600
Retry-After: Sat, 18 May 1996 06:59:37 GMT
```

# Server: string

Contains the name and version number of the server. For example:

```
Server: NCSA/1.3
```

If security holes are discovered in a particular server, the **Server** header information may be used to indicate a site's vulnerability. For that reason, it's a good idea for servers to make it easy for administrators to suppress sending this header in the server configuration, if their server has a well-known bug.

# Set-Cookie: name=value options

Contains a name/value pair of information to retain for this URL. For browsers supporting Netscape persistent cookies—not included in the HTTP standard. For example:

```
Set-Cookie: acct=03845324
```

Options are:

| Option | Meaning |
|---|---|
| expires = *date* | The cookie becomes invalid after the specified date. |
| path = *pathname* | The URL range for which the cookie is valid. |
| domain = *domain_name* | The domain name range for which the cookie is valid. |
| secure | Return the cookie only under a secure connection. |

## Vary: *headers*

Specifies that the entity has multiple sources and may therefore vary according to specified list of request header(s).

```
Vary: Accept-Language,Accept-Encoding
```

Multiple headers can be listed, separated by commas. An asterisk ( * ) means that another factor, other than the request headers, may affect the document that is returned.

## Warning: *code host string*

Indicates information additional to that in the status code, for use by caching proxies. For example:

```
Warning: Response stale
```

The host field contains the name or pseudonym of the server host, with an optional port number. The two-digit warning codes and their recommended descriptive strings are:

| Code | String | Meaning |
|---|---|---|
| 10 | Response stale | The response data is known to be stale. |
| 11 | Revalidation failed | The response data is known to be stale because the proxy failed to revalidate the data. |
| 12 | Disconnected operation | The cache is disconnected from the network. |
| 13 | Heuristic expiration | The data is older than 24 hours, and the cache heuristically chose a freshness lifetime greater than 24 hours. |
| 14 | Transformation applied | The proxy has changed the encoding or media type of the document, as specified by the `Content-Encoding` or `Content-Type` headers. |
| 99 | Miscellaneous warning | Arbitrary information to be logged or presented to the user. |

## WWW-Authenticate: scheme realm

A request for authentication, used with the 401 (Unauthorized) response code. It specifies the authorization scheme and realm of authorization required from a client at the requested URI. Many different authorization realms can exist on a server. A common authorization scheme is BASIC, which requires a username and password. For example:

```
WWW-Authenticate: BASIC realm="Admin"
```

When returned to the client, this header indicates that the BASIC type of authorization data in the appropriate realm should be returned in the client's `Authorization` header.

# Entity Headers

Entity headers are used in both client requests and server responses. They supply information about the entity body in an HTTP message.

## Allow: methods

Contains a comma-separated list of methods that are allowed at a specified URI. In a server response it is used with code 405 (Method Not Allowed) to inform the client of valid methods available for the requested information. For example:

```
Allow: GET, HEAD
```

Some methods may not apply to a URL, and the server must verify that the methods supplied by the client makes sense with the given URL.

## Content-Base: url

Specifies the base URL for resolving relative URLs. The base URL must be written as an absolute URL. For example:

```
Content-Base: http://www.ora.com/products/
```

## Content-Encoding: encoding_schemes

Specifies the encoding scheme(s) used for the transferred entity-body. Values are *gzip* (or *x-gzip*) and *compress* (or *x-compress*). If multiple encoding schemes are specified (in a comma-separated list), they must be listed in the order in which they were applied to the source data.

The server should attempt to use an encoding scheme used by the client's `Accept-Encoding` header. The client may use this information to determine how to decode the document after it is transferred.

See the description of the `Accept-Encoding` header earlier in this appendix for a listing of possible values. For example:

```
Content-Encoding: x-gzip
```

## Content-Language: languages

Specifies the language(s) that the transferred entity-body is intended for. Languages are represented by their two-letter abbreviations (e.g., *en* for English, *fr* for French). The server should attempt to use a language specified by the client's `Accept-Language` header. (See Appendix B for a listing of possible values.) This header is useful when a client specifies a preference for one language over another for a given URL. For example:

```
Content-Language: fr
```

## Content-Length: n

This header specifies the length of the data (in bytes) of the transferred entity-body. For example:

```
Content-Length:  47293
```

Due to the dynamic nature of some requests, the content length is sometimes unknown and this header is omitted.

## Content-Location: url

Supplies the URL for the entity, in cases where a document has multiple entities with separately accessible locations. The URL can be either an absolute or relative URL. For example:

```
Content-Location: http://www.ora.com/products/
```

See the section "Retrieving Content" in Chapter 3 for more information.

## Content-MD5: digest

Supplies an MD5 digest of the entity, for checking the integrity of the message upon receipt.

## Content-Range: bytes n-n/m

Specifies where the accompanying partial entity-body should be inserted, and the total size of the full entity-body. For example:

```
Content-Range: bytes 6143-7166/15339
```

See the section "Retrieving Content" in Chapter 3 for more information.

## Content-Transfer-Encoding: scheme

Specifies any transformations that occurred to the data for transport over the network. For example:

```
Content-Transfer-Encoding: base64
```

Between web servers and clients, this header is usually not needed, since no encoding is needed. Possible encoding schemes are:

| Transfer Encoding | Format |
| --- | --- |
| 7bit | Data represented by short lines of US-ASCII data. |
| 8bit | Data represented by short lines, but may contain non-ASCII data. (High-order bit may be set.) |
| binary | Data may not be in short lines, and can be non-ASCII characters. |
| base64 | Data is encoded in base64 ASCII. (See Section 5.2 of RFC 1521 for details.) |
| quoted-printable | Special characters replaced with an equal sign (=) followed by the ASCII value in hex. (See Section 5.1 of RFC 1521 for complete details.) |

## Content-Type: type/subtype

Describes the media type and subtype of an entity-body. It uses the same values as the client's Accept header, and the server should return media types that conform with the client's preferred formats. For example:

```
Content-type: text/html
```

See the discussion of media types in Chapter 3 for more information.

## ETag: entity_tag

Defines the entity tag for use with the If-Match and If-None-Match request headers. See the discussion of client caching in Chapter 3 for more information.

## Expires: date

Specifies the time when a document may change, or when its information becomes invalid. After that time, the document may or may not change or be deleted. The value is a date and time in a valid format as described for the Date header. For example:

```
Expires: Sat, 20 May 1995 03:32:38 GMT
```

This is useful for cache management. The **Expires** header means that it is unlikely that the document will change before the given time. This does not imply that the document will be changed or deleted at that time. It is only an advisory that the document will not be modified until the specified time.

See the discussion on client caching in Chapter 3 for more information.

### Last-Modified: date

Specifies when the specified URL was last modified. The value is a date and time in a valid format as described for the **Date** header. If a client has a copy of the URL in its cache that is older than the last-modified date, it should be refreshed. See the discussion on client caching in Chapter 3 for more information. For example:

```
Last-Modified: Sat, 20 May 1995 03:32:38 GMT
```

### Location: url

Specifies the new location of a document, usually with response code 201 (Created), 301 (Moved Permanently), or 302 (Moved Temporarily). The URL given must be written as an absolute URL. For example:

```
Location: http://www.ora.com/contacts.html
```

### URI: uri

Specifies the new location of a document, usually with response code 201 (Created), 301 (Moved Permanently), or 302 (Moved Temporarily). For example:

```
URI: <http://www.ora.com/contacts.html>
```

An optional vary parameter may also be used in this header, indicating multiple documents at the URI in the following categories: type, language, version, encoding, charset, and user-agent. Sending these parameters in a server response prompts the client to specify its preferences appropriately in the new request. The use of the URI header is deprecated in HTTP 1.1 in favor of the **Location**, **Content-Location**, and **Vary** headers.

# Summary of Support Across HTTP Versions

The following is a listing of all HTTP headers supported by each version of HTTP so far.

## HTTP 0.9

| Method | General | Request | Entity | Response |
|--------|---------|---------|--------|----------|
| GET | none | none | none | none |

## HTTP 1.0

| Method | General | Request | Entity | Response |
|--------|---------|---------|--------|----------|
| GET | Connection | Accept | Allow | Location |
| HEAD | Date | Accept-charset | Content-encoding | Retry-after |
| POST | MIME-version | Accept-encoding | Content-language | Server |
| PUT | Pragma | Accept-language | Content-length | WWW-Authenticate |
| DELETE | | Authorization | Content-type | |
| LINK | | From | Expires | |
| UNLINK | | If-modified-since | Last-modified | |
| | | Referer | Link | |
| | | User-agent | Title | |
| | | | URI | |

## HTTP 1.1

| Method | General | Request | Entity | Response |
|--------|---------|---------|--------|----------|
| OPTIONS | Cache-control | Accept | Allow | Age |
| GET | Connection | Accept-charset | Content-base | Location |
| HEAD | Date | Accept-encoding | Content-encoding | Proxy-authenticate |
| POST | Pragma | Accept-language | Content-language | Public |
| PUT | Transfer-encoding | Authorization | Content-length | Retry-after |
| DELETE | Upgrade | From | Content-location | Server |
| TRACE | Via | Host | Content-md5 | URI |
| PATCH | | If-Modified-Since | Content-range | Vary |
| LINK | | If-match | Content-type | Warning |
| UNLINK | | If-none-match | Content-version | WWW-Authenticate |

| Method | General | Request | Entity | Response |
|---|---|---|---|---|
| | | If-range | Derived-from | |
| | | If-unmodified-since | Etag | |
| | | Max-forwards | Expires | |
| | | Range | Last-modified | |
| | | Referer | Link | |
| | | User-agent | | |

# B

# *Reference Tables*

This appendix contains several tables that will be useful when negotiating HTTP content. Covered in this appendix are:

*Media Types*

> Whenever an entity-body is sent via HTTP, a media type must be sent using the `Content-type` header. Also, web clients can use the `Accept` header to define which media types the client can handle.

*Character Encoding*

> In URL-encoded data (as described in Chapter 3, *Learning HTTP*), any "special" characters such as spaces and punctuation must be encoded with a % escape sequence.

*Languages*

> Entity-bodies can be sent with a `Content-language` header, to declare what language the entity is written in. Clients can declare which languages they can handle, using the `Accept-language` header.

*Character Sets*

> Clients can use the `Accept-charset` header to declare which character sets they are capable of handling.

## *Media Types*

Listed below are media types that are registered with the Internet Assigned Number Authority (IANA). According to the HTTP specification, use of nonregistered media types is discouraged.

The IANA media list is available in RFC 1700. A more readable document describing the assigned media types is available at *ftp://ftp.isi.edu/in-notes/iana/assignments/media-types/*.

A variety of methods is used to identify the media type of a document. The easiest method, but the least accurate, is to map well-known file extensions with a media type. For example, a file that ends in ".GIF" would map to "image/gif". However, in usual practice, there is no verification that the file is in fact a GIF file.

A more accurate method would examine the structure or data format of the file and map it to a media type. For some media types, magic numbers allow this to happen. For example, all GIF files begin with the three uppercase letters of GIF, and all JPEG files begin with 0xFFD8 (hexadecimal notation). This method, however, is more time consuming.

Under some filesystems, media types may be mapped by examining the file *type/ creator* attribute of the file. While this is easily achieved under MacOS's HFS, other filesystems (DOS, NTFS, BSD) do not have these file attributes.

*Table B-1. Internet Media Types*

| Type | Subtype | Type | Subtype |
|------|---------|------|---------|
| text | plain | application | andrew-inset |
| text | richtext | application | slate |
| text | enriched | application | wita |
| text | tab-separated-values | application | dec-dx |
| text | html | application | dca-rft |
| text | sgml | application | activemessage |
| multipart | mixed | application | rtf |
| multipart | alternative | application | applefile |
| multipart | digest | application | mac-binhex40 |
| multipart | parallel | application | news-message-id |
| multipart | appledouble | application | news-transmission |
| multipart | header-set | application | wordperfect5.1 |
| multipart | form-data | application | pdf |
| multipart | related | application | zip |
| multipart | report | application | macwriteii |
| multipart | voice-message | application | msword |
| message | rfc822 | application | remote-printing |
| message | partial | application | mathematica |
| message | external-body | application | cybercash |
| message | news | application | commonground |
| message | http | application | iges |
| application | octet-stream | application | riscos |
| application | postscript | application | eshop |
| application | oda | application | x400-bp |
| application | atomicmail | application | sgml |

*Table B-1. Internet Media Types (continued)*

| Type | Subtype | Type | Subtype |
|------|---------|------|---------|
| application | cals-1840 | image | gif |
| application | vnd.framemaker | image | ief |
| application | vnd.mif | image | g3fax |
| application | vnd.ms-excel | image | tiff |
| application | vnd.ms-powerpoint | image | cgm |
| application | vnd.ms-project | image | naplps |
| application | vnd.ms-works | image | vnd.dwg |
| application | vnd.ms-tnef | image | vnd.svf |
| application | vnd.svd | image | vnd.dxf |
| application | vnd.music-niff | audio | basic |
| application | vnd.ms-artgalry | audio | 32kadpcm |
| application | vnd.truedoc | video | mpeg |
| application | vnd.koan | video | quicktime |
| image | jpeg | video | vnd.vivo |

# Character Encoding

When the client sends data to a CGI program using the **Content-type** of *application/x-www-form-urlencoded*, certain special characters are encoded to eliminate ambiguity. Table B-2 shows which characters are transformed and which are not transformed. For more information on URLs, see RFC 1738.

*Table B-2. Character Encoding*

| ASCII | Symbol | CGI representation | ASCII | Symbol | CGI representation |
|-------|--------|--------------------|-------|--------|--------------------|
| < 32 | | *always encode with* **%xx** *where* **xx** *is the hexadecimal representation of the character* | 42 | * | * |
| | | | 43 | + | %2B |
| | | | 44 | , | %2C |
| | | | 45 | – | – |
| 32 | | + or %20 | 46 | . | . |
| 33 | ! | %21 | 47 | / | %2F |
| 34 | " | %22 | 48 | 0 | 0 |
| 35 | # | %23 | 49 | 1 | 1 |
| 36 | $ | %24 | 50 | 2 | 2 |
| 37 | % | %25 | 51 | 3 | 3 |
| 38 | & | %26 | 52 | 4 | 4 |
| 39 | ' | %27 | 53 | 5 | 5 |
| 40 | ( | %28 | 54 | 6 | 6 |
| 41 | ) | %29 | 55 | 7 | 7 |

*Table B-2. Character Encoding (continued)*

| ASCII | Symbol | CGI representation | ASCII | Symbol | CGI representation |
|-------|--------|--------------------|-------|--------|--------------------|
| 56 | 8 | 8 | 94 | ^ | %5E |
| 57 | 9 | 9 | 95 | _ | _ |
| 58 | : | %3A | 96 | ` | %60 |
| 59 | ; | %3B | 97 | a | a |
| 60 | < | %3C | 98 | b | b |
| 61 | = | %3D | 99 | c | c |
| 62 | > | %3E | 100 | d | d |
| 63 | ? | %3F | 101 | e | e |
| 64 | @ | %40 | 102 | f | f |
| 65 | A | A | 103 | g | g |
| 66 | B | B | 104 | h | h |
| 67 | C | C | 105 | i | i |
| 68 | D | D | 106 | j | j |
| 69 | E | E | 107 | k | k |
| 70 | F | F | 108 | l | l |
| 71 | G | G | 109 | m | m |
| 72 | H | H | 110 | n | n |
| 73 | I | I | 111 | o | o |
| 74 | J | J | 112 | p | p |
| 75 | K | K | 113 | q | q |
| 76 | L | L | 114 | r | r |
| 77 | M | M | 115 | s | s |
| 78 | N | N | 116 | t | t |
| 79 | O | O | 117 | u | u |
| 80 | P | P | 118 | v | v |
| 81 | Q | Q | 119 | w | w |
| 82 | R | R | 120 | x | x |
| 83 | S | S | 121 | y | y |
| 84 | T | T | 122 | z | z |
| 85 | U | U | 123 | { | %7B |
| 86 | V | V | 124 | \| | %7C |
| 87 | W | W | 125 | } | %7D |
| 88 | X | X | 126 | ~ | %7E |
| 89 | Y | Y | 127 |  | %7F |
| 90 | Z | Z | > 127 |  | *always encode with* |
| 91 | [ | %5B |  |  | *%xx where xx is the* |
| 92 | \ | %5C |  |  | *hexadecimal repre-* |
| 93 | ] | %5D |  |  | *sentation of the* |
|  |  |  |  |  | *character* |

# *Languages*

A language tag is of the form of:

```
<primary-tag> <-subtag>
```

where zero or more subtags are allowed. The primary-tag specifies the language, and the subtag specifies parameters to the language, like dialect information, country identification, or script variations. RFC 1766 contains the complete documentation of languages and parameter usage. The key values for the primary-tag and subtag are outlined in Tables B-3 and B-4, respectively.

Examples:

*de*

> (German)

*en*

> (English)

*en-us*

> (English, USA)

Table B-3 lists the primary langauge tags as defined in ISO 639.

*Table B-3. Primary Language Types*

| Primary Tag | Language | Primary Tag | Language |
|---|---|---|---|
| aa | Afar | cs | Czech |
| ab | Abkhazian | cy | Welsh |
| af | Afrikaans | da | Danish |
| am | Amharic | de | German |
| ar | Arabic | dz | Bhutani |
| as | Assamese | el | Greek |
| ay | Aymara | en | English |
| az | Azerbaijani | eo | Esperanto |
| ba | Bashkir | es | Spanish |
| be | Byelorussian | et | Estonian |
| bg | Bulgarian | eu | Basque |
| bh | Bihari | fa | Persian |
| bi | Bislama | fi | Finnish |
| bn | Bengali; Bangla | fj | Fiji |
| bo | Tibetan | fo | Faeroese |
| br | Breton | fr | French |
| ca | Catalan | fy | Frisian |
| co | Corsican | ga | Irish |

*Table B-3. Primary Language Types (continued)*

| Primary Tag | Language | Primary Tag | Language |
|---|---|---|---|
| gd | Scots, Gaelic | ml | Malayalam |
| gl | Galician | mn | Mongolian |
| gn | Guarani | mo | Moldavian |
| gu | Gujarati | mr | Marathi |
| ha | Hausa | ms | Malay |
| hi | Hindi | mt | Maltese |
| hr | Croatian | my | Burmese |
| hu | Hungarian | na | Nauru |
| hy | Armenian | ne | Nepali |
| ia | Interlingua | nl | Dutch |
| ie | Interlingue | no | Norwegian |
| ik | Inupiak | oc | Occitan |
| in | Indonesian | om | (Afan) Oromo |
| is | Icelandic | or | Oriya |
| it | Italian | pa | Punjabi |
| iw | Hebrew | pl | Polish |
| ja | Japanese | ps | Pashto, Pushto |
| ji | Yiddish | pt | Portuguese |
| jw | Javanese | qu | Quechua |
| ka | Georgian | rm | Rhaeto-Romance |
| kk | Kazakh | rn | Kirundi |
| kl | Greenlandic | ro | Romanian |
| km | Cambodian | ru | Russian |
| kn | Kannada | rw | Kinyarwanda |
| ko | Korean | sa | Sanskrit |
| ks | Kashmiri | sd | Sindhi |
| ku | Kurdish | sg | Sangro |
| ky | Kirghiz | sh | Serbo-Croatian |
| la | Latin | si | Singhalese |
| ln | Lingala | sk | Slovak |
| lo | Laothian | sl | Slovenian |
| lt | Lithuanian | sm | Samoan |
| lv | Latvian, Lettish | sn | Shona |
| mg | Malagasy | so | Somali |
| mi | Maori | sq | Albanian |
| mk | Macedonian | sr | Serbian |

*Table B-3. Primary Language Types (continued)*

| Primary Tag | Language | Primary Tag | Language |
|---|---|---|---|
| ss | Siswati | tr | Turkish |
| st | Sesotho | ts | Tsonga |
| su | Sudanese | tt | Tatar |
| sv | Swedish | tw | Twi |
| sw | Swahili | uk | Ukrainian |
| ta | Tamil | ur | Urdu |
| te | Tegulu | uz | Uzbek |
| tg | Tajik | vi | Vietnamese |
| th | Thai | vo | Volapuk |
| ti | Tigrinya | wo | Wolof |
| tk | Turkmen | xh | Xhosa |
| tl | Tagalog | yo | Yoruba |
| tn | Setswana | zh | Chinese |
| to | Tonga | zu | Zulu |

Table B-4 lists the language subtypes as defined in ISO 3166.

*Table B-4. Language Subtypes*

| Subtype | Country | Subtype | Country |
|---|---|---|---|
| AD | Andorra | BB | Barbados |
| AE | United Arab Emirates | BD | Bangladesh |
| AF | Afghanistan | BE | Belgium |
| AG | Antigua and Barbuda | BF | Burkina Faso |
| AI | Anguilla | BG | Bulgaria |
| AL | Albania | BH | Bahrain |
| AM | Armenia | BI | Burundi |
| AN | Netherland Antilles | BJ | Benin |
| AO | Angola | BM | Bermuda |
| AQ | Antarctica | BN | Brunei Darussalam |
| AR | Argentina | BO | Bolivia |
| AS | American Samoa | BR | Brazil |
| AT | Austria | BS | Bahamas |
| AU | Australia | BT | Buthan |
| AW | Aruba | BV | Bouvet Island |
| AZ | Azerbaidjan | BW | Botswana |
| BA | Bosnia-Herzegovina | BY | Belarus |

*Table B-4. Language Subtypes (continued)*

| Subtype | Country | Subtype | Country |
|---------|---------|---------|---------|
| BZ | Belize | FR | France |
| CA | Canada | FX | France (European Ter.) |
| CC | Cocos (Keeling) Isl. | GA | Gabon |
| CF | Central African Rep. | GB | Great Britain (UK) |
| CG | Congo | GD | Grenada |
| CH | Switzerland | GE | Georgia |
| CI | Ivory Coast | GH | Ghana |
| CK | Cook Islands | GI | Gibraltar |
| CL | Chile | GL | Greenland |
| CM | Cameroon | GP | Guadeloupe (Fr.) |
| CN | China | GQ | Equatorial Guinea |
| CO | Colombia | GF | Guyana (Fr.) |
| CR | Costa Rica | GM | Gambia |
| CS | Czechoslovakia | GN | Guinea |
| CU | Cuba | GR | Greece |
| CV | Cape Verde | GT | Guatemala |
| CX | Christmas Island | GU | Guam (US) |
| CY | Cyprus | GW | Guinea Bissau |
| CZ | Czech Republic | GY | Guyana |
| DE | Germany | HK | Hong Kong |
| DJ | Djibouti | HM | Heard & McDonald Isl. |
| DK | Denmark | HN | Honduras |
| DM | Dominica | HR | Croatia |
| DO | Dominican Republic | HT | Haiti |
| DZ | Algeria | HU | Hungary |
| EC | Ecuador | ID | Indonesia |
| EE | Estonia | IE | Ireland |
| EG | Egypt | IL | Israel |
| EH | Western Sahara | IN | India |
| ES | Spain | IO | British Indian O. Terr. |
| ET | Ethiopia | IQ | Iraq |
| FI | Finland | IR | Iran |
| FJ | Fiji | IS | Iceland |
| FK | Falkland Isl. (Malvinas) | IT | Italy |
| FM | Micronesia | JM | Jamaica |
| FO | Faroe Islands | JO | Jordan |

*Table B-4. Language Subtypes (continued)*

| Subtype | Country | Subtype | Country |
|---------|---------|---------|---------|
| JP | Japan | MT | Malta |
| KE | Kenya | MU | Mauritius |
| KG | Kirgistan | MV | Maldives |
| KH | Cambodia | MW | Malawi |
| KI | Kiribati | MX | Mexico |
| KM | Comoros | MY | Malaysia |
| KN | St. Kitts Nevis Anguilla | MZ | Mozambique |
| KP | Korea (North) | NA | Namibia |
| KR | Korea (South) | NC | New Caledonia (Fr.) |
| KW | Kuwait | NE | Niger |
| KY | Cayman Islands | NF | Norfolk Island |
| KZ | Kazachstan | NG | Nigeria |
| LA | Laos | NI | Nicaragua |
| LB | Lebanon | NL | Netherlands |
| LC | Saint Lucia | NO | Norway |
| LI | Liechtenstein | NP | Nepal |
| LK | Sri Lanka | NR | Nauru |
| LR | Liberia | NT | Neutral Zone |
| LS | Lesotho | NU | Niue |
| LT | Lithuania | NZ | New Zealand |
| LU | Luxembourg | OM | Oman |
| LV | Latvia | PA | Panama |
| LY | Libya | PE | Peru |
| MA | Morocco | PF | Polynesia (Fr.) |
| MC | Monaco | PG | Papua New Guinea |
| MD | Moldavia | PH | Philippines |
| MG | Madagascar | PK | Pakistan |
| MH | Marshall Islands | PL | Poland |
| ML | Mali | PM | St. Pierre & Miquelon |
| MM | Myanmar | PN | Pitcairn |
| MN | Mongolia | PT | Portugal |
| MO | Macau | PR | Puerto Rico (US) |
| MP | Northern Mariana Isl. | PW | Palau |
| MQ | Martinique (Fr.) | PY | Paraguay |
| MR | Mauritania | QA | Qatar |
| MS | Montserrat | RE | Reunion (Fr.) |

*Table B-4. Language Subtypes (continued)*

| Subtype | Country | Subtype | Country |
|---------|---------|---------|---------|
| RO | Romania | TN | Tunisia |
| RU | Russian Federation | TO | Tonga |
| RW | Rwanda | TP | East Timor |
| SA | Saudi Arabia | TR | Turkey |
| SB | Solomon Islands | TT | Trinidad & Tobago |
| SC | Seychelles | TV | Tuvalu |
| SD | Sudan | TW | Taiwan |
| SE | Sweden | TZ | Tanzania |
| SG | Singapore | UA | Ukraine |
| SH | St. Helena | UG | Uganda |
| SI | Slovenia | UK | United Kingdom |
| SJ | Svalbard & Jan Mayen Isl. | UM | US Minor Outlying Isl. |
| SK | Slovak Republic | US | United States |
| SL | Sierra Leone | UY | Uruguay |
| SM | San Marino | UZ | Uzbekistan |
| SN | Senegal | VA | Vatican City State |
| SO | Somalia | VC | St.Vincent & Grenadines |
| SR | Suriname | VE | Venezuela |
| ST | St. Tome and Principe | VG | Virgin Islands (British) |
| SU | Soviet Union | VI | Virgin Islands (US) |
| SV | El Salvador | VN | Vietnam |
| SY | Syria | VU | Vanuatu |
| SZ | Swaziland | WF | Wallis & Futuna Islands |
| TC | Turks & Caicos Islands | WS | Samoa |
| TD | Chad | YE | Yemen |
| TF | French Southern Terr. | YU | Yugoslavia |
| TG | Togo | ZA | South |
| TH | Thailand | ZM | Zambia |
| TJ | Tadjikistan | ZR | Zaire |
| TK | Tokelau | ZW | Zimbabwe |
| TM | Turkmenistan | | |

# *Character Sets*

Table B-5 lists the character sets that may be used with the `Accept-language` and `Content-language` HTTP headers. This list does not describe all of the possible character sets of international languages that can appear in the headers. For a comprehensive list of character sets, their aliases, and pointers to more descriptive documents, refer to RFC 1700.

*Table B-5. Character Sets*

| Character Sets | Language | Source |
| --- | --- | --- |
| US-ASCII | American Standard Code for Information Exchange | RFC 1345 |
| ISO-8859-1 | Latin Alphabet No. 1 | RFC 1345 |
| ISO-8859-2 | Latin Alphabet No. 2 | RFC 1345 |
| ISO-8859-3 | Latin Alphabet No. 3 | RFC 1345 |
| ISO-8859-4 | Latin Alphabet No. 4 | RFC 1345 |
| ISO-8859-5 | Latin/Cyrillic Alphabet | RFC 1345 |
| ISO-8859-6 | Latin/Arabic Alphabet | RFC 1345 |
| ISO-8859-7 | Latin/Greek Alphabet | RFC 1345 |
| ISO-8859-8 | Latin/Hebrew Alphabet | RFC 1345 |
| ISO-8859-9 | Latin Alphabet No. 5 | RFC 1345 |
| ISO-2022-JP | Japanese | RFC 1468 |
| ISO-2022-JP-2 | Extension of Japanese in ISO-2022-JP | RFC 1554 |
| ISO-2022-KR | Korean | RFC1557 |
| UNICODE-1-1 | Unicode for MIME | RFC 1641 |
| UNICODE-1-1-UTF-7 | 7-bit UCS Transformation Format | RFC 1642 |
| UNICODE-1-1-UTF-8 | 8-bit UCS Transformation Format | N/A |

# C

# *The Robot Exclusion*
# *Standard*

As we've mentioned earlier in this book, automated clients, or robots, might be considered an invasion of resources by many servers. A robot is defined as a web client that may retrieve documents in an automated, rapid-fire succession. Examples of robots are indexers for search engines, content mirroring programs, and link traversal programs. While many server administrators welcome robots—how else will they be listed by search engines and attract potential customers?—others would prefer that they stay out.

The Robot Exclusion Standard was devised in 1994 to give administrators an opportunity to make their preferences known. It describes how a web server administrator can designate certain areas of a website as "off limits" for certain (or all) web robots. The creator of the document, Martijn Koster, maintains this document at *http://info.webcrawler.com/mak/projects/robots/norobots.html* and also provides an informational RFC at *http://info.webcrawler.com/mak/projects/robots/ norobots-rfc.txt*. The informational RFC adds some additional features to those in the original 1994 document.

The success of the Robot Exclusion Standard depends on web application programmers being good citizens and heeding it carefully. While it can't serve as a locked door, it can serve as a clear "Do Not Disturb" sign. You ignore it at the peril of (at best) being called a cad, and (at worst) being explicitly locked out if you persist, and having angry complaints sent to your boss or system administrator or both. This appendix gives you the basic idea behind the Robot Exclusion Standard, but you should also check the RFC itself.

In a nutshell, the Robot Exclusion Standard declares that a web server administrator should create a document accessible at the relative URL */robots.txt*. For example, a remote client would access a *robots.txt* file at the server *hypothetical.ora.com* using the following URL:

```
http://hypothetical.ora.com/robots.txt
```

If the web server returns a status of 200 (OK) for the URL, the client should parse and interpret the resulting entity-body (described below). In other cases, status codes in the range of 300-399 indicate URL redirections, which should be followed by the client. Status codes of 401 (Unauthorized) or 403 (Forbidden) indicate access restrictions and the client should avoid the entire site. A 404 (Not Found) indicates that the administrator did not specify any Robot Exclusion Standard and the entire site is okay to visit.

Here's the good news if you use LWP for your programs: LWP::RobotUA takes care of all this for you. While it's still good to know about the standard, you can rest easy—yet another perk of using LWP. See Chapter 5 for an example using LWP::RobotUA.

## *Syntax for the /robots.txt File*

When clients receive the *robots.txt* file, they need to parse it to determine whether they are allowed access to the site. There are three basic directives that can be in the *robots.txt* file: `User-agent`, `Allow`, and `Disallow`.

The `User-agent` directive specifies that subsequent `Allow` and `Disallow` statements apply to it. The robot should use a case-insensitive comparison of this value with its own user agent name. Version numbers are not used in the comparison.

If the *robots.txt* file specifies a * as a `User-Agent`, it indicates all robots, not any particular robot. So if an administrator wants to shut out all robots from an entire site, the *robots.txt* file only needs the following two lines:

```
User-agent: *
Disallow: /
```

The `Allow` and `Disallow` directives indicate areas of the site that the previously-listed `User-agent` is allowed or denied access. Instead of listing all the URLs that the `User-Agent` is allowed and disallowed, the directive specifies the general prefix that describes what is allowed or disallowed. For example:

```
Disallow: /index
```

would match both `/index.html` and `/index/summary.html`, while:

```
Disallow: /index/
```

would match only URLs in `/index/`. In the extreme case,

```
Disallow: /
```

specifies the entire web site.

Multiple **User-agents** can be specified within a *robots.txt* file. For example,

```
User-agent: friendly-indexer
User-agent: search-thingy
Disallow: /cgi-bin/
Allow: /
```

specifies that the allow and disallow statements apply to both the **friendly-indexer** and **search-thingy** robots.

The *robots.txt* file moves from general to specific; that is, subsequent listings can override previous ones. For example:

```
User-agent: *
Disallow: /
User-agent: search-thingy
Allow: /
```

would specify that all robots should go away, except the *search-thingy* robot.

# *Index*

## *Symbols*

& (ampersand), 20, 37
= (equal sign), 37
% (percent sign), 37
+ (plus sign), 20

## *Numbers*

100 range HTTP status codes, 47, 101
200 range HTTP status codes, 48, 101
300 range HTTP status codes, 48, 101
400 range HTTP status codes, 49–51, 102
500 range HTTP status codes, 51, 102

## *A*

abs( ), 111
absolute URLs, 91, 111
accept( ), 66–68, 70
Accept header, 56, 177
Accept-Charset header, 177
Accept-Encoding header, 177
Accept-Language header, 178
Accept-Ranges header, 59, 181
add_content( ), 100, 102
Age header, 182
agent( ), 96
Allow header, 184
ampersand (&), 20, 37

application/x-www-form-urlencoded
media type, 19, 35–37,
193–194
as_string( ), 98, 100, 103, 113
authorization/authentication, 44, 85
Authorization header, 62–63, 178
digest authentication, 46, 185
LWP functions for, 96
Proxy-Authenticate header, 182
Proxy-Authorization header, 181
WWW-Authenticate header, 62, 184

## *B*

base( ), 102, 111
BASIC authorization, 62, 178
bind( ), 66–68
body, response (see entity-body)
BottomMargin attribute, 109
browsers, vii, 3
bugs, 6
byte ranges, 45, 59

## *C*

Cache-Control header, 57, 172
caching, 57–59, 172
CGI programs, 17–20
HTTP codes for errors in, 51, 102
character encoding (see encoding)

## About the Author

Clinton Wong works in the Internet/Web Engineering group at Intel Corporation where his work focuses on proxy servers, web servers, and firewalls. He graduated from Purdue University in 1996 with a B.S. in computer science and a minor in psychology. In his spare time, Clinton enjoys reading about the social impact of technology, listening to an eclectic collection of music, drinking various flavors of coffee, and appreciating (sometimes unintentional) works of art.

## Colophon

The bird featured on the cover of *Web Client Programming with Perl* is a white pelican. White pelicans are among the world's largest birds. To creatures not belonging to the order *pelicanus erythrorynchos*,[*] the white pelican's profile probably appears preposterous with an enormous pouched bill with a hook on the end, large-proportioned body, and stubby legs with webbed feet. But those who have witnessed pelicans circling in flight at dizzying heights or gliding through water in pursuit of a catfish can attest to their grace in motion.

The adult white pelican is 4–6 feet long with a giant wingspread of 8–9½ feet. Usual weight is 10–17 pounds but can reach 30 pounds. The tips of the wings are black. The large pouched bill is orange or salmon-colored. Eyes are orange-yellow; the legs and feet are orange-red. Feet are totipalmate, which means that all four toes, including the back one, are united by a web of skin. Unlike many birds, the male and female have the same coloring and plumage.

Contrary to popular belief, pelicans do not store fish in their bills. They thrust their heads under water, using the pouch as a dip net for catching fish. The pouch can hold 17 pints of water. Fish are actually stored in the esophagus when the pelican travels.

The white pelican flies with head drawn back and bill resting on the breast. The birds fly at heights up to 8,000 feet. By using thermal currents they can circle for hours.

White pelicans nest on isolated islands in lakes of inland Canada and the U.S. They winter in coastal California and along the Pacific coast to Guatemala. The largest nesting colony in North America is at Chase Lake National Wildlife Refuge in North Dakota.

---

[*] From the Greek *pelicus*, an ax (probably from the shape of its bill); *erythros*, red; and *rynchos*, beak.

Pelicans can live to a great age. The accepted official record is 52 years, though the Emperor Maximilian of Mexico is said to have had a pelican who always accompanied his troops when on the march; that pelican is said to have lived for 80 years.

Edie Freedman designed the cover of this book, using a 19th-century engraving from the Dover Pictorial Archive. The cover layout was produced with Quark XPress 3.3 using the ITC Garamond font.

The inside layout was designed by Nancy Priest and implemented in FrameMaker by Mike Sierra. The text and heading fonts are ITC Garamond Light and Garamond Book. The illustrations that appear in the book were created in Macromedia Freehand 5.0 by Chris Reilley. This colophon was written by Kismet McDonough-Chan.

 # More Titles from O'Reilly

## Perl

### Programming Perl, 2nd Edition

*By Larry Wall, Tom Christiansen, & Randal L. Schwartz*
*2nd Edition September 1996*
*676 pages, ISBN 1-56592-149-6*

 *Programming Perl,* second edition, is the authoritative guide to Perl version 5, the scripting utility that has established itself as the programming tool of choice for the World Wide Web, UNIX system administration, and a vast range of other applications. Version 5 of Perl includes object-oriented programming facilities. The book is coauthored by Larry Wall, the creator of Perl. Perl is a language for easily manipulating text, files, and processes. It provides a more concise and readable way to do many jobs that were formerly accomplished (with difficulty) by programming with C or one of the shells. Perl is likely to be available wherever you choose to work. And if it isn't, you can get it and install it easily and free of charge.

This heavily revised second edition of *Programming Perl* contains a full explanation of the features in Perl version 5.003. It covers version 5.003 syntax, functions, library modules, references, debugging, and object-oriented programming.

### Learning Perl

*By Randal L. Schwartz, Foreword by Larry Wall*
*1st Edition November 1993*
*274 pages, ISBN 1-56592-042-2*

 *Learning Perl* is ideal for system administrators, programmers, and anyone else wanting a down-to-earth introduction to this useful language. Written by a Perl trainer, its aim is to make a competent, hands-on Perl programmer out of the reader as quickly as possible. The book takes a tutorial approach and includes hundreds of short code examples, along with some lengthy ones. The relatively inexperienced programmer will find *Learning Perl* easily accessible. Each chapter of the book includes practical programming exercises. Solutions are provided for all exercises.

### CGI Programming on the World Wide Web

*By Shishir Gundavaram*
*1st Edition March 1996*
*450 pages, ISBN 1-56592-168-2*

 This book offers a comprehensive explanation of CGI and related techniques for people who hold on to the dream of providing their own information servers on the Web. It starts at the beginning, explaining the value of CGI and how it works, then moves swiftly into the subtle details of programming.

### Perl 5 Desktop Reference

*By Johan Vromans*
*1st Edition February 1996*
*44 pages, ISBN 1-56592-187-9*

 This is the standard quick-reference guide for the Perl programming language. It provides a complete overview of the language, from variables to input and output, from flow control to regular expressions, from functions to document formats—all packed into a convenient, carry-around booklet. Updated to cover Perl version 5.003.

### Mastering Regular Expressions

*By Jeffrey E. F. Friedl*
*1st Edition January 1997*
*368 pages, ISBN 1-56592-257-3*

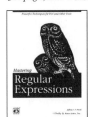 Regular expressions, a powerful tool for manipulating text and data, are found in scripting languages, editors, programming environments, and specialized tools. In this book, author Jeffrey Friedl leads you through the steps of crafting a regular expression that gets the job done. He examines a variety of tools and uses them in an extensive array of examples, dedicating an entire chapter to Perl.

## O'REILLY™

*TO ORDER:* **800-998-9938** • **order@ora.com** • **http://www.ora.com/**
*OUR PRODUCTS ARE AVAILABLE AT A BOOKSTORE OR SOFTWARE STORE NEAR YOU.*
*FOR INFORMATION:* **800-998-9938** • **707-829-0515** • **info@ora.com**

# Developing Web Content

## Building Your Own WebSite

By Susan B. Peck & Stephen Arrants
1st Edition July 1996
514 pages, ISBN 1-56592-232-8

This is a hands-on reference for Windows® 95 and Windows NT™ desktop users who want to host their own site on the Web or on a corporate intranet. You'll also learn how to connect your web to information in other Windows applications, such as word processing documents and databases. Packed with examples and tutorials on every aspect of Web management. Includes the highly acclaimed WebSite™ 1.1 on CD-ROM.

## Web Client Programming with Perl

By Clinton Wong
1st Edition March 1997 (est.)
250 pages (est.), ISBN 1-56592-214-X

Web Client Programming with Perl teaches you how to extend scripting skills to the Web. This book teaches you the basics of how browsers communicate with servers and how to write your own customized Web clients to automate common tasks. It is intended for those who are motivated to develop software that offers a more flexible and dynamic response than a standard Web browser.

## JavaScript: The Definitive Guide, Second Edition

By David Flanagan
2nd Edition January 1997
672 pages, ISBN 1-56592-234-4

In this second edition, the author of the best-selling, *Java in a Nutshell* describes the server-side JavaScript application, LiveWire, developed by Netscape and Sun Microsystems.

Using LiveWire, developers can easily convert JavaScript applications and any HTML pages containing JavaScript code, into platform-independent byte codes ready to run on any Netscape 2.0 Server. The book describes the version of JavaScript shipped with Navigator 2.0, 2.0.1, and 2.0.2, and also the much-changed version of JavaScript shipped with Navigator 3.0. LiveConnect, used for communication between JavaScript and Java applets, and addresses commonly encountered bugs onJavaScript objects.

## HTML: The Definitive Guide, Second Edition

By Chuck Musciano & Bill Kennedy
2nd Edition April 1997 (est.)
520 pages (est.), ISBN 1-56592-235-2

The second edition covers the most up-to-date version of the HTML standard (the proposed HTML version 3.2), Netscape 4.0 and Internet Explorer 3.0, plus all the common extensions, especially Netscape extensions. The authors address all the current version's elements, explaining how they work and interact with each other. Includes a style guide that helps you to use HTML to accomplish a variety of tasks, from simple online documentation to complex marketing and sales presentations. Readers of the first edition can find the updates for the second edition on the Web at www.ora.com.

## Designing for the Web: Getting Started in a New Medium

By Jennifer Niederst with Edie Freedman
1st Edition April 1996
180 pages, ISBN 1-56592-165-8

*Designing for the Web* gives you the basics you need to hit the ground running. Although geared toward designers, it covers information and techniques useful to anyone who wants to put graphics online. It explains how to work with HTML documents from a designer's point of view, outlines special problems with presenting information online, and walks through incorporating images into Web pages, with emphasis on resolution and improving efficiency.

## WebMaster in a Nutshell

By Stephen Spainhour & Valerie Quercia
1st Edition October 1996
378 pages, ISBN 1-56592-229-8

Web content providers and administrators have many sources of information, both in print and online. *WebMaster in a Nutshell* pulls it all together into one slim volume—for easy desktop access.

This quick-reference covers HTML, CGI, Perl, HTTP, server configuration, and tools for Web administration.

## O'REILLY™

TO ORDER: *800-998-9938* • *order@ora.com* • *http://www.ora.com/*
OUR PRODUCTS ARE AVAILABLE AT A BOOKSTORE OR SOFTWARE STORE NEAR YOU.
FOR INFORMATION: *800-998-9938* • *707-829-0515* • *info@ora.com*

# World Wide Web Journal

## Fourth International World Wide Web Conference Proceedings

*A publication of O'Reilly & Associates and the World Wide Web Consortium (W3C)*
*Winter 1995/96*
*748 pages, ISBN 1-56592-169-0*

The *World Wide Web Journal* provides timely, in-depth coverage of the W3C's technological developments, such as protocols for security, replication and caching, HTML and SGML, and content labeling. It also explores the broader issues of the Web with Web luminaries and articles on controversial legal issues such as censorship and intellectual property rights. Whether you follow Web developments for strategic planning, application programming, or Web page authoring and designing, you'll find the in-depth information you need here.

The *World Wide Web Journal* is published quarterly. This issue contains 57 refereed technical papers presented at the Fourth International World Wide Web Conference, held December 1995 in Boston, Massachusetts. It also includes the two best papers from regional conferences.

## Key Specifications of the World Wide Web

*A publication of O'Reilly & Associates and the World Wide Web Consortium (W3C)*
*Spring 1996*
*356 pages, ISBN 1-56592-190-9*

The key specifications that describe the architecture of the World Wide Web and how it works are maintained online at the World Wide Web Consortium. This issue of the *World Wide Web Journal* collects these key papers in a single volume as an important reference for the Webmaster, application programmer, or technical manager.

In this valuable reference, you'll find the definitive specifications for the core technologies in the Web: Hypertext Markup Language (HTML), Hypertext Transfer Protocol (HTTP), and Uniform Resource Locators (URLs), plus the emerging standards for portable graphics (PNG), content selection (PICS), and style sheets (CSS).

## The Web After Five Years

*A publication of O'Reilly & Associates and the World Wide Web Consortium (W3C)*
*Summer 1996, 226 pp, ISBN 1-56592-210-7*

As the Web explodes across the technology scene, it's increasingly difficult to keep track of myriad new protocols, standards, and applications. The *World Wide Web Journal* is your direct connection to the work of the World Wide Web Consortium.

This issue is a reflection on the web after five years. In an interview with Tim Berners-Lee, the inventor of the Web and Director of the W3C, we learn that the Web was built to be an interactive, intercreative, two-way medium from the beginning. At the opposite scale, as a mass medium, are urgent questions about the Web's size, character, and users. These issues are addressed in selections from the MIT/W3C Workshop on Web Demographics and Internet Survey Methodology, along with commerce-related papers selected from the Fifth International World Wide Web Conference, which took place from May 6–10 in Paris.

## Building an Industrial Strength Web

*A publication of O'Reilly & Associates and the World Wide Web Consortium (W3C)*
*Fall 1996, 244 pp, ISBN 1-56592-211-5*

Issue 4 focuses on the infrastructure needed to create and maintain an "Industrial Strength Web," from network protocols to application design. Included are the first standard versions of core Web protocols: HTTP/1.1, Digest Authentica-tion, State Management (Cookies), and PICS. This issue also provides guides to the specs, highlighting new features, papers explaining modifications to 1.1 (sticky and compressed headers), extensibility, support for collaborative authoring, and using distributed objects.

## Advancing HTML: Style and Substance

*A publication of O'Reilly & Associates and the World Wide Web Consortium (W3C)*
*Winter 1996/97*
*254 pages, ISBN 1-56592-264-6*

Issue 5 is a guide to the specifications and tools that buttress the user interface to the World Wide Web. It includes the latest HTML 3.2 and CSS1 specs, papers on gif animation, JavaScript, Web accessibility, usability engineering, multimedia design, and a report on Amaya.

# O'REILLY™

TO ORDER: **800-998-9938** • **order@ora.com** • **http://www.ora.com/**
OUR PRODUCTS ARE AVAILABLE AT A BOOKSTORE OR SOFTWARE STORE NEAR YOU.
FOR INFORMATION: **800-998-9938** • **707-829-0515** • **info@ora.com**

# Java Programming

## Exploring Java

By Patrick Niemeyer & Joshua Peck
1st Edition May 1996
426 pages, ISBN 1-56592-184-4

The ability to create animated World Wide Web pages has sparked the rush to Java. But what has also made this new language so important is that it's truly portable. *Exploring Java* introduces the basics of Java, the hot new object-oriented programming language for networked applications. The code runs on any machine that provides a Java interpreter, be it Windows 95, Windows NT, the Macintosh, or any flavor of UNIX.

But that's only the beginning! This book shows you how to quickly get up to speed writing Java applets (programs executed within web browsers) and other applications, including networking programs, content and protocol handlers, and security managers. *Exploring Java* is the first book in a new Java documentation series from O'Reilly that will keep pace with the rapid Java developments. Covers Java's latest Beta release.

## Java in a Nutshell

By David Flanagan
1st Edition February 1996
460 pages, ISBN 1-56592-183-6

*Java in a Nutshell* is a complete quick-reference guide to Java, the hot new programming language from Sun Microsystems. This comprehensive volume contains descriptions of all of the classes in the Java 1.0 API, with a definitive listing of all methods and variables. It also contains an accelerated introduction to Java for C and C++ programmers who want to learn the language *fast*.

Java in a Nutshell introduces the Java programming language and contains many practical examples that show programmers how to write Java applications and applets. It is also an indispensable quick reference designed to wait faithfully by the side of every Java programmer's keyboard. It puts all the information Java programmers need right at their fingertips.

## Java Virtual Machine

By Troy Downing & Jon Meyer
1st Edition March 1997
440 pages (est.), ISBN 1-56592-194-1

This book is a comprehensive programming guide for the Java Virtual Machine (JVM). It gives readers a strong overview and reference of the JVM so that they may create their own implementations of the JVM or write their own compilers that create Java object code. The book is divided into two sections: the first includes information on the semantics and structure of the JVM; the second is a reference of the JVM instructions, or "opcodes." The programming guide includes numerous examples written in Java assembly language. A Java assembler is provided with the book, so the examples can all be compiled and executed. The reference section offers a complete description of the instruction set of the VM and the class file format, including a description of the byte-code verifier.

## Java Language Reference

By Mark Grand
1st Edition January 1997
448 pages, ISBN 1-56592-204-2

*Java Language Reference* is an indispensable tool for Java programmers. Part of O'Reilly's new Java documentation series, the book details every aspect of the Java programming language, from the definition of data types to the syntax of expressions and control structures.

Using numerous examples to illustrate various fine points of the language, this book helps you understand all of the subtle nuances of Java so you can ensure that your programs run exactly as expected. This edition describes Java Version 1.0.2. It covers the syntax (presented in easy-to-understand railroad diagrams), object-oriented programming, exception handling, multithreaded programming, and differences between Java and C/C++.

# O'REILLY™

TO ORDER: **800-998-9938** • *order@ora.com* • *http://www.ora.com/*
OUR PRODUCTS ARE AVAILABLE AT A BOOKSTORE OR SOFTWARE STORE NEAR YOU.
FOR INFORMATION: **800-998-9938** • **707-829-0515** • *info@ora.com*

# Java Programming *continued*

## Java Fundamental Classes Reference

By Mark Grand
*1st Edition May 1997 (est.)*
*880 pages (est.), ISBN 1-56592-241-7*

The *Java Fundamental Classes Reference* provides complete reference documentation for the Java fundamental classes. These classes contain architecture-independent methods that serve as Java's gateway to the real world and provide access to resources such as the network, the windowing system, and the host filesystem. This book takes you beyond what you'd expect from a standard reference manual. Classes and methods are, of course, described in detail. But the book does much more. It offers tutorial-style explanations of the important classes in the Java Core API and includes lots of sample code to help you learn by example.

## Java AWT Reference

By John Zukowski
*1st Edition March 1997 (est.)*
*1100 pages (est.), ISBN 1-56592-240-9*

With AWT, you can create windows, draw, work with images, and use components like buttons, scrollbars, and pulldown menus. *Java* AWT Reference covers the classes that comprise the java.awt, java.awt.image, and java.applet packages. These classes provide the functionality that allows a Java application to provide user interaction in a graphical environment.

The *Java AWT Reference* provides complete reference documentation on the Abstract Windowing Toolkit (AWT), a large collection of classes for building graphical user interfaces in Java. Part of O'Reilly's new Java documentation series, this edition describes Version 1.0.2 of the Java Developer's Kit. This book takes you beyond what you'd expect from a standard reference manual. It offers a comprehensive explanation of how AWT components fit together with easy-to-use reference material on every AWT class and lots of sample code to help you learn by example.

## Java Threads

By Scott Oaks and Henry Wong
*1st Edition January 1997*
*252 pages, ISBN 1-56592-216-6*

Threaded programming being essential to Java, any new Java program that is at all substantial is multithreaded. The concept of threaded programming isn't new; however, as widespread as threads are, the number of developers who have worked with them is fairly small. *Java Threads* is a comprehensive guide to the intracacies of threaded programming in Java, covering everything from the most basic synchronization techniques to advanced topics like writing your own thread scheduler.

*Java Threads* uncovers the one tricky but essential aspect of Java programming and provides techniques, perhaps unfamiliar to most developers, for avoiding deadlock, lock starvation, and other topics. With many useful examples, you'll find this book essential if sophisticated Java programming is part of your future.

## Java Network Programming

By Elliotte Rusty Harold
*1st Edition February 1997*
*448 pages, ISBN 1-56592-227-1*

Most Java programmers have yet to take advantage of Java's networking capabilities because they have limited themselves to relatively simple applets. *Java Network Programming* is a complete introduction to developing network programs, both applets and applications, using Java; covering everything from networking fundamentals to remote method invocation (RMI). It also covers what you can do without explicitly writing network code, how you can accomplish your goals using URLs and the basic capabilites of applets.

*Java Network Programming* includes chapters on TCP and UDP sockets, multicasting protocal and content handlers and servlets, part of the new Server API. Once you start taking advantage of Java's networking features, the possibilities are limited only by imagination!

# O'REILLY™

*TO ORDER:* **800-998-9938** • **order@ora.com** • **http://www.ora.com/**
*OUR PRODUCTS ARE AVAILABLE AT A BOOKSTORE OR SOFTWARE STORE NEAR YOU.*
*FOR INFORMATION:* **800-998-9938** • **707-829-0515** • **info@ora.com**

# How to stay in touch with O'Reilly

## 1. Visit Our Award-Winning Web Site
### http://www.ora.com/

★ "Top 100 Sites on the Web" —*PC Magazine*
★ "Top 5% Web sites" —*Point Communications*
★ "3-Star site" —*The McKinley Group*

Our web site contains a library of comprehensive product information (including book excerpts and tables of contents), downloadable software, background articles, interviews with technology leaders, links to relevant sites, book cover art, and more. File us in your Bookmarks or Hotlist!

## 2. Join Our Email Mailing Lists
### New Product Releases
To receive automatic email with brief descriptions of all new O'Reilly products as they are released, send email to:
**listproc@online.ora.com**
Put the following information in the first line of your message (*not* in the Subject field):
**subscribe ora-news "Your Name"of "Your Organization"** (for example: subscribe ora-news Kris Webber of Fine Enterprises)

### O'Reilly Events
If you'd also like us to send information about trade show events, special promotions, and other O'Reilly events, send email to: **listproc@online.ora.com**
Put the following information in the first line of your message (*not* in the Subject field):
**subscribe ora-events "Your Name" of "Your Organization"**

## 3. Get Examples from Our Books via FTP

There are two ways to access an archive of example files from our books:

### Regular FTP
- ftp to:
  **ftp.ora.com**
  (login: anonymous
  password: your email address)
- Point your web browser to:
  **ftp://ftp.ora.com/**

### FTPMAIL
- Send an email message to:
  **ftpmail@online.ora.com**
  (Write "help" in the message body)

## 4. Visit Our Gopher Site
- Connect your gopher to:
  **gopher.ora.com**

- Point your web browser to:
  **gopher://gopher.ora.com/**

- Telnet to:
  **gopher.ora.com
  login: gopher**

## 5. Contact Us via Email
**order@ora.com**
To place a book or software order online. Good for North American and international customers.

**subscriptions@ora.com**
To place an order for any of our newsletters or periodicals.

**books@ora.com**
General questions about any of our books.

**software@ora.com**
For general questions and product information about our software. Check out O'Reilly Software Online at **http://software.ora.com/** for software and technical support information. Registered O'Reilly software users send your questions to: **website-support@ora.com**

**cs@ora.com**
For answers to problems regarding your order or our products.

**booktech@ora.com**
For book content technical questions or corrections.

**proposals@ora.com**
To submit new book or software proposals to our editors and product managers.

**international@ora.com**
For information about our international distributors or translation queries. For a list of our distributors outside of North America check out:
**http://www.ora.com/www/order/country.html**

O'Reilly & Associates, Inc.
101 Morris Street, Sebastopol, CA 95472 USA
TEL 707-829-0515 or 800-998-9938
(6am to 5pm PST)
FAX 707-829-0104

## O'REILLY™
TO ORDER: **800-998-9938** • **order@ora.com** • **http://www.ora.com/**
*OUR PRODUCTS ARE AVAILABLE AT A BOOKSTORE OR SOFTWARE STORE NEAR YOU.*
FOR INFORMATION: **800-998-9938** • **707-829-0515** • **info@ora.com**

# Titles from O'Reilly

*Please note that upcoming titles are displayed in italic.*

## WEB PROGRAMMING

*Apache: The Definitive Guide*
Building Your Own Web
  Conferences
Building Your Own Website
*Building Your Own Win-CGI
  Programs*
CGI Programming for the World
  Wide Web
Designing for the Web
HTML: The Definitive Guide
JavaScript: The Definitive Guide,
  2nd Ed.
Learning Perl
Programming Perl, 2nd Ed.
Mastering Regular Expressions
WebMaster in a Nutshell
*Web Security & Commerce*
*Web Client Programming with
  Perl*
World Wide Web Journal

## USING THE INTERNET

Smileys
The Future Does Not Compute
The Whole Internet User's Guide
  & Catalog
The Whole Internet for Win 95
Using Email Effectively
Bandits on the Information
  Superhighway

## JAVA SERIES

Exploring Java
*Java AWT Reference*
*Java Fundamental Classes
  Reference*
Java in a Nutshell
*Java Language Reference*
*Java Network Programming*
Java Threads
*Java Virtual Machine*

## SOFTWARE

WebSite™ 1.1
WebSite Professional™
Building Your Own Web
  Conferences
WebBoard™
PolyForm™
*Statisphere™*

## SONGLINE GUIDES

NetActivism       *NetResearch*
Net Law           *NetSuccess*
NetLearning       *NetTravel*
*Net Lessons*

## SYSTEM ADMINISTRATION

Building Internet Firewalls
Computer Crime: A
  Crimefighter's Handbook
Computer Security Basics
DNS and BIND, 2nd Ed.
Essential System Administration,
  2nd Ed.
Getting Connected: The Internet
  at 56K and Up
*Internet Server Administration
  with Windows NT*
Linux Network Administrator's
  Guide
Managing Internet Information
  Services
Managing NFS and NIS
Networking Personal Computers
  with TCP/IP
Practical UNIX & Internet
  Security. 2nd Ed.
PGP: Pretty Good Privacy
sendmail, 2nd Ed.
*sendmail Desktop Reference*
System Performance Tuning
TCP/IP Network Administration
termcap & terminfo
Using & Managing UUCP
Volume 8: X Window System
  Administrator's Guide
*Web Security & Commerce*

## UNIX

Exploring Expect
*Learning VBScript*
Learning GNU Emacs, 2nd Ed.
Learning the bash Shell
Learning the Korn Shell
Learning the UNIX Operating
  System
Learning the vi Editor
Linux in a Nutshell
Making TeX Work
Linux Multimedia Guide
Running Linux, 2nd Ed.
SCO UNIX in a Nutshell
*sed & awk, 2nd Edition*
*Tcl/Tk Tools*
UNIX in a Nutshell: System V
  Edition
UNIX Power Tools
Using csh & tsch
When You Can't Find Your UNIX
  System Administrator
*Writing GNU Emacs Extensions*

## WEB REVIEW STUDIO SERIES

Gif Animation Studio
Shockwave Studio

## WINDOWS

Dictionary of PC Hardware and
  Data Communications Terms
Inside the Windows 95 Registry
*Inside the Windows 95 File
  System*
*Win95 & WinNT Annoyances*
*Windows NT File System
  Internals*
*Windows NT in a Nutshell*

## PROGRAMMING

Advanced Oracle PL/SQL
  Programming
Applying RCS and SCCS
C++: The Core Language
Checking C Programs with lint
DCE Security Programming
Distributing Applications Across
  DCE & Windows NT
Encyclopedia of Graphics File
  Formats, 2nd Ed.
Guide to Writing DCE
  Applications
lex & yacc
Managing Projects with make
*Mastering Oracle Power Objects*
*Oracle Design: The Definitive
  Guide*
Oracle Performance Tuning, 2nd
  Ed.
Oracle PL/SQL Programming
Porting UNIX Software
POSIX Programmer's Guide
POSIX.4: Programming for the
  Real World
Power Programming with RPC
Practical C Programming
Practical C++ Programming
Programming Python
Programming with curses
Programming with GNU Software
Pthreads Programming
Software Portability with imake,
  2nd Ed.
Understanding DCE
Understanding Japanese
  Information Processing
UNIX Systems Programming for
  SVR4

## BERKELEY 4.4 SOFTWARE DISTRIBUTION

4.4BSD System Manager's
  Manual
4.4BSD User's Reference Manual
4.4BSD User's Supplementary
  Documents
4.4BSD Programmer's Reference
  Manual
4.4BSD Programmer's
  Supplementary Documents
X Programming
Vol. 0: X Protocol Reference
  Manual
Vol. 1: Xlib Programming Manual
Vol. 2: Xlib Reference Manual
Vol. 3M: X Window System User's
  Guide, Motif Edition
Vol. 4M: X Toolkit Intrinsics
  Programming Manual, Motif
  Edition
Vol. 5: X Toolkit Intrinsics
  Reference Manual
Vol. 6A: Motif Programming
  Manual
Vol. 6B: Motif Reference Manual
Vol. 6C: Motif Tools
Vol. 8 : X Window System
  Administrator's Guide
Programmer's Supplement for
  Release 6
X User Tools
The X Window System in a
  Nutshell

## CAREER & BUSINESS

Building a Successful Software
  Business
The Computer User's Survival
  Guide
Love Your Job!
Electronic Publishing on CD-
  ROM

## TRAVEL

Travelers' Tales: Brazil
Travelers' Tales: Food
Travelers' Tales: France
Travelers' Tales: Gutsy Women
Travelers' Tales: India
Travelers' Tales: Mexico
Travelers' Tales: Paris
Travelers' Tales: San Francisco
Travelers' Tales: Spain
Travelers' Tales: Thailand
Travelers' Tales: A Woman's
  World

## O'REILLY™

TO ORDER: **800-998-9938** • **order@ora.com** • **http://www.ora.com/**
*OUR PRODUCTS ARE AVAILABLE AT A BOOKSTORE OR SOFTWARE STORE NEAR YOU.*
FOR INFORMATION: **800-998-9938** • **707-829-0515** • **info@ora.com**

# International Distributors

## UK, Europe, Middle East and Northern Africa (except France, Germany, Switzerland, & Austria)

**INQUIRIES**

International Thomson Publishing Europe
Berkshire House
168-173 High Holborn
London WC1V 7AA, United Kingdom
Telephone: 44-171-497-1422
Fax: 44-171-497-1426
Email: itpint@itps.co.uk

**ORDERS**

International Thomson Publishing Services, Ltd.
Cheriton House, North Way
Andover, Hampshire SP10 5BE,
United Kingdom
Telephone: 44-264-342-832
  (UK orders)
Telephone: 44-264-342-806
  (outside UK)
Fax: 44-264-364418 (UK orders)
Fax: 44-264-342761 (outside UK)
UK & Eire orders: itpuk@itps.co.uk
International orders: itpint@itps.co.uk

## France

Editions Eyrolles
61 bd Saint-Germain
75240 Paris Cedex 05
France
Fax: 33-01-44-41-11-44

**FRENCH LANGUAGE BOOKS**

All countries except Canada
Phone: 33-01-44-41-46-16
Email: geodif@eyrolles.com

**ENGLISH LANGUAGE BOOKS**

Phone: 33-01-44-41-11-87
Email: distribution@eyrolles.com

## Australia

WoodsLane Pty. Ltd.
7/5 Vuko Place, Warriewood NSW 2102
P.O. Box 935, Mona Vale NSW 2103
Australia
Telephone: 61-2-9970-5111
Fax: 61-2-9970-5002
Email: info@woodslane.com.au

## Germany, Switzerland, and Austria

**INQUIRIES**

O'Reilly Verlag
Balthasarstr. 81
D-50670 Köln
Germany
Telephone: 49-221-97-31-60-0
Fax: 49-221-97-31-60-8
Email: anfragen@oreilly.de

**ORDERS**

International Thomson Publishing
Königswinterer Straße 418
53227 Bonn, Germany
Telephone: 49-228-97024 0
Fax: 49-228-441342
Email: order@oreilly.de

## Asia (except Japan & India)

**INQUIRIES**

International Thomson Publishing Asia
60 Albert Street #15-01
Albert Complex
Singapore 189969
Telephone: 65-336-6411
Fax: 65-336-7411

**ORDERS**

Telephone: 65-336-6411
Fax: 65-334-1617
thomson@signet.com.sg

## New Zealand

WoodsLane New Zealand Ltd.
21 Cooks Street (P.O. Box 575)
Wanganui, New Zealand
Telephone: 64-6-347-6543
Fax: 64-6-345-4840
Email: info@woodslane.com.au

## Japan

O'Reilly Japan, Inc.
Kiyoshige Building 2F
12-Banchi, Sanei-cho
Shinjuku-ku
Tokyo 160 Japan
Telephone: 81-3-3356-5227
Fax: 81-3-3356-5261
Email: kenji@ora.com

## India

Computer Bookshop (India) PVT. LTD.
190 Dr. D.N. Road, Fort
Bombay 400 001
India
Telephone: 91-22-207-0989
Fax: 91-22-262-3551
Email: cbsbom@giasbm01.vsnl.net.in

## The Americas

O'Reilly & Associates, Inc.
101 Morris Street
Sebastopol, CA 95472 U.S.A.
Telephone: 707-829-0515
Telephone: 800-998-9938 (U.S. & Canada)
Fax: 707-829-0104
Email: order@ora.com

## Southern Africa

International Thomson Publishing
Southern Africa
Building 18, Constantia Park
240 Old Pretoria Road
P.O. Box 2459
Halfway House, 1685 South Africa
Telephone: 27-11-805-4819
Fax: 27-11-805-3648